C-1346 CAREER EXAMINATION SERIES

This is your PASSBOOK for...

Library Director

Test Preparation Study Guide Questions & Answers

NLC®

NATIONAL LEARNING CORPORATION®

National Learning Corporation

212 Michael Drive, Syosset, NY 11791
(516) 921-8888 • www.passbooks.com
E-mail: info@passbooks.com

PUBLISHED IN THE UNITED STATES OF AMERICA

PASSBOOK® SERIES

THE *PASSBOOK® SERIES* has been created to prepare applicants and candidates for the ultimate academic battlefield – the examination room.

At some time in our lives, each and every one of us may be required to take an examination – for validation, matriculation, admission, qualification, registration, certification, or licensure.

Based on the assumption that every applicant or candidate has met the basic formal educational standards, has taken the required number of courses, and read the necessary texts, the *PASSBOOK® SERIES* furnishes the one special preparation which may assure passing with confidence, instead of failing with insecurity. Examination questions – together with answers – are furnished as the basic vehicle for study so that the mysteries of the examination and its compounding difficulties may be eliminated or diminished by a sure method.

This book is meant to help you pass your examination provided that you qualify and are serious in your objective.

The entire field is reviewed through the huge store of content information which is succinctly presented through a provocative and challenging approach – the question-and-answer method.

A climate of success is established by furnishing the correct answers at the end of each test.

You soon learn to recognize types of questions, forms of questions, and patterns of questioning. You may even begin to anticipate expected outcomes.

You perceive that many questions are repeated or adapted so that you can gain acute insights, which may enable you to score many sure points.

You learn how to confront new questions, or types of questions, and to attack them confidently and work out the correct answers.

You note objectives and emphases, and recognize pitfalls and dangers, so that you may make positive educational adjustments.

Moreover, you are kept fully informed in relation to new concepts, methods, practices, and directions in the field.

You discover that you are actually taking the examination all the time: you are preparing for the examination by "taking" an examination, not by reading extraneous and/or supererogatory textbooks.

In short, this PASSBOOK®, used directedly, should be an important factor in helping you to pass your test.

LIBRARY DIRECTOR

DUTIES:

Directs the administration of a library. Plans, develops, implements, directs, and coordinates the programs and activities of a public library; evaluates the effectiveness of the library's services in relation to the changing needs of the community; recommends necessary library services to the board; prepares preliminary budget estimates and submits a budget to the library board; represents the library at community and group meetings; supervises all library personnel and the maintenance of buildings and grounds; perform related duties as required.

SCOPE OF THE WRITTEN TEST

The written test will be designed to test for knowledge, skills, and/or abilities in such areas as:

1. Library science;
2. Public and community relations;
3. Supervision;
4. Administration;
5. Program planning and evaluation; and
6. Budgeting.

HOW TO TAKE A TEST

I. YOU MUST PASS AN EXAMINATION

A. WHAT EVERY CANDIDATE SHOULD KNOW

Examination applicants often ask us for help in preparing for the written test. What can I study in advance? What kinds of questions will be asked? How will the test be given? How will the papers be graded?

As an applicant for a civil service examination, you may be wondering about some of these things. Our purpose here is to suggest effective methods of advance study and to describe civil service examinations.

Your chances for success on this examination can be increased if you know how to prepare. Those "pre-examination jitters" can be reduced if you know what to expect. You can even experience an adventure in good citizenship if you know why civil service exams are given.

B. WHY ARE CIVIL SERVICE EXAMINATIONS GIVEN?

Civil service examinations are important to you in two ways. As a citizen, you want public jobs filled by employees who know how to do their work. As a job seeker, you want a fair chance to compete for that job on an equal footing with other candidates. The best-known means of accomplishing this two-fold goal is the competitive examination.

Exams are widely publicized throughout the nation. They may be administered for jobs in federal, state, city, municipal, town or village governments or agencies.

Any citizen may apply, with some limitations, such as the age or residence of applicants. Your experience and education may be reviewed to see whether you meet the requirements for the particular examination. When these requirements exist, they are reasonable and applied consistently to all applicants. Thus, a competitive examination may cause you some uneasiness now, but it is your privilege and safeguard.

C. HOW ARE CIVIL SERVICE EXAMS DEVELOPED?

Examinations are carefully written by trained technicians who are specialists in the field known as "psychological measurement," in consultation with recognized authorities in the field of work that the test will cover. These experts recommend the subject matter areas or skills to be tested; only those knowledges or skills important to your success on the job are included. The most reliable books and source materials available are used as references. Together, the experts and technicians judge the difficulty level of the questions.

Test technicians know how to phrase questions so that the problem is clearly stated. Their ethics do not permit "trick" or "catch" questions. Questions may have been tried out on sample groups, or subjected to statistical analysis, to determine their usefulness.

Written tests are often used in combination with performance tests, ratings of training and experience, and oral interviews. All of these measures combine to form the best-known means of finding the right person for the right job.

II. HOW TO PASS THE WRITTEN TEST

A. NATURE OF THE EXAMINATION

To prepare intelligently for civil service examinations, you should know how they differ from school examinations you have taken. In school you were assigned certain definite pages to read or subjects to cover. The examination questions were quite detailed and usually emphasized memory. Civil service exams, on the other hand, try to discover your present ability to perform the duties of a position, plus your potentiality to learn these duties. In other words, a civil service exam attempts to predict how successful you will be. Questions cover such a broad area that they cannot be as minute and detailed as school exam questions.

In the public service similar kinds of work, or positions, are grouped together in one "class." This process is known as *position-classification.* All the positions in a class are paid according to the salary range for that class. One class title covers all of these positions, and they are all tested by the same examination.

B. FOUR BASIC STEPS

1) Study the announcement

How, then, can you know what subjects to study? Our best answer is: "Learn as much as possible about the class of positions for which you've applied." The exam will test the knowledge, skills and abilities needed to do the work.

Your most valuable source of information about the position you want is the official exam announcement. This announcement lists the training and experience qualifications. Check these standards and apply only if you come reasonably close to meeting them.

The brief description of the position in the examination announcement offers some clues to the subjects which will be tested. Think about the job itself. Review the duties in your mind. Can you perform them, or are there some in which you are rusty? Fill in the blank spots in your preparation.

Many jurisdictions preview the written test in the exam announcement by including a section called "Knowledge and Abilities Required," "Scope of the Examination," or some similar heading. Here you will find out specifically what fields will be tested.

2) Review your own background

Once you learn in general what the position is all about, and what you need to know to do the work, ask yourself which subjects you already know fairly well and which need improvement. You may wonder whether to concentrate on improving your strong areas or on building some background in your fields of weakness. When the announcement has specified "some knowledge" or "considerable knowledge," or has used adjectives like "beginning principles of..." or "advanced ... methods," you can get a clue as to the number and difficulty of questions to be asked in any given field. More questions, and hence broader coverage, would be included for those subjects which are more important in the work. Now weigh your strengths and weaknesses against the job requirements and prepare accordingly.

3) Determine the level of the position

Another way to tell how intensively you should prepare is to understand the level of the job for which you are applying. Is it the entering level? In other words, is this the position in which beginners in a field of work are hired? Or is it an intermediate or advanced level? Sometimes this is indicated by such words as "Junior" or "Senior" in the class title. Other jurisdictions use Roman numerals to designate the level – Clerk I, Clerk II, for example. The word "Supervisor" sometimes appears in the title. If the level is not indicated by the title, check the description of duties. Will you be working under very close supervision, or will you have responsibility for independent decisions in this work?

4) Choose appropriate study materials

Now that you know the subjects to be examined and the relative amount of each subject to be covered, you can choose suitable study materials. For beginning level jobs, or even advanced ones, if you have a pronounced weakness in some aspect of your training, read a modern, standard textbook in that field. Be sure it is up to date and has general coverage. Such books are normally available at your library, and the librarian will be glad to help you locate one. For entry-level positions, questions of appropriate difficulty are chosen – neither highly advanced questions, nor those too simple. Such questions require careful thought but not advanced training.

If the position for which you are applying is technical or advanced, you will read more advanced, specialized material. If you are already familiar with the basic principles of your field, elementary textbooks would waste your time. Concentrate on advanced textbooks and technical periodicals. Think through the concepts and review difficult problems in your field.

These are all general sources. You can get more ideas on your own initiative, following these leads. For example, training manuals and publications of the government agency which employs workers in your field can be useful, particularly for technical and professional positions. A letter or visit to the government department involved may result in more specific study suggestions, and certainly will provide you with a more definite idea of the exact nature of the position you are seeking.

III. KINDS OF TESTS

Tests are used for purposes other than measuring knowledge and ability to perform specified duties. For some positions, it is equally important to test ability to make adjustments to new situations or to profit from training. In others, basic mental abilities not dependent on information are essential. Questions which test these things may not appear as pertinent to the duties of the position as those which test for knowledge and information. Yet they are often highly important parts of a fair examination. For very general questions, it is almost impossible to help you direct your study efforts. What we can do is to point out some of the more common of these general abilities needed in public service positions and describe some typical questions.

1) General information

Broad, general information has been found useful for predicting job success in some kinds of work. This is tested in a variety of ways, from vocabulary lists to questions about current events. Basic background in some field of work, such as sociology or economics, may be sampled in a group of questions. Often these are principles which have become familiar to most persons through exposure rather than through formal training. It is difficult to advise you how to study for these questions; being alert to the world around you is our best suggestion.

2) Verbal ability

An example of an ability needed in many positions is verbal or language ability. Verbal ability is, in brief, the ability to use and understand words. Vocabulary and grammar tests are typical measures of this ability. Reading comprehension or paragraph interpretation questions are common in many kinds of civil service tests. You are given a paragraph of written material and asked to find its central meaning.

3) Numerical ability

Number skills can be tested by the familiar arithmetic problem, by checking paired lists of numbers to see which are alike and which are different, or by interpreting charts and graphs. In the latter test, a graph may be printed in the test booklet which you are asked to use as the basis for answering questions.

4) Observation

A popular test for law-enforcement positions is the observation test. A picture is shown to you for several minutes, then taken away. Questions about the picture test your ability to observe both details and larger elements.

5) Following directions

In many positions in the public service, the employee must be able to carry out written instructions dependably and accurately. You may be given a chart with several columns, each column listing a variety of information. The questions require you to carry out directions involving the information given in the chart.

6) Skills and aptitudes

Performance tests effectively measure some manual skills and aptitudes. When the skill is one in which you are trained, such as typing or shorthand, you can practice. These tests are often very much like those given in business school or high school courses. For many of the other skills and aptitudes, however, no short-time preparation can be made. Skills and abilities natural to you or that you have developed throughout your lifetime are being tested.

Many of the general questions just described provide all the data needed to answer the questions and ask you to use your reasoning ability to find the answers. Your best preparation for these tests, as well as for tests of facts and ideas, is to be at your physical and mental best. You, no doubt, have your own methods of getting into an exam-taking mood and keeping "in shape." The next section lists some ideas on this subject.

IV. KINDS OF QUESTIONS

Only rarely is the "essay" question, which you answer in narrative form, used in civil service tests. Civil service tests are usually of the short-answer type. Full instructions for answering these questions will be given to you at the examination. But in case this is your first experience with short-answer questions and separate answer sheets, here is what you need to know:

1) Multiple-choice Questions

Most popular of the short-answer questions is the "multiple choice" or "best answer" question. It can be used, for example, to test for factual knowledge, ability to solve problems or judgment in meeting situations found at work.

A multiple-choice question is normally one of three types—

- It can begin with an incomplete statement followed by several possible endings. You are to find the one ending which *best* completes the statement, although some of the others may not be entirely wrong.
- It can also be a complete statement in the form of a question which is answered by choosing one of the statements listed.

- It can be in the form of a problem – again you select the best answer.

Here is an example of a multiple-choice question with a discussion which should give you some clues as to the method for choosing the right answer:

When an employee has a complaint about his assignment, the action which will *best* help him overcome his difficulty is to

A. discuss his difficulty with his coworkers
B. take the problem to the head of the organization
C. take the problem to the person who gave him the assignment
D. say nothing to anyone about his complaint

In answering this question, you should study each of the choices to find which is best. Consider choice "A" – Certainly an employee may discuss his complaint with fellow employees, but no change or improvement can result, and the complaint remains unresolved. Choice "B" is a poor choice since the head of the organization probably does not know what assignment you have been given, and taking your problem to him is known as "going over the head" of the supervisor. The supervisor, or person who made the assignment, is the person who can clarify it or correct any injustice. Choice "C" is, therefore, correct. To say nothing, as in choice "D," is unwise. Supervisors have and interest in knowing the problems employees are facing, and the employee is seeking a solution to his problem.

2) True/False Questions

The "true/false" or "right/wrong" form of question is sometimes used. Here a complete statement is given. Your job is to decide whether the statement is right or wrong.

SAMPLE: A roaming cell-phone call to a nearby city costs less than a non-roaming call to a distant city.

This statement is wrong, or false, since roaming calls are more expensive.

This is not a complete list of all possible question forms, although most of the others are variations of these common types. You will always get complete directions for answering questions. Be sure you understand *how* to mark your answers – ask questions until you do.

V. RECORDING YOUR ANSWERS

Computer terminals are used more and more today for many different kinds of exams.

For an examination with very few applicants, you may be told to record your answers in the test booklet itself. Separate answer sheets are much more common. If this separate answer sheet is to be scored by machine – and this is often the case – it is highly important that you mark your answers correctly in order to get credit.

An electronic scoring machine is often used in civil service offices because of the speed with which papers can be scored. Machine-scored answer sheets must be marked with a pencil, which will be given to you. This pencil has a high graphite content which responds to the electronic scoring machine. As a matter of fact, stray dots may register as answers, so do not let your pencil rest on the answer sheet while you are pondering the correct answer. Also, if your pencil lead breaks or is otherwise defective, ask for another.

Since the answer sheet will be dropped in a slot in the scoring machine, be careful not to bend the corners or get the paper crumpled.

The answer sheet normally has five vertical columns of numbers, with 30 numbers to a column. These numbers correspond to the question numbers in your test booklet. After each number, going across the page are four or five pairs of dotted lines. These short dotted lines have small letters or numbers above them. The first two pairs may also have a "T" or "F" above the letters. This indicates that the first two pairs only are to be used if the questions are of the true-false type. If the questions are multiple choice, disregard the "T" and "F" and pay attention only to the small letters or numbers.

Answer your questions in the manner of the sample that follows:

32. The largest city in the United States is
    A. Washington, D.C.
    B. New York City
    C. Chicago
    D. Detroit
    E. San Francisco

1) Choose the answer you think is best. (New York City is the largest, so "B" is correct.)
2) Find the row of dotted lines numbered the same as the question you are answering. (Find row number 32)
3) Find the pair of dotted lines corresponding to the answer. (Find the pair of lines under the mark "B.")
4) Make a solid black mark between the dotted lines.

VI. BEFORE THE TEST

Common sense will help you find procedures to follow to get ready for an examination. Too many of us, however, overlook these sensible measures. Indeed, nervousness and fatigue have been found to be the most serious reasons why applicants fail to do their best on civil service tests. Here is a list of reminders:

- Begin your preparation early – Don't wait until the last minute to go scurrying around for books and materials or to find out what the position is all about.
- Prepare continuously – An hour a night for a week is better than an all-night cram session. This has been definitely established. What is more, a night a week for a month will return better dividends than crowding your study into a shorter period of time.
- Locate the place of the exam – You have been sent a notice telling you when and where to report for the examination. If the location is in a different town or otherwise unfamiliar to you, it would be well to inquire the best route and learn something about the building.
- Relax the night before the test – Allow your mind to rest. Do not study at all that night. Plan some mild recreation or diversion; then go to bed early and get a good night's sleep.
- Get up early enough to make a leisurely trip to the place for the test – This way unforeseen events, traffic snarls, unfamiliar buildings, etc. will not upset you.
- Dress comfortably – A written test is not a fashion show. You will be known by number and not by name, so wear something comfortable.

- Leave excess paraphernalia at home – Shopping bags and odd bundles will get in your way. You need bring only the items mentioned in the official notice you received; usually everything you need is provided. Do not bring reference books to the exam. They will only confuse those last minutes and be taken away from you when in the test room.
- Arrive somewhat ahead of time – If because of transportation schedules you must get there very early, bring a newspaper or magazine to take your mind off yourself while waiting.
- Locate the examination room – When you have found the proper room, you will be directed to the seat or part of the room where you will sit. Sometimes you are given a sheet of instructions to read while you are waiting. Do not fill out any forms until you are told to do so; just read them and be prepared.
- Relax and prepare to listen to the instructions
- If you have any physical problem that may keep you from doing your best, be sure to tell the test administrator. If you are sick or in poor health, you really cannot do your best on the exam. You can come back and take the test some other time.

VII. AT THE TEST

The day of the test is here and you have the test booklet in your hand. The temptation to get going is very strong. Caution! There is more to success than knowing the right answers. You must know how to identify your papers and understand variations in the type of short-answer question used in this particular examination. Follow these suggestions for maximum results from your efforts:

1) Cooperate with the monitor

The test administrator has a duty to create a situation in which you can be as much at ease as possible. He will give instructions, tell you when to begin, check to see that you are marking your answer sheet correctly, and so on. He is not there to guard you, although he will see that your competitors do not take unfair advantage. He wants to help you do your best.

2) Listen to all instructions

Don't jump the gun! Wait until you understand all directions. In most civil service tests you get more time than you need to answer the questions. So don't be in a hurry. Read each word of instructions until you clearly understand the meaning. Study the examples, listen to all announcements and follow directions. Ask questions if you do not understand what to do.

3) Identify your papers

Civil service exams are usually identified by number only. You will be assigned a number; you must not put your name on your test papers. Be sure to copy your number correctly. Since more than one exam may be given, copy your exact examination title.

4) Plan your time

Unless you are told that a test is a "speed" or "rate of work" test, speed itself is usually not important. Time enough to answer all the questions will be provided, but this does not mean that you have all day. An overall time limit has been set. Divide the total time (in minutes) by the number of questions to determine the approximate time you have for each question.

5) Do not linger over difficult questions

If you come across a difficult question, mark it with a paper clip (useful to have along) and come back to it when you have been through the booklet. One caution if you do this – be sure to skip a number on your answer sheet as well. Check often to be sure that you have not lost your place and that you are marking in the row numbered the same as the question you are answering.

6) Read the questions

Be sure you know what the question asks! Many capable people are unsuccessful because they failed to *read* the questions correctly.

7) Answer all questions

Unless you have been instructed that a penalty will be deducted for incorrect answers, it is better to guess than to omit a question.

8) Speed tests

It is often better NOT to guess on speed tests. It has been found that on timed tests people are tempted to spend the last few seconds before time is called in marking answers at random – without even reading them – in the hope of picking up a few extra points. To discourage this practice, the instructions may warn you that your score will be "corrected" for guessing. That is, a penalty will be applied. The incorrect answers will be deducted from the correct ones, or some other penalty formula will be used.

9) Review your answers

If you finish before time is called, go back to the questions you guessed or omitted to give them further thought. Review other answers if you have time.

10) Return your test materials

If you are ready to leave before others have finished or time is called, take ALL your materials to the monitor and leave quietly. Never take any test material with you. The monitor can discover whose papers are not complete, and taking a test booklet may be grounds for disqualification.

VIII. EXAMINATION TECHNIQUES

1) Read the general instructions carefully. These are usually printed on the first page of the exam booklet. As a rule, these instructions refer to the timing of the examination; the fact that you should not start work until the signal and must stop work at a signal, etc. If there are any *special* instructions, such as a choice of questions to be answered, make sure that you note this instruction carefully.

2) When you are ready to start work on the examination, that is as soon as the signal has been given, read the instructions to each question booklet, underline any key words or phrases, such as *least, best, outline, describe* and the like. In this way you will tend to answer as requested rather than discover on reviewing your paper that you *listed without describing*, that you selected the *worst* choice rather than the *best* choice, etc.

3) If the examination is of the objective or multiple-choice type – that is, each question will also give a series of possible answers: A, B, C or D, and you are called upon to select the best answer and write the letter next to that answer on your answer paper – it is advisable to start answering each question in turn. There may be anywhere from 50 to 100 such questions in the three or four hours allotted and you can see how much time would be taken if you read through all the questions before beginning to answer any. Furthermore, if you come across a question or group of questions which you know would be difficult to answer, it would undoubtedly affect your handling of all the other questions.

4) If the examination is of the essay type and contains but a few questions, it is a moot point as to whether you should read all the questions before starting to answer any one. Of course, if you are given a choice – say five out of seven and the like – then it is essential to read all the questions so you can eliminate the two that are most difficult. If, however, you are asked to answer all the questions, there may be danger in trying to answer the easiest one first because you may find that you will spend too much time on it. The best technique is to answer the first question, then proceed to the second, etc.

5) Time your answers. Before the exam begins, write down the time it started, then add the time allowed for the examination and write down the time it must be completed, then divide the time available somewhat as follows:
   - If 3-1/2 hours are allowed, that would be 210 minutes. If you have 80 objective-type questions, that would be an average of 2-1/2 minutes per question. Allow yourself no more than 2 minutes per question, or a total of 160 minutes, which will permit about 50 minutes to review.
   - If for the time allotment of 210 minutes there are 7 essay questions to answer, that would average about 30 minutes a question. Give yourself only 25 minutes per question so that you have about 35 minutes to review.

6) The most important instruction is to *read each question* and make sure you know what is wanted. The second most important instruction is to *time yourself properly* so that you answer every question. The third most important instruction is to *answer every question*. Guess if you have to but include something for each question. Remember that you will receive no credit for a blank and will probably receive some credit if you write something in answer to an essay question. If you guess a letter – say "B" for a multiple-choice question – you may have guessed right. If you leave a blank as an answer to a multiple-choice question, the examiners may respect your feelings but it will not add a point to your score. Some exams may penalize you for wrong answers, so in such cases *only*, you may not want to guess unless you have some basis for your answer.

7) Suggestions
   a. Objective-type questions
      1. Examine the question booklet for proper sequence of pages and questions
      2. Read all instructions carefully
      3. Skip any question which seems too difficult; return to it after all other questions have been answered
      4. Apportion your time properly; do not spend too much time on any single question or group of questions

5. Note and underline key words – *all, most, fewest, least, best, worst, same, opposite,* etc.
6. Pay particular attention to negatives
7. Note unusual option, e.g., unduly long, short, complex, different or similar in content to the body of the question
8. Observe the use of "hedging" words – *probably, may, most likely,* etc.
9. Make sure that your answer is put next to the same number as the question
10. Do not second-guess unless you have good reason to believe the second answer is definitely more correct
11. Cross out original answer if you decide another answer is more accurate; do not erase until you are ready to hand your paper in
12. Answer all questions; guess unless instructed otherwise
13. Leave time for review

b. Essay questions
1. Read each question carefully
2. Determine exactly what is wanted. Underline key words or phrases.
3. Decide on outline or paragraph answer
4. Include many different points and elements unless asked to develop any one or two points or elements
5. Show impartiality by giving pros and cons unless directed to select one side only
6. Make and write down any assumptions you find necessary to answer the questions
7. Watch your English, grammar, punctuation and choice of words
8. Time your answers; don't crowd material

8) Answering the essay question

Most essay questions can be answered by framing the specific response around several key words or ideas. Here are a few such key words or ideas:

M's: manpower, materials, methods, money, management
P's: purpose, program, policy, plan, procedure, practice, problems, pitfalls, personnel, public relations

a. Six basic steps in handling problems:
1. Preliminary plan and background development
2. Collect information, data and facts
3. Analyze and interpret information, data and facts
4. Analyze and develop solutions as well as make recommendations
5. Prepare report and sell recommendations
6. Install recommendations and follow up effectiveness

b. Pitfalls to avoid
1. *Taking things for granted* – A statement of the situation does not necessarily imply that each of the elements is necessarily true; for example, a complaint may be invalid and biased so that all that can be taken for granted is that a complaint has been registered

2. *Considering only one side of a situation* – Wherever possible, indicate several alternatives and then point out the reasons you selected the best one
3. *Failing to indicate follow up* – Whenever your answer indicates action on your part, make certain that you will take proper follow-up action to see how successful your recommendations, procedures or actions turn out to be
4. *Taking too long in answering any single question* – Remember to time your answers properly

IX. AFTER THE TEST

Scoring procedures differ in detail among civil service jurisdictions although the general principles are the same. Whether the papers are hand-scored or graded by machine we have described, they are nearly always graded by number. That is, the person who marks the paper knows only the number – never the name – of the applicant. Not until all the papers have been graded will they be matched with names. If other tests, such as training and experience or oral interview ratings have been given, scores will be combined. Different parts of the examination usually have different weights. For example, the written test might count 60 percent of the final grade, and a rating of training and experience 40 percent. In many jurisdictions, veterans will have a certain number of points added to their grades.

After the final grade has been determined, the names are placed in grade order and an eligible list is established. There are various methods for resolving ties between those who get the same final grade – probably the most common is to place first the name of the person whose application was received first. Job offers are made from the eligible list in the order the names appear on it. You will be notified of your grade and your rank as soon as all these computations have been made. This will be done as rapidly as possible.

People who are found to meet the requirements in the announcement are called "eligibles." Their names are put on a list of eligible candidates. An eligible's chances of getting a job depend on how high he stands on this list and how fast agencies are filling jobs from the list.

When a job is to be filled from a list of eligibles, the agency asks for the names of people on the list of eligibles for that job. When the civil service commission receives this request, it sends to the agency the names of the three people highest on this list. Or, if the job to be filled has specialized requirements, the office sends the agency the names of the top three persons who meet these requirements from the general list.

The appointing officer makes a choice from among the three people whose names were sent to him. If the selected person accepts the appointment, the names of the others are put back on the list to be considered for future openings.

That is the rule in hiring from all kinds of eligible lists, whether they are for typist, carpenter, chemist, or something else. For every vacancy, the appointing officer has his choice of any one of the top three eligibles on the list. This explains why the person whose name is on top of the list sometimes does not get an appointment when some of the persons lower on the list do. If the appointing officer chooses the second or third eligible, the No. 1 eligible does not get a job at once, but stays on the list until he is appointed or the list is terminated.

X. HOW TO PASS THE INTERVIEW TEST

The examination for which you applied requires an oral interview test. You have already taken the written test and you are now being called for the interview test – the final part of the formal examination.

You may think that it is not possible to prepare for an interview test and that there are no procedures to follow during an interview. Our purpose is to point out some things you can do in advance that will help you and some good rules to follow and pitfalls to avoid while you are being interviewed.

What is an interview supposed to test?

The written examination is designed to test the technical knowledge and competence of the candidate; the oral is designed to evaluate intangible qualities, not readily measured otherwise, and to establish a list showing the relative fitness of each candidate – as measured against his competitors – for the position sought. Scoring is not on the basis of "right" and "wrong," but on a sliding scale of values ranging from "not passable" to "outstanding." As a matter of fact, it is possible to achieve a relatively low score without a single "incorrect" answer because of evident weakness in the qualities being measured.

Occasionally, an examination may consist entirely of an oral test – either an individual or a group oral. In such cases, information is sought concerning the technical knowledges and abilities of the candidate, since there has been no written examination for this purpose. More commonly, however, an oral test is used to supplement a written examination.

Who conducts interviews?

The composition of oral boards varies among different jurisdictions. In nearly all, a representative of the personnel department serves as chairman. One of the members of the board may be a representative of the department in which the candidate would work. In some cases, "outside experts" are used, and, frequently, a businessman or some other representative of the general public is asked to serve. Labor and management or other special groups may be represented. The aim is to secure the services of experts in the appropriate field.

However the board is composed, it is a good idea (and not at all improper or unethical) to ascertain in advance of the interview who the members are and what groups they represent. When you are introduced to them, you will have some idea of their backgrounds and interests, and at least you will not stutter and stammer over their names.

What should be done before the interview?

While knowledge about the board members is useful and takes some of the surprise element out of the interview, there is other preparation which is more substantive. It *is* possible to prepare for an oral interview – in several ways:

1) Keep a copy of your application and review it carefully before the interview

This may be the only document before the oral board, and the starting point of the interview. Know what education and experience you have listed there, and the sequence and dates of all of it. Sometimes the board will ask you to review the highlights of your experience for them; you should not have to hem and haw doing it.

2) Study the class specification and the examination announcement

Usually, the oral board has one or both of these to guide them. The qualities, characteristics or knowledges required by the position sought are stated in these documents. They offer valuable clues as to the nature of the oral interview. For example, if the job involves supervisory responsibilities, the announcement will usually indicate that knowledge of modern supervisory methods and the qualifications of the candidate as a supervisor will be tested. If so, you can expect such questions, frequently in the form of a hypothetical situation which you are expected to solve. NEVER go into an oral without knowledge of the duties and responsibilities of the job you seek.

3) Think through each qualification required

Try to visualize the kind of questions you would ask if you were a board member. How well could you answer them? Try especially to appraise your own knowledge and background in each area, *measured against the job sought*, and identify any areas in which you are weak. Be critical and realistic – do not flatter yourself.

4) Do some general reading in areas in which you feel you may be weak

For example, if the job involves supervision and your past experience has NOT, some general reading in supervisory methods and practices, particularly in the field of human relations, might be useful. Do NOT study agency procedures or detailed manuals. The oral board will be testing your understanding and capacity, not your memory.

5) Get a good night's sleep and watch your general health and mental attitude

You will want a clear head at the interview. Take care of a cold or any other minor ailment, and of course, no hangovers.

What should be done on the day of the interview?

Now comes the day of the interview itself. Give yourself plenty of time to get there. Plan to arrive somewhat ahead of the scheduled time, particularly if your appointment is in the fore part of the day. If a previous candidate fails to appear, the board might be ready for you a bit early. By early afternoon an oral board is almost invariably behind schedule if there are many candidates, and you may have to wait. Take along a book or magazine to read, or your application to review, but leave any extraneous material in the waiting room when you go in for your interview. In any event, relax and compose yourself.

The matter of dress is important. The board is forming impressions about you – from your experience, your manners, your attitude, and your appearance. Give your personal appearance careful attention. Dress your best, but not your flashiest. Choose conservative, appropriate clothing, and be sure it is immaculate. This is a business interview, and your appearance should indicate that you regard it as such. Besides, being well groomed and properly dressed will help boost your confidence.

Sooner or later, someone will call your name and escort you into the interview room. *This is it.* From here on you are on your own. It is too late for any more preparation. But remember, you asked for this opportunity to prove your fitness, and you are here because your request was granted.

What happens when you go in?

The usual sequence of events will be as follows: The clerk (who is often the board stenographer) will introduce you to the chairman of the oral board, who will introduce you to the other members of the board. Acknowledge the introductions before you sit down. Do not be surprised if you find a microphone facing you or a stenotypist sitting by. Oral interviews are usually recorded in the event of an appeal or other review.

Usually the chairman of the board will open the interview by reviewing the highlights of your education and work experience from your application – primarily for the benefit of the other members of the board, as well as to get the material into the record. Do not interrupt or comment unless there is an error or significant misinterpretation; if that is the case, do not hesitate. But do not quibble about insignificant matters. Also, he will usually ask you some question about your education, experience or your present job – partly to get you to start talking and to establish the interviewing "rapport." He may start the actual questioning, or turn it over to one of the other members. Frequently, each member undertakes the questioning on a particular area, one in which he is perhaps most competent, so you can expect each member to participate in the examination. Because time is limited, you may also expect some rather abrupt switches in the direction the questioning takes, so do not be upset by it. Normally, a board member will not pursue a single line of questioning unless he discovers a particular strength or weakness.

After each member has participated, the chairman will usually ask whether any member has any further questions, then will ask you if you have anything you wish to add. Unless you are expecting this question, it may floor you. Worse, it may start you off on an extended, extemporaneous speech. The board is not usually seeking more information. The question is principally to offer you a last opportunity to present further qualifications or to indicate that you have nothing to add. So, if you feel that a significant qualification or characteristic has been overlooked, it is proper to point it out in a sentence or so. Do not compliment the board on the thoroughness of their examination – they have been sketchy, and you know it. If you wish, merely say, "No thank you, I have nothing further to add." This is a point where you can "talk yourself out" of a good impression or fail to present an important bit of information. Remember, *you close the interview yourself.*

The chairman will then say, "That is all, Mr. ______, thank you." Do not be startled; the interview is over, and quicker than you think. Thank him, gather your belongings and take your leave. Save your sigh of relief for the other side of the door.

How to put your best foot forward

Throughout this entire process, you may feel that the board individually and collectively is trying to pierce your defenses, seek out your hidden weaknesses and embarrass and confuse you. Actually, this is not true. They are obliged to make an appraisal of your qualifications for the job you are seeking, and they want to see you in your best light. Remember, they must interview all candidates and a non-cooperative candidate may become a failure in spite of their best efforts to bring out his qualifications. Here are 15 suggestions that will help you:

1) Be natural – Keep your attitude confident, not cocky

If you are not confident that you can do the job, do not expect the board to be. Do not apologize for your weaknesses, try to bring out your strong points. The board is interested in a positive, not negative, presentation. Cockiness will antagonize any board member and make him wonder if you are covering up a weakness by a false show of strength.

2) Get comfortable, but don't lounge or sprawl

Sit erectly but not stiffly. A careless posture may lead the board to conclude that you are careless in other things, or at least that you are not impressed by the importance of the occasion. Either conclusion is natural, even if incorrect. Do not fuss with your clothing, a pencil or an ashtray. Your hands may occasionally be useful to emphasize a point; do not let them become a point of distraction.

3) Do not wisecrack or make small talk

This is a serious situation, and your attitude should show that you consider it as such. Further, the time of the board is limited – they do not want to waste it, and neither should you.

4) Do not exaggerate your experience or abilities

In the first place, from information in the application or other interviews and sources, the board may know more about you than you think. Secondly, you probably will not get away with it. An experienced board is rather adept at spotting such a situation, so do not take the chance.

5) If you know a board member, do not make a point of it, yet do not hide it

Certainly you are not fooling him, and probably not the other members of the board. Do not try to take advantage of your acquaintanceship – it will probably do you little good.

6) Do not dominate the interview

Let the board do that. They will give you the clues – do not assume that you have to do all the talking. Realize that the board has a number of questions to ask you, and do not try to take up all the interview time by showing off your extensive knowledge of the answer to the first one.

7) Be attentive

You only have 20 minutes or so, and you should keep your attention at its sharpest throughout. When a member is addressing a problem or question to you, give him your undivided attention. Address your reply principally to him, but do not exclude the other board members.

8) Do not interrupt

A board member may be stating a problem for you to analyze. He will ask you a question when the time comes. Let him state the problem, and wait for the question.

9) Make sure you understand the question

Do not try to answer until you are sure what the question is. If it is not clear, restate it in your own words or ask the board member to clarify it for you. However, do not haggle about minor elements.

10) Reply promptly but not hastily

A common entry on oral board rating sheets is "candidate responded readily," or "candidate hesitated in replies." Respond as promptly and quickly as you can, but do not jump to a hasty, ill-considered answer.

11) Do not be peremptory in your answers

A brief answer is proper – but do not fire your answer back. That is a losing game from your point of view. The board member can probably ask questions much faster than you can answer them.

12) Do not try to create the answer you think the board member wants

He is interested in what kind of mind you have and how it works – not in playing games. Furthermore, he can usually spot this practice and will actually grade you down on it.

13) Do not switch sides in your reply merely to agree with a board member

Frequently, a member will take a contrary position merely to draw you out and to see if you are willing and able to defend your point of view. Do not start a debate, yet do not surrender a good position. If a position is worth taking, it is worth defending.

14) Do not be afraid to admit an error in judgment if you are shown to be wrong

The board knows that you are forced to reply without any opportunity for careful consideration. Your answer may be demonstrably wrong. If so, admit it and get on with the interview.

15) Do not dwell at length on your present job

The opening question may relate to your present assignment. Answer the question but do not go into an extended discussion. You are being examined for a *new* job, not your present one. As a matter of fact, try to phrase ALL your answers in terms of the job for which you are being examined.

Basis of Rating

Probably you will forget most of these "do's" and "don'ts" when you walk into the oral interview room. Even remembering them all will not ensure you a passing grade. Perhaps you did not have the qualifications in the first place. But remembering them will help you to put your best foot forward, without treading on the toes of the board members.

Rumor and popular opinion to the contrary notwithstanding, an oral board wants you to make the best appearance possible. They know you are under pressure – but they also want to see how you respond to it as a guide to what your reaction would be under the pressures of the job you seek. They will be influenced by the degree of poise you display, the personal traits you show and the manner in which you respond.

ABOUT THIS BOOK

This book contains tests divided into Examination Sections. Go through each test, answering every question in the margin. We have also attached a sample answer sheet at the back of the book that can be removed and used. At the end of each test look at the answer key and check your answers. On the ones you got wrong, look at the right answer choice and learn. Do not fill in the answers first. Do not memorize the questions and answers, but understand the answer and principles involved. On your test, the questions will likely be different from the samples. Questions are changed and new ones added. If you understand these past questions you should have success with any changes that arise. Tests may consist of several types of questions. We have additional books on each subject should more study be advisable or necessary for you. Finally, the more you study, the better prepared you will be. This book is intended to be the last thing you study before you walk into the examination room. Prior study of relevant texts is also recommended. NLC publishes some of these in our Fundamental Series. Knowledge and good sense are important factors in passing your exam. Good luck also helps. So now study this Passbook, absorb the material contained within and take that knowledge into the examination. Then do your best to pass that exam.

EXAMINATION SECTION

EXAMINATION SECTION
TEST 1

DIRECTIONS: Each question or incomplete statement is followed by several suggested answers or completions. Select the one that BEST answers the question or completes the statement. *PRINT THE LETTER OF THE CORRECT ANSWER IN THE SPACE AT THE RIGHT.*

1. Electronic library catalogs and periodical indexes differ from Web search engines in each of the following ways, EXCEPT that 1.____

   A. they put cataloged and indexed information through an editorial and publishing process
   B. they contain information that is cataloged and indexed by computers
   C. they can be searched by subject headings that are assigned by the indexer
   D. they include only information that has been selected by an indexer

2. The contents of a typical reference book are about ______ than the book's copyright date 2.____

   A. a year newer
   B. a year older
   C. two years older
   D. three years older

3. An acceptable use policy 3.____

   A. identifies access-blocking rules for filtering software
   B. explains First Amendment protections of freedom of speech in the library
   C. defines a curriculum for teaching users ethical and responsible computer use
   D. states the rules that govern computer, network and/or Internet use and the consequences of violations

4. Which of the following would NOT be a reason for a library staff's decision to develop an expert system? 4.____

   A. There is high staff turnover
   B. The problem is repetitive and expensive.
   C. Human experts are widely available.
   D. The problem is complex.

5. Elements of a library security plan, organized by a library security officer, typically include 5.____

   I. acceptable use policy/policies for online resources
   II. a survey of the library's collections
   III. standard operating procedures for dealing with theft
   IV. a review of the physical layout

   A. I and II
   B. I and III
   C. II, III and IV
   D. I, II, III and IV

6. Some library systems contain auxiliary systems programs that are initiated at startup and executed in the background to perform a task when needed-for example, checking incoming e-mail messages for addresses that cannot be found. These programs are known as 6.____

A. bots
B. crawlers
C. macros
D. daemons

7. The programming interface that enables a Web browser to be an interface to information services other than Web sites is a(n) 7.____

A. DOI
B. CGI
C. OPAC
D. GUI

8. HTML is most appropriate for delivering 8.____

A. business-to-business e-commerce
B. documents that originated from paper
C. dynamic data
D. static information

9. The semantic relationship between the words "bibliography" and "heading" is 9.____

A. generic
B. passive
C. associative
D. partitive

10. The Online Computer Library Center (OCLC) has established a set of input standards for entering bibliographic data into its online union catalog. Data generated by the cataloging system that cannot be altered by the cataloger is denoted 10.____

A. R
B. SS
C. X
D. O

11. What is the term for the form of the book as it is used today? 11.____

A. Incipit
B. Folio
C. Index
D. Codex

12. In indexing, a parenthetical qualifier is likely to be used for each of the following, EXCEPT to 12.____

A. distinguish homographs
B. give the context of an obscure word or phrase

C. indicate the intended use or meaning of the term in the indexing language
D. specify the academic discipline in which a subject is studied

13. The common measurement of the internal speed of a computer's processor is 13.____

A. megahertz (MHz)
B. bits per second (bps)
C. kilobytes per second (Kbps)
D. gigabytes (GB)

14. In ______ classification, each subject is developed to the point of indivisibility and a notation assigned for every subdivision 14.____

A. hierarchical
B. enumerative
C. synthetic
D. dichotomous

15. In Walford's *Guide to Reference Material,* religion is included in the same volume as 15.____

A. literature
B. social sciences
C. humanities
D. generalia

16. A group of librarians is meeting to determine the selection of electronic journals for a library's collection. One of the MOST likely disadvantages of including the existing electronic resources coordinator in this group is that she may not 16.____

A. have the expertise for many of the subjects
B. understand the issues or technology involved
C. have the motivation or commitment
D. be in a position to develop access interfaces

17. Which of the following is NOT a general review publication? 17.____

A. *Quill & Quire*
B. *CHOICE*
C. *Lambda Book Report*
D. *Booklist*

18. In networking, a cable is plugged into the ______ of each workstation on the network. 18.____

A. NIC
B. GUI
C. LAN
D. twisted pair

19. The PDF format is MOST typically used to transmit and store 19.____

A. static data
B. business-to-business e-commerce documents
C. visually rich content
D. database output

20. The turnover rate for media items in a library is usually measured in 20.____

A. hours
B. days
C. weeks
D. months

21. Which of the following is considered the basis of a "collection-centered" method for evaluating a library collection? 21.____

A. Percent of relative use (PRU)
B. In-house use studies
C. Comparison to recommended lists
D. Interlibrary loan statistics

22. In a MARC record for an electronic journal database, the ______ field contains the URL to the database, but not to any specific journal title. 22.____

A. 538
B. 710
C. 856
D. 949

23. Which of the following is a device used to scan and audibly read the information printed on a written page? 23.____

A. Screen-reading software
B. OCR software
C. Kurzweil Reader
D. TTY

24. A regional public library has ordered a packaged electronic journals database. The vendor asks for the "class" of the library's network. The systems librarian doesn't quite know how to answer this. She knows that the network accommodates 256 IP addresses. This network would be considered a class 24.____

A. A
B. B
C. C
D. D

25. From the library's point of view, a license agreement with an electronic journal publisher or packager should 25.____

I. indemnify the publisher against third-party claims
II. permit access to users who are off-site
III. provide for archiving of content if publication or service ceases
IV. define hardware, browser, and networking requirements

A. I and II
B. I and IV
C. II, III and IV
D. I, II, III and IV

KEY (CORRECT ANSWERS)

1. B
2. B
3. D
4. C
5. C
6. D
7. B
8. D
9. D
10. B
11. D
12. C
13. A
14. B
15. B
16. A
17. C
18. A
19. C
20. B
21. C
22. C
23. C
24. C
25. C

TEST 2

DIRECTIONS: Each question or incomplete statement is followed by several suggested answers or completions. Select the one that BEST answers the question or completes the statement. *PRINT THE LETTER OF THE CORRECT ANSWER IN THE SPACE AT THE RIGHT.*

1. The Digital Millenium Copyright Act of 1998 provides for each of the following, EXCEPT a(n) 1.___

   A. prohibition against circumventing technological measures used to protect copyrighted works
   B. limitation of liability for online service providers
   C. prohibition against altering information imbedded in digital works by copyright owners
   D. extension of the term of copyright to the author's lifetime plus 70 years

2. In the URL *http://www.sparkslib.org:80/index.html,* the *80* is a reference to a 2.___

   A. parameter
   B. file
   C. port
   D. protocol

3. Which of the following assistive technologies offers patrons who have difficulty hearing a means of communicating with library staff members? 3.___

   A. Touchpad or trackball controller
   B. TTY
   C. On-screen keyboard
   D. Screen-reading software

4. A user wants access to SEC filings of public companies on the Internet, including prospectuses, annual reports, 10K reports, and 10Q reports. The user should be directed to 4.___

   A. www.sec.gov
   B. the Thomas Register
   C. Lexis/Nexis
   D. EDGAR

5. Which of the following is a term for a software program that searches intelligently for information on the World Wide Web? 5.___

   A. Daemon
   B. Pathfinder
   C. Crawler
   D. Sorter

6. In a MARC record for an electronic journal that is separately cataloged, the complement to the 530 note is the linking entry field for a link to another format. This is the _______ field. 6.___

   A. 538 B. 776 C. 856 D. 949

7. What is the term for a complete revision of a Dewey Decimal class? 7.____

A. Reconstruction
B. Phoenix
C. Rebridgement
D. Overhaul

8. Which of the following network topologies tends to be faster and involve the least amount of cabling? 8.____

A. Ring
B. Matrix
C. Bus
D. Star

9. The method of choice for most libraries in authenticating access to electronic journals databases is 9.____

A. User ID
B. IP address
C. Password
D. User ID and password

10. Which of the following is one of S.R. Ranganathan's Five Laws of Library Science? 10.____

A. The pen is mightier than the sword.
B. Save the time of the reader.
C. Every reader knows the book he/she wants to read already; it's just a matter of finding it.
D. Information longs to be free.

11. The semantic relationship between the words "chapbook" and "pamphlet" is 11.____

A. hierarchic
B. locative
C. associative
D. synonymous

12. Which of the following is NOT a leading vendor of library management software? 12.____

A. Logos
B. Endeavor
C. Auto-Graphics
D. Sirsi

13. A systems librarian discovers old magnetic tapes in storage, which came from an obsolete computer system. The only way to read the data in the new library system is to write a special program. This method of bringing old data into new systems is referred to as data 13.____

A. copying
B. conversion
C. reformatting
D. migration

14. Which of the following is LEAST likely to be categorized as a social science? 14.__

A. History
B. Law
C. Journalism
D. Anthropology

15. What is the term for a classified display in a thesaurus of indexing terms that shows the complete hierarchy of descriptors, from the broadest to the most specific, usually by indention? 15.__

A. Tree structure
B. Indexing matrix
C. Dichotomous key
D. Cant

16. Which of the following storage media has the greatest storage capacity? 16.__

A. ZIP disk
B. CD-RW
C. CD-ROM
D. DVD-ROM

17. A ______ license with an electronic database publisher is a unilateral license who terms are accepted with the software package is opened. 17.__

A. shrink-wrap
B. force majeure
C. click-wrap
D. pay-per-view

18. One way to limit search results in Web search engines and directories is to use phrase searching, which involves 18.__

A. using Boolean terms such as AND or NOT
B. putting quotation marks around the search words
C. putting parentheses around the search words
D. putting an asterisk after the search words

19. In book sales, the largest discounts offered by publishers are typically ______ discounts. 19.__

A. trade
B. cash
C. library
D. convention

20. Reference software is NOT the most appropriate learning tool when users want to 20.__

A. investigate topics that may be beyond their reading capabilities
B. browse a number of topics
C. learn how to perform a specific task
D. ask a specific question

21. The holdings of all the libraries in a library system, in which libraries owning at least one copy of an item are identified by name and/or location symbol, are always accessible from the 21.____

A. union catalog
B. bibliographic database
C. OPAC
D. reference desk

22. An overview article on a particular topic is MOST likely to be found in a(n) 22.____

A. encyclopedia
B. index
C. gazetteer
D. dictionary

23. In the MARC record, the same digits are assigned across fields in the second and third character positions of the tag to indicate data of the same type. For example, tags reading "X51" contain information about 23.____

A. personal names
B. topical terms
C. bibliographic titles
D. geographic names

24. Generally, XML is NOT 24.____

A. capable of storing context as well as content
B. considered to be the optimal format for file compression and delivery
C. able to display dynamic information as a document
D. an excellent standard for business-to-business applications such as invoices and purchase orders

25. The USA Patriot Act provides that law enforcement agencies can compel libraries to 25.____

I. produce circulation records
II. provide Internet usage records
III. remain silent about the existence of any warrants served on the library
IV. reveal patron registration information

A. I and II
B. I, II and III
C. II and III
D. I, II, III and IV

KEY (CORRECT ANSWERS)

1. D
2. C
3. B
4. D
5. C
6. B
7. B
8. C
9. B
10. B
11. D
12. A
13. D
14. C
15. A
16. D
17. A
18. B
19. A
20. C
21. A
22. A
23. D
24. B
25. D

EXAMINATION SECTION
TEST 1

DIRECTIONS: Each question or incomplete statement is followed by several suggested answers or completions. Select the one that BEST answers the question or completes the statement. *PRINT THE LETTER OF THE CORRECT ANSWER IN THE SPACE AT THE RIGHT.*

1. A library is in the process of conducting an annual performance evaluation. Which of the following would be an output measure that might be used in this process? 1.____

   A. Staff expenditures
   B. User satisfaction survey results
   C. Ratio of computer workstations to daily average users
   D. Ratio of interlibrary loan lending to borrowing

2. The ______ record is a separate record attached to the bibliographic record for a serial title in which the receipt of individual issues or parts is entered on an ongoing basis. 2.____

   A. holdings
   B. check-in
   C. item
   D. periodical

3. Of the following, which research tool would be most appropriate for finding where an author uses specific words or phrases? 3.____

   A. Abstract
   B. Gazetteer
   C. Dictionary
   D. Concordance

4. In library cataloging, a separately published part of a bibliographic resource, usually representing a subject category within the whole and indicated by a topical heading or an alphanumeric heading, is a(n) 4.____

   A. class
   B. scope
   C. notch
   D. section

5. The main advantage to paying an electronic journal publisher on a per-article basis, rather than subscribing to a package or database, is that 5.____

   A. hardware, browser, and networking requirements are simpler
   B. the library pays only for what it uses
   C. costs are shifted entirely to the user
   D. costs are more predictable over time

6. The Dublin Core Metadata Initiative, an international effort to develop standard mechanisms for searching online resources, has named 15 core metadata elements to be used to direct searches. Which of the following is NOT one of these? 6.____

   A. Editor B. Rights C. Date D. Format

7. "Converting" electronic records means that 7.___

A. there is a change to the underlying bit stream, but there is no change in the representation or intellectual content of the records
B. they are moved from a proprietary legacy system that lacks software functionality to an open system
C. they have been transferred from old storage media to new storage media with the same format specifications and without any loss in structure, content, or context
D. they have been exported or imported from one software environment to another without the loss of structure, content, or context even though the underlying bit stream has likely been altered

8. The 3XX fields in the MARC system contain 8.___

A. physical descriptions
B. main entries
C. subject added entries
D. titles, editions, and imprints

9. In Internet user, instead of being taken to a desired Web page, instead is taken to a page that says *Error Message 404.* What has happened? 9.___

A. Either the server is busy, or the site has moved.
B. Special permission is needed to access the site.
C. The file has been moved or deleted, or the URL in incorrect.
D. The syntax used in the URL is incorrect.

10. An anthology is compiled by 6 authors. According to the MLA format, how many of the author's names should be included in a citation? 10.___

A. 0
B. 1
C. 2
D. 6

11. Which of the following is NOT an advantage of using HTML as a format for file preservation? 11.___

A. Extensive authoring tools
B. Improving tools for conversion-to-HTML
C. Good standard for delivering simple text
D. Can be viewed in any browser

12. In the MARC record, the same digits are assigned across fields in the second and third character positions of the tag to indicate data of the same type. For example, tags reading "X10" contain information about 12.___

A. topical terms
B. bibliographic titles
C. uniform titles
D. corporate names

13. A librarian wants to subscribe to an e-mail newsletter that contains annotations of information technology articles and other items written by a team of librarians and library staff. She is wary, however, of having her inbox clogged with unread material that arrives too frequently for her to read it all, and would prefer to have the newsletter arrive monthly. The librarian should subscribe to 13.____

A. *Free Pint*
B. *Edupage*
C. *Current Cites*
D. *NewsScan*

14. A journal's "impact factor," a measure of its relative importance, is most often defined as the ______ in a given year. 14.____

A. number of electronic queries coming from a library database
B. frequency of citations to its articles
C. number of top-rated professionals or scholars who publish in it
D. times the full-text is displayed on a library terminal

15. ______ is the online database designed and maintained since 1995 by the Library of Congress to make legislative information accessible to the public 15.____

A. CQ
B. NARA
C. THOMAS
D. FindLaw

16. The main software protocol that manages data on the Internet is 16.____

A. TCP/IP
B. HTTP
C. HTML
D. FTP

17. Which of the following is a repeatable MARC field? 17.____

A. 100
B. 246
C. 250
D. 260

18. A user seeking articles about transportation should be directed to Wilson's ______ Index. 18.____

A. Social Sciences
B. Business Periodicals
C. Applied Science and Technology
D. General Science

19. In the library literature, materials designated with the collecting level "4" in relation to a given subject are considered 19.____

A. "out of scope"
B. sources of basic information
C. comprehensive and authoritative
D. useful for the support of research in the given subject

20. In Web addresses, the hashmark is used to 20.____

A. create a link to another location in the same document
B. identify a port
C. create a link to another Web page
D. differentiate numerical characters

21. The content of a Web site is difficult to navigate, and users tend to get confused when trying to find information. The resource assessment guideline that needs to be addressed is 21.____

A. Documentation and Credibility
B. Ease of Use, Navigation, and Accessibility
C. User Interface and Design
D. Content

22. To extend the accessibility of any material that can be displayed at a library workstation to those with extremely poor vision, ______ can be used. 22.____

A. screen reading software
B. screen magnifying software
C. TTY
D. an on-screen keyboard

23. The software application needed to read files in Portable Document Format (PDF) is known as 23.____

A. Acrobat Reader
B. Real Page
C. Pagemaker
D. techexplorer Hypermedia Browser

24. In data that is prepared in the cataloging-in-publication (CIP) format and distributed in MARC format prior to a work's publication, the element that typically appears after the notes about bibliographical references or previous editions is the 24.____

A. Library of Congress classification number
B. statement of responsibility
C. ISBN
D. Dewey Decimal classification number

25. The reason for the slow pace of initial acceptance of WORM (write once, read many) technology in library archiving is that 25.____

A. the amount of storage available on the disks is too variable to offer predictable capacity
B. disks are not standardized and can be read only on the type of drive used to write them
C. the data cannot be altered once it is stored
D. the longevity of the disk media is still unknown

KEY (CORRECT ANSWERS)

1. D	6. A	11. A	16. A	21. B
2. B	7. D	12. D	17. B	22. A
3. D	8. A	13. C	18. C	23. A
4. D	9. C	14. B	19. D	24. C
5. B	10. B	15. C	20. A	25. B

TEST 2

DIRECTIONS: Each question or incomplete statement is followed by several suggested answers or completions. Select the one that BEST answers the question or completes the statement. *PRINT THE LETTER OF THE CORRECT ANSWER IN THE SPACE AT THE RIGHT.*

1. Which of the following is NOT an aggregator service? 1.____

   A. ScienceDirect
   B. JSTOR
   C. Britannica
   D. Blackwell's Electronic Journal Navigator

2. Technical service librarians are usually concerned with any of the following, EXCEPT 2.____

   A. repairing damaged materials
   B. checking in journals
   C. cataloging books
   D. checking books out

3. Materials that are published electronically are identified by their 3.____

   A. EAD
   B. DOI
   C. XLS
   D. ISBN

4. Which of the following is an example of "mobile code" that allows a Web designer to incorporate computer programs, such as Flash pages, into Web page content? 4.____

   A. Packet
   B. Worm
   C. Warez
   D. Applet

5. The abbreviation "NOP" on a publisher's invoice usually means the requested item 5.____

   A. is on back order
   B. is not in print
   C. the requested item is not published by the vendor
   D. has not yet been published, but will be in the future

6. A well-designed online catalog or bibliographic database allows the user to employ limiting parameters to restrict the retrieval or entries including the terms included in the search statement. Which of the following is NOT a common example of these "limiters?" 6.____

   A. Spelling
   B. Publication date
   C. Full-text
   D. Locally held

7. Which of the following is LEAST likely to be a guideline followed in setting up an electronic reserves (ER) system in an academic library? 7.____

A. Restrict access to authorized users off-site, but maintain open access on-site.
B. Limit offsite access by course and/or instructor name.
C. Remove or suppress access at the end of every session.
D. Post copyright warning notices.

8. Subsystems of the Internet include 8.____

I. the World Wide Web
II. Newsgroups
III. Telnet
IV. e-mail

A. I only
B. I, II and III
C. II and III
D. I, II, III and IV

9. Binary scanning at 300 dots per inch (dpi) is usually considered adequate for 9.____

A. halftones
B. illustrated text
C. typed or laser-printed archival documents
D. published text/line art

10. The systems librarian's responsibilities typically include each of the following, EXCEPT 10.____

A. development and maintenance of hardware and software
B. Webmaster
C. training staff in the use of library systems
D. interlibrary loan processing

11. A records survey is LEAST likely to be used for the purpose of determining the _______ of archival records. 11.____

A. quality
B. content
C. physical quantities
D. provenance

12. In the searching of an electronic database, which of the following might cause a "false drop?" 12.____

A. The omission of older information
B. Too-frequent updating of the database
C. A word with more than one meaning
D. Restrictions on database use

13. A group of librarians is meeting to determine the selection of electronic journals for a library's collection. One of the MOST likely disadvantages of including the reference librarian in this group is that he may not 13.___

A. have close contact with users
B. be accustomed to the collaborative approach
C. be able to relinquish his primary responsibilities for long enough periods of time
D. have experience selecting and supporting electronic resources

14. Most Internet service providers (ISPs) are built on ______ lines. 14.___

A. 56 Kbps
B. ISDN
C. T-1
D. T-3

15. Which of the following is a term used to denote a hard copy enlargement of an image on microform? 15.___

A. Blowback
B. Macroform
C. Aperture card
D. Blowup

16. On the Web or in an online bibliography, well-designed search software is capable of 16.___

I. searching more than one database simultaneously
II. removing duplicate record s from results when searching multiple databases
III. viewing search terms highlighted in results
IV. printing, e-mailing, and downloading results in various formats

A. I only
B. I and III
C. III only
D. I, II, III and IV

17. Subject heading systems do NOT 17.___

A. assist searchers in understanding how a specific subject fits into a larger structure of knowledge
B. divide knowledge over 30 broad categories
C. describe what a book or article is about
D. allow people to search by subject area

18. In order to ensure the integrity of digital archive, the origin and chain of custody of a particular file or record most be preserved. This feature of information integrity is known as 18.___

A. content
B. provenance
C. content
D. fixity

19. The creation of a Web page could involve 19.____

I. using a dedicated Web authoring software program
II. converting a word-processed document to HTML
III. converting a magazine article, with images, to PDF
IV. use the Web authoring capability of a portal

A. I and II
B. I, II and IV
C. II and III
D. II, III and IV

20. What is the general term for an indexable concept that is assigned to add depth to subject indexing, and that is not listed in the thesaurus of indexing terms because it either represents a proper name or a concept that is not yet authorized for inclusion in the bibliographic database? 20.____

A. assigner
B. identifier
C. descriptor
D. ideogram

21. The *World of Learning* is an example of a(n) 21.____

A. concordance
B. encyclopedia
C. abstract
D. directory

22. In the United States, the professional association for academic libraries and librarians is the 22.____

A. Association of College and Research Libraries (ACRL)
B. Association of Specialized and Cooperative Library Agencies (ASCLA)
C. American Library Association (ALA)
D. National Commission on Libraries and Information Science (NCLIS)

23. The module of the library automation system that is used by the public for interacting with the system is the 23.____

A. circulation module
B. serials module
C. OPAC
D. cataloging module

24. Which of the following is a synthetic classification system? 24.____

A. Dewey Decimal
B. Colon classification
C. Library of Congress classification
D. Sears List

25. Library issues concerning the USA Patriot Act include 25.___
    I. civil liberties related to privacy and confidentiality
    II. denial of access to information
    III. fair use
    IV. copyright law

A. I and II
B. II only
C. II, III and IV
D. I, II, III and IV

KEY (CORRECT ANSWERS)

1.	C	6.	A	11.	A	16.	D	21.	D
2.	D	7.	A	12.	C	17.	B	22.	A
3.	B	8.	D	13.	C	18.	B	23.	C
4.	D	9.	C	14.	C	19.	B	24.	B
5.	C	10.	D	15.	A	20.	B	25.	A

EXAMINATION SECTION

TEST 1

DIRECTIONS: Each question or incomplete statement is followed by several suggested answers or completions. Select the one that BEST answers the question or completes the statement. *PRINT THE LETTER OF THE CORRECT ANSWER IN THE SPACE AT THE RIGHT.*

1. When conducting a needs assessment for the purpose of education planning, an agency's FIRST step is to identify or provide 1.____
   A. a profile of population characteristics
   B. barriers to participation
   C. existing resources
   D. profiles of competing resources

2. Research has demonstrated that of the following, the MOST effective medium for communicating with external publics is(are) 2.____
   A. video news releases B. television
   C. radio D. newspapers

3. Basic ideas behind the effort to influence the attitudes and behaviors of a constituency include each of the following EXCEPT the idea that 3.____
   A. words, rather than actions or events, are most likely to motivate
   B. demands for action are a usual response
   C. self-interest usually figures heavily into public involvement
   D. the reliability of change programs is difficult to assess

4. An agency representative is trying to craft a pithy message to constituents in order to encourage the use of agency program resources. 4.____
   Choosing an audience for such messages is easiest when the message
   A. is project- or behavior-based B. is combined with other messages
   C. is abstract D. has a broad appeal

5. Of the following factors, the MOST important to the success of an agency's external education or communication programs is the 5.____
   A. amount of resources used to implement them
   B. public's prior experiences with the agency
   C. real value of the program to the public
   D. commitment of the internal audience

6. A representative for a state agency is being interviewed by a reporter from a local news network. The representative is being asked to defend a program that is extremely unpopular in certain parts of the municipality. 6.____
   When a constituency is known to be opposed to a position, the MOST useful communication strategy is to present

A. only the arguments that are consistent with constituents' views
B. only the agency's side of the issue
C. both sides of the argument as clearly as possible
D. both sides of the argument, omitting key information about the opposing position

7. The MOST significant barriers to effective agency community relations include 7.____
I. widespread distrust of communication strategies
II. the media's "watchdog" stance
III. public apathy
IV. statutory opposition

The CORRECT answer is:
A. I only B. I and II C. II and III D. III and IV

8. In conducting an education program, many agencies use workshops and seminars in a classroom setting. 8.____
Advantages of classroom-style teaching over other means of educating the public include each of the following, EXCEPT
A. enabling an instructor to verify learning through testing and interaction with the target audience
B. enabling hands-on practice and other participatory learning techniques
C. ability to reach an unlimited number of participants in a given length of time
D. ability to convey the latest, most up-to-date information

9. The _____ model of community relations is characterized by an attempt to persuade the public to adopt the agency's point of view. 9.____
A. two-way symmetric B. two-way asymmetric
C. public information D. press agency/publicity

10. Important elements of an internal situation analysis include the 10.____
I. list of agency opponents II. communication audit
III. updated organizational almanac IV. stakeholder analysis

The CORRECT answer is:
A. I and II B. I, II, and III C. II and III D. I, II, III and IV

11. Government agency information efforts typically involve each of the following objectives, EXCEPT to 11.____
A. implement changes in the policies of government agencies to align with public opinion
B. communicate the work of agencies
C. explain agency techniques in a way that invites input from citizens
D. provide citizen feedback to government administrators

12. Factors that are likely to influence the effectiveness of an educational campaign include the 12.____
I. level of homogeneity among intended participants
II. number and types of media used
III. receptivity of the intended participants
IV. level of specificity in the message or behavior to be taught

The CORRECT answer is:
A. I and II B. I, II, and III C. II and III D. I, II, III, and IV

13. An agency representative is writing instructional objectives that will later help to measure the effectiveness of an educational program. 13.____
Which of the following verbs, included in an objective, would be MOST helpful for the purpose of measuring effectiveness?
A. Know B. Identify C. Learn D. Comprehend

14. A state education agency wants to encourage participation in a program that has just received a boost through new federal legislation. The program is intended to include participants from a wide variety of socioeconomic and other demographic characteristics. The agency wants to launch a broad-based program that will inform virtually every interested party in the state about the program's new circumstances. 14.____
In attempting to deliver this message to such a wide-ranging constituency, the agency's BEST practice would be to
A. broadcast the same message through as many different media channels as possible
B. focus on one discrete segment of the public at a time
C. craft a message whose appeal is as broad as the public itself
D. let the program's achievements speak for themselves and rely on word-of-mouth

15. Advantages associated with using the World Wide Web as an educational tool include 15.____
I. an appeal to younger generations of the public
II. visually-oriented, interactive learning
III. learning that is not confined by space, time, or institutional association
IV. a variety of methods for verifying use and learning

The CORRECT answer is:
A. I only B. I and II C. I, II, and III D. I, II, II, and IV

16. In agencies involved in health care, community relations is a critical function because it 16.____
A. serves as an intermediary between the agency and consumers
B. generates a clear mission statement for agency goals and priorities
C. ensures patient privacy while satisfying the media's right to information
D. helps marketing professionals determine the wants and needs of agency constituents

17. After an extensive campaign to promote its newest program to constituents, an agency learns that most of the audience did not understand the intended message. 17.____
MOST likely, the agency has
A. chosen words that were intended to inform, rather than persuade
B. not accurately interpreted what the audience really needed to know
C. overestimated the ability of the audience to receive and process the message
D. compensated for noise that may have interrupted the message

18. The necessary elements that lead to conviction and motivation in the minds of participants in an educational or information program include each of the following, EXCEPT the _____ of the message. 18.____
A. acceptability
B. intensity
C. single-channel appeal
D. pervasiveness

19. Printed materials are often at the core of educational programs provided by public agencies. 19.____
The PRIMARY disadvantage associated with print is that it
A. does not enable comprehensive treatment of a topic
B. is generally unreliable in term of assessing results
C. is often the most expensive medium available
D. is constrained by time

20. Traditional thinking on public opinion holds that there is about _____ percent of the public who are pivotal to shifting the balance and momentum of opinion—they are concerned about an issue, but not fanatical, and interested enough to pay attention to a reasoned discussion. 20.____
A. 2
B. 10
C. 33
D. 51

21. One of the most useful guidelines for influencing attitude change among people is to 21.____
A. invite the target audience to come to you, rather than approaching them
B. use moral appeals as the primary approach
C. use concrete images to enable people to see the results of behaviors or indifference
D. offer tangible rewards to people for changes in behavior

22. An agency is attempting to evaluate the effectiveness of its educational program. For this purpose, it wants to observe several focus groups discussing the same program. 22.____
Which of the following would NOT be a guideline for the use of focus groups?
A. Focus groups should only include those who have participated in the program.
B. Be sure to accurately record the discussion.
C. The same questions should be asked at each focus group meeting.
D. It is often helpful to have a neutral, non-agency employee facilitate discussions.

23. Research consistently shows that _____ is the determinant most likely to make a newspaper editor run a news release. 23.____
    A. novelty B. prominence C. proximity D. conflict

24. Which of the following is NOT one of the major variables to take into account when considering a population-needs assessment? 24.____
    A. State of program development
    B. Resources available
    C. Demographics
    D. Community attitudes

25. The FIRST step in any communications audit is to 25.____
    A. develop a research instrument
    B. determine how the organization currently communicates
    C. hire a contractor
    D. determine which audience to assess

KEY (CORRECT ANSWERS)

1.	A	11.	A
2.	D	12.	D
3.	A	13.	B
4.	A	14.	B
5.	D	15.	C
6.	C	16.	A
7.	D	17.	B
8.	C	18.	C
9.	B	19.	B
10.	C	20.	B

21.	C
22.	A
23.	C
24.	C
25.	D

TEST 2

DIRECTIONS: Each question or incomplete statement is followed by several suggested answers or completions. Select the one that BEST answers the question or completes the statement. *PRINT THE LETTER OF THE CORRECT ANSWER IN THE SPACE AT THE RIGHT.*

1. A public relations practitioner at an agency has just composed a press release highlighting a program's recent accomplishments and success stories. 1.____
In pitching such releases to print outlets, the practitioner should
I. e-mail, mail, or send them by messenger
II. address them to "editor" or "news director"
III. have an assistant call all media contacts by telephone
IV. ask reporters or editors how they prefer to receive them

The CORRECT answer is:
A. I and II B. I and IV C. II, III, and IV D. III only

2. The "output goals" of an educational program are MOST likely to include 2.____
A. specified ratings of services by participants on a standardized scale
B. observable effects on a given community or clientele
C. the number of instructional hours provided
D. the number of participants served

3. An agency wants to evaluate satisfaction levels among program participants, and mails out questionnaires to everyone who has been enrolled in the last year. 3.___
The PRIMARY problem associated with this method of evaluative research is that it
A. poses a significant inconvenience for respondents
B. is inordinately expensive
C. does not allow for follow-up or clarification questions
D. usually involves a low response rate

4. A communications audit is an important tool for measuring 4.____
A. the depth of penetration of a particular message or program
B. the cost of the organization's information campaigns
C. how key audiences perceive an organization
D. the commitment of internal stakeholders

5. The "ABCs" of written learning objectives include each of the following, EXCEPT 5.____
A. Audience B. Behavior C. Conditions D. Delineation

6. When attempting to change the behaviors of constituents, it is important to keep in mind that 6.____
   I. most people are skeptical of communications that try to get them to change their behaviors
   II. in most cases, a person selects the media to which he exposes himself
   III. people tend to react defensively to messages or programs that rely on fear as a motivating factor
   IV. programs should aim for the broadest appeal possible in order to include as many participants as possible

   The CORRECT answer is:
   A. I and II B. I, II and III C. II and III D. I, II, III, and IV

7. The “laws” of public opinion include the idea that it is 7.____
   A. useful for anticipating emergencies
   B. not sensitive to important events
   C. basically determined by self-interest
   D. sustainable through persistent appeals

8. Which of the following types of evaluations is used to measure public attitudes before and after an information/educational program? 8.____
   A. Retrieval study B. Copy test
   C. Quota sampling D. Benchmark study

9. The PRIMARY source for internal communications is(are) usually 9.____
   A. flow charts B. meetings
   C. voice mail D. printed publications

10. An agency representative is putting together informational materials—brochures and a newsletter—outlining changes in one of the state’s biggest benefits programs. 10.____
   In assembling print materials as a medium for delivering information to the public, the representative should keep in mind each of the following trends:
   I. For various reasons, the reading capabilities of the public are in general decline
   II. Without tables and graphs to help illustrate the changes, it is unlikely that the message will be delivered effectively
   III. Professionals and career-oriented people are highly receptive to information written in the form of a journal article or empirical study
   IV. People tend to be put off by print materials that use itemized and bulleted (●) lists

   The CORRECT answer is:
   A. I and II B. I, II and III C. II and III D. I, II, III, and IV

11. Which of the following steps in a problem-oriented information campaign would typically be implemented FIRST? 11.____
    A. Deciding on tactics
    B. Determining a communications strategy
    C. Evaluating the problem's impact
    D. Developing an organizational strategy

12. A common pitfall in conducting an educational program is to 12.____
    A. aim it at the wrong target audience
    B. overfund it
    C. leave it in the hands of people who are in the business of education, rather than those with expertise in the business of the organization
    D. ignore the possibility that some other organization is meeting the same educational need for the target audience

13. The key factors that affect the credibility of an agency's educational program include 13.____
    A. organization
    B. scope
    C. sophistication
    D. penetration

14. Research on public opinion consistently demonstrates that it is 14.____
    A. easy to move people toward a strong opinion on anything, as long as they are approached directly through their emotions
    B. easier to move people away from an opinion they currently hold than to have them form an opinion about something they have not previously cared about
    C. easy to move people toward a strong opinion on anything, as long as the message appeals to their reason and intellect
    D. difficult to move people toward a strong opinion on anything, no matter what the approach

15. In conducting an education program, many agencies use meetings and conferences to educate an audience about the organization and its programs. Advantages associated with this approach include 15.____
    I. a captive audience that is known to be interested in the topic
    II. ample opportunities for verifying learning
    III. cost-efficient meeting space
    IV. the ability to provide information on a wider variety of subjects

    The CORRECT answer is:
    A. I and II
    B. I, III and IV
    C. II and III
    D. I, II, III and IV

16. An agency is attempting to evaluate the effectiveness of its educational programs. For this purpose, it wants to observe several focus groups discussing particular programs. 16.____
    For this purpose, a focus group should never number more than _____ participants.
    A. 5
    B. 10
    C. 15
    D. 20

17. A _____ speech is written so that several agency members can deliver it to different audiences with only minor variations. 17._____
   A. basic B. printed C. quota D. pattern

18. Which of the following statements about public opinion is generally considered to be FALSE? 18._____
   A. Opinion is primarily reactive rather than proactive.
   B. People have more opinions about goals than about the means by which to achieve them.
   C. Facts tend to shift opinion in the accepted direction when opinion is not solidly structured.
   D. Public opinion is based more on information than desire.

19. An agency is trying to promote its educational program. 19._____
   As a general rule, the agency should NOT assume that
   A. people will only participate if they perceive an individual benefit
   B. promotions need to be aimed at small, discrete groups
   C. if the program is good, the audience will find out about it
   D. a variety of methods, including advertising, special events, and direct mail, should be considered

20. In planning a successful educational program, probably the first and most important question for an agency to ask is: 20._____
   A. What will be the content of the program?
   B. Who will be served by the program?
   C. When is the best time to schedule the program?
   D. Why is the program necessary?

21. Media kits are LEAST likely to contain 21._____
   A. fact sheets B. memoranda
   C. photographs with captions D. news releases

22. The use of pamphlets and booklets as media for communication with the public often involves the disadvantage that 22._____
   A. the messages contained within them are frequently nonspecific
   B. it is difficult to measure their effectiveness in delivering the message
   C. there are few opportunities for people to refer to them
   D. color reproduction is poor

23. The MOST important prerequisite of a good educational program is an 23._____
   A. abundance of resources to implement it
   B. individual staff unit formed for the purpose of program delivery
   C. accurate needs assessment
   D. uneducated constituency

24. After an education program has been delivered, an agency conducts a program evaluation to determine whether its objectives have been met. General rules about how to conduct such an education program valuation include each of the following, EXCEPT that it 24.____
    A. must be done immediately after the program has been implemented
    B. should be simple and easy to use
    C. should be designed so that tabulation of responses can take place quickly and inexpensively
    D. should solicit mostly subjective, open-ended responses if the audience was large

25. Using electronic media such as television as means of educating the public is typically recommended ONLY for agencies that 25.____
    I. have a fairly simple message to begin with
    II. want to reach the masses, rather than a targeted audience
    III. have substantial financial resources
    IV. accept that they will not be able to measure the results of the campaign with much precision

    The CORRECT answer is:
    A. I and II B. I, II and III C. II and IV D. I, II, III and IV

KEY (CORRECT ANSWERS)

1. B
2. C
3. D
4. C
5. D

6. B
7. C
8. D
9. D
10. A

11. C
12. D
13. A
14. D
15. B

16. B
17. D
18. D
19. C
20. D

21. B
22. B
23. C
24. D
25. D

EXAMINATION SECTION

TEST 1

DIRECTIONS: Each question or incomplete statement is followed by several suggested answers or completions. Select the one that BEST answers the question or completes the statement. *PRINT THE LETTER OF THE CORRECT ANSWER IN THE SPACE AT THE RIGHT.*

1. In public agencies, communications should be based PRIMARILY on a 1.____
   A. two-way flow from the top down and from the bottom up, most of which should be given in writing to avoid ambiguity
   B. multi-direction flow among all levels and with outside persons
   C. rapid, internal one-way flow from the top down
   D. two-way flow of information, most of which should be given orally for purposes of clarity

2. In some organizations, changes in policy or procedures are often communicated by word of mouth from supervisors to employees with no prior discussion or exchange of viewpoints with employees. 2.____
   This procedure often produces employee dissatisfaction CHIEFLY because
   A. information is mostly unusable since a considerable amount of time is required to transmit information
   B. lower-level supervisors tend to be excessively concerned with minor details
   C. management has failed to seek employees' advice before making changes
   D. valuable staff time is lost between decision-making and the implementation of decisions

3. For good letter writing, you should try to visualize the person to whom you are writing, especially if you know him. 3.____
   Of the following rules, it is LEAST helpful in such visualization to think of
   A. the person's likes and dislikes, his concerns, and his needs
   B. what you would be likely to say if speaking in person
   C. what you would expect to be asked if speaking in person
   D. your official position in order to be certain that your words are proper

4. One approach to good informal letter writing is to make letters and conversational. 4.____
   All of the following practices will usually help to do this EXCEPT:
   A. If possible, use a style which is similar to the style used when speaking
   B. Substitute phrases for single words (e.g., *at the present time for now*)
   C. Use contractions of words (e.g., *you're* for *you are*)
   D. Use ordinary vocabulary when possible

5. All of the following rules will aid in producing clarity in report-writing EXCEPT: 5.____
   A. Give specific details or examples, if possible
   B. Keep related words close together in each sentence
   C. Present information in sequential order
   D. Put several thoughts or ideas in each paragraph

6. The one of the following statements about public relations which is MOST accurate is that 6.____
   A. in the long run, appearance gains better results than performance
   B. objectivity is decreased if outside public relations consultants are employed
   C. public relations is the responsibility of every employee
   D. public relations should be based on a formal publicity program

7. The form of communication which is usually considered to be MOST personally directed to the intended recipient is the 7.____
   A. brochure B. film C. letter D. radio

8. In general, a document that presents an organization's views or opinions on a particular topic is MOST accurately known as a 8.____
   A. tear sheet B. position paper
   C. flyer D. journal

9. Assume that you have been asked to speak before an organization of persons who oppose a newly announced program in which you are involved. You feel tense about talking to this group. 9.____
   Which of the following rules generally would be MOST useful in gaining rapport when speaking before the audience?
   A. Impress them with your experience
   B. Stress all areas of disagreement
   C. Talk to the group as to one person
   D. Use formal grammar and language

10. An organization must have an effective public relations program since, at its best, public relations is a bridge to change. 10.____
    All of the following statements about communication and human behavior have validity EXCEPT:
    A. People are more likely to talk about controversial matters with like-minded people than with those holding other views
    B. The earlier an experience, the more powerful its effect since it influences how later experiences will be interpreted
    C. In periods of social tension, official sources gain increased believability
    D. Those who are already interested in a topic are the ones who are most open to receive new communications about it

11. An employee should be encouraged to talk easily and frankly when he is dealing with his supervisor. 11.____
In order to encourage such free communication, it would be MOST appropriate for a supervisor to behave in a(n)
   A. sincere manner; assure the employee that you will deal with him honestly and openly
   B. official manner; you are a supervisor and must always act formally with subordinates
   C. investigative manner; you must probe and question to get to a basis of trust
   D. unemotional manner; the employee's emotions and background should play no part in your dealings with him

12. Research findings show that an increase in free communication within an agency GENERALLY results in which one of the following? 12.____
   A. Improved morale and productivity
   B. Increased promotional opportunities
   C. An increase in authority
   D. A spirit of honesty

13. Assume that you are a supervisor and your superiors have given you a new-type procedure to be followed. 13.____
Before passing this information on to your subordinates, the one of the following actions that you should take FIRST is to
   A. ask your superiors to send out a memorandum to the entire staff
   B. clarify the procedure in your own mind
   C. set up a training course to provide instruction on the new procedure
   D. write a memorandum to your subordinates

14. Communication is necessary for an organization to be effective. 14.____
The one of the following which is LEAST important for most communication systems is that
   A. messages are sent quickly and directly to the person who needs them to operate
   B. information should be conveyed understandably and accurately
   C. the method used to transmit information should be kept secret so that security can be maintained
   D. senders of messages must know how their messages are received and acted upon

15. Which one of the following is the CHIEF advantage of listening willingly to subordinates and encouraging them to talk freely and honestly? 15.____
It
   A. reveals to supervisors the degree to which ideas that are passed down are accepted by subordinates
   B. reduces the participation of subordinates in the operation of the department
   C. encourages subordinates to try for promotion
   D. enables supervisors to learn more readily what the *grapevine* is saying

16. A supervisor may be informed through either oral or written reports. Which one of the following is an ADVANTAGE of using oral reports? 16.____
    A. There is no need for a formal record of the report.
    B. An exact duplicate of the report is not easily transmitted to others.
    C. A good oral report requires little time for preparation.
    D. An oral report involves two-way communication between a subordinate and his supervisor.

17. Of the following, the MOST important reason why supervisors should communicate effectively with the public is to 17.____
    A. improve the public's understanding of information that is important for them to know
    B. establish a friendly relationship
    C. obtain information about the kinds of people who come to the agency
    D. convince the public that services are adequate

18. Supervisors should generally NOT use phrases like *too hard*, *too easy*, and *a lot* PRINCIPALLY because such phrases 18.____
    A. may be offensive to some minority groups
    B. are too informal
    C. mean different things to different people
    D. are difficult to remember

19. The ability to communicate clearly and concisely is an important element in effective leadership. Which of the following statements about oral and written communication is GENERALLY true? 19.____
    A. Oral communication is more time-consuming.
    B. Written communication is more likely to be misinterpreted.
    C. Oral communication is useful only in emergencies.
    D. Written communication is useful mainly when giving information to fewer than twenty people.

20. Rumors can often have harmful and disruptive effects on an organization. Which one of the following is the BEST way to prevent rumors from becoming a problem? 20.____
    A. Refuse to act on rumors, thereby making them less believable.
    B. Increase the amount of information passed along by the *grapevine*.
    C. Distribute as much factual information as possible.
    D. Provide training in report writing.

21. Suppose that a subordinate asks you about a rumor he has heard. The rumor deals with a subject which your superiors consider *confidential*. Which of the following BEST describes how you should answer the subordinate? Tell 21.____

A. the subordinate that you don't make the rules and that he should speak to higher ranking officials
B. the subordinate that you will ask your superior for information
C. him only that you cannot comment on the matter
D. him the rumor is not true

22. Supervisors often find it difficult to *get their message across* when instructing newly appointed employees in their various duties. 22.____
The MAIN reason for this is generally that the
A. duties of the employees have increased
B. supervisor is often so expert in his area that he fails to see it from the learner's point of view
C. supervisor adapts his instruction to the slowest learner in the group
D. new employees are younger, less concerned with job security and more interested in fringe benefits

23. Assume that you are discussing a job problem with an employee under your supervision. During the discussion, you see that the man's eyes are turning away from you and that he is not paying attention. 23.____
In order to get the man's attention, you should FIRST
A. ask him to look you in the eye
B. talk to him about sports
C. tell him he is being very rude
D. change your tone of voice

24. As a supervisor, you may find it necessary to conduct meetings with your subordinates. 24.____
Of the following, which would be MOST helpful in assuring that a meeting accomplishes the purpose for which it was called?
A. Give notice of the conclusions you would like to reach at the start of the meeting.
B. Delay the start of the meeting until everyone is present.
C. Write down points to be discussed in proper sequence.
D. Make sure everyone is clear on whatever conclusions have been reached and on what must be done after the meeting.

25. Every supervisor will occasionally be called upon to deliver a reprimand to a subordinate. If done properly, this can greatly help an employee improve his performance. 25.____
Which one of the following is NOT a good practice to follow when giving a reprimand?
A. Maintain your composure and temper
B. Reprimand a subordinate in the presence of other employees so they can learn the same lesson
C. Try to understand why the employee was not able to perform satisfactorily
D. Let your knowledge of the man involved determine the exact nature of the reprimand

KEY (CORRECT ANSWERS)

1.	C	11.	A
2.	B	12.	A
3.	D	13.	B
4.	B	14.	C
5.	D	15.	A
6.	C	16.	D
7.	C	17.	A
8.	B	18.	C
9.	C	19.	B
10.	C	20.	C

21.	B
22.	B
23.	D
24.	D
25.	B

TEST 2

DIRECTIONS: Each question or incomplete statement is followed by several suggested answers or completions. Select the one that BEST answers the question or completes the statement. *PRINT THE LETTER OF THE CORRECT ANSWER IN THE SPACE AT THE RIGHT.*

1. Usually one thinks of communication as a single step, essentially that of transmitting an idea. 1.____
Actually, however, this is only part of a total process, the FIRST step of which should be
   A. the prompt dissemination of the idea to those who may be affected by it
   B. motivating those affected to take the required action
   C. clarifying the idea in one's own mind
   D. deciding to whom the idea is to be communicated

2. Research studies on patterns of informal communication have concluded that most individuals in a group tend to be passive recipients of news, while a few make it their business to spread it around in an organization. 2.____
With this conclusion in mind, it would be MOST correct for the supervisor to attempt to identify these few individuals and
   A. give them the complete facts on important matters in advance of others
   B. inform the other subordinates of the identity of these few individuals so that their influence may be minimized
   C. keep them straight on the facts on important matters
   D. warn them to cease passing along any information to others

3. The one of the following which is the PRINCIPAL advantage of making an oral report is that it 3.____
   A. affords an immediate opportunity for two-way communication between the subordinate and superior
   B. is an easy method for the superior to use in transmitting information to others of equal rank
   C. saves the time of all concerned
   D. permits more precise pinpointing of praise or blame by means of follow-up questions by the superior

4. An agency may sometimes undertake a public relations program of a defensive nature. 4.____
With reference to the use of defensive public relations, it would be MOST correct to state that it
   A. is bound to be ineffective since defensive statements, even though supported by factual data, can never hope to even partly overcome the effects of prior unfavorable attacks
   B. proves that the agency has failed to establish good relationships with newspapers, radio stations, or other means of publicity

C. shows that the upper echelons of the agency have failed to develop sound public relations procedures and techniques
D. is sometimes required to aid morale by protecting the agency from unjustified criticism and misunderstanding of policies or procedures

5. Of the following factors which contribute to possible undesirable public attitudes towards an agency, the one which is MOST susceptible to being changed by the efforts of the individual employee in an organization is that 5.____
A. enforcement of unpopular regulations as offended many individuals
B. the organization itself has an unsatisfactory reputation
C. the public is not interested in agency matters
D. there are many errors in judgment committed by individual subordinates

6. It is not enough for an agency's services to be of a high quality; attention must also be given to the acceptability of these services to the general public. 6.____
This statement is GENERALLY
A. *false*; a superior quality of service automatically wins public support
B. *true*; the agency cannot generally progress beyond the understanding and support of the public
C. *false*; the acceptance by the public of agency services determines their quality
D. *true*; the agency is generally unable to engage in any effective enforcement activity without public support

7. Sustained agency participation in a program sponsored by a community organization is MOST justified when 7.____
A. the achievement of agency objectives in some area depends partly on the activity of this organization
B. the community organization is attempting to widen the base of participation in all community affairs
C. the agency is uncertain as to what the community wants
D. the agency is uncertain as to what the community wants

8. Of the following, the LEAST likely way in which a records system may serve a supervisor is in 8.____
A. developing a sympathetic and cooperative public attitude toward the agency
B. improving the quality of supervision by permitting a check on the accomplishment of subordinates
C. permit a precise prediction of the exact incidences in specific categories for the following year
D. helping to take the guesswork out of the distribution of the agency

9. Assuming that the *grapevine* in any organization is virtually indestructible, the one of the following which it is MOST important for management to understand is: 9.____
   A. What is being spread by means of the *grapevine* and the reason for spreading it
   B. What is being spread by means of the *grapevine* and how it is being spread
   C. Who is involved in spreading the information that is on the *grapevine*
   D. Why those who are involved in spreading the information are doing so

10. When the supervisor writes a report concerning an investigation to which he has been assigned, it should be LEAST intended to provide 10.____
   A. a permanent official record of relevant information gathered
   B. a summary of case findings limited to facts which tend to indicate the guilt of a suspect
   C. a statement of the facts on which higher authorities may base a corrective or disciplinary action
   D. other investigators with information so that they may continue with other phases of the investigation

11. In survey work, questionnaires rather than interviews are sometimes used. The one of the following which is a DISADVANTAGE of the questionnaire method as compared with the interview is the 11.____
   A. difficulty of accurately interpreting the results
   B. problem of maintaining anonymity of the participant
   C. fact that it is relatively uneconomical
   D. requirement of special training for the distribution of questionnaires

12. in his contacts with the public, an employee should attempt to create a good climate of support for his agency. 12.____
This statement is GENERALLY
   A. *false*; such attempts are clearly beyond the scope of his responsibility
   B. *true*; employees of an agency who come in contact with the public have the opportunity to affect public relations
   C. *false*; such activity should be restricted to supervisors trained in public relations techniques
   D. *true*; the future expansion of the agency depends to a great extent on continued public support of the agency

13. The repeated use by a supervisor of a call for volunteers to get a job done is objectionable MAINLY because it 13.____
   A. may create a feeling of animosity between the volunteers and the non-volunteers
   B. may indicate that the supervisor is avoiding responsibility for making assignments which will be most productive
   C. is an indication that the supervisor is not familiar with the individual capabilities of his men
   D. is unfair to men who, for valid reasons, do not, or cannot volunteer

14. Of the following statements concerning subordinates' expressions to a supervisor of their opinions and feelings concerning work situations, the one which is MOST correct is that 14.____
   A. by listening and responding to such expressions the supervisor encourages the development of complaints
   B. the lack of such expressions should indicate to the supervisor that there is a high level of job satisfaction
   C. the more the supervisor listens to and responds to such expressions, the more he demonstrates lack of supervisory ability
   D. by listening and responding to such expressions, the supervisor will enable many subordinates to understand and solve their own problems on the job

15. In attempting to motivate employees, rewards are considered preferable to punishment PRIMARILY because 15.____
   A. punishment seldom has any effect on human behavior
   B. punishment usually results in decreased production
   C. supervisors find it difficult to punish
   D. rewards are more likely to result in willing cooperation

16. In an attempt to combat the low morale in his organization, a high level supervisor publicized an *open-door policy* to allow employees who wished to do so to come to him with their complaints.
Which of the following is LEAST likely to account for the fact that no employee came in with a complaint? 16.____
   A. Employees are generally reluctant to go over the heads of their immediate supervisor.
   B. The employees did not feel that management would help them.
   C. The low morale was not due to complaints associated with the job.
   D. The employees felt that they had more to lose than to gain.

17. It is MOST desirable to use written instructions rather than oral instructions for a particular job when 17.____
   A. a mistake on the job will not be serious
   B. the job can be completed in a short time
   C. there is no need to explain the job minutely
   D. the job involves many details

18. If you receive a telephone call regarding a matter which your office does not handle, you should FIRST 18.____
   A. give the caller the telephone number of the proper office so that he can dial again
   B. offer to transfer the caller to the proper office
   C. suggest that the caller re-dial since he probably dialed incorrectly
   D. tell the caller he has reached the wrong office and then hang up

19. When you answer the telephone, the MOST important reason for identifying yourself and your organization is to 19.____
   A. give the caller time to collect his or her thoughts
   B. impress the caller with your courtesy
   C. inform the caller that he or she has reached the right number
   D. set a business-like tone at the beginning of the conversation

20. As soon as you pick up the phone, a very angry caller begins immediately to complain about city agencies and *red tape*. He says that he has been shifted to two or three different offices. It turs out that he is seeking information which is not immediately available to you. You believe, you know, however, where it can be found. 20.____
   Which of the following actions is the BEST one for you to take?
   A. To eliminate all confusion, suggest that the caller write the agency stating explicitly what he wants.
   B. Apologize by telling the caller how busy city agencies now are, but also tell him directly that you do not have the information he needs.
   C. Ask for the caller's telephone number and assure him you will call back after you have checked further.
   D. Give the caller the name and telephone number of the person who might be able to help, but explain that you are not positive he will get results/

21. Which of the following approaches usually provides the BEST communication in the objectives and values of a new program which is to be introduced? 21.____
   A. A general written description of the program by the program manager for review by those who share responsibility
   B. An effective verbal presentation by the program manager to those affected
   C. Development of the plan and operational approach in carrying out the program by the program manager assisted by his key subordinates
   D. Development of the plan by the program manager's supervisor

22. What is the BEST approach for introducing change? 22.____
   A
   A. combination of written and also verbal communication to all personnel affected by the change
   B. general bulletin to all personnel
   C. meeting pointing out all the values of the new approach
   D. written directive to key personnel

23. Of the following, committees are BEST used for 23.____
   A. advising the head of the organization
   B. improving functional work
   C. making executive decisions
   D. making specific planning decisions

24. An effective discussion leader is one who 24.____
   A. announces the problem and his preconceived solution at the start of the discussion
   B. guides and directs the discussion according to pre-arranged outline
   C. interrupts or corrects confused participants to save time
   D. permits anyone to say anything at any time

25. The human relations movement in management theory is basically concerned with 25.____
   A. counteracting employee unrest
   B. eliminating the *time and motion* man
   C. interrelationships among individuals in organizations
   D. the psychology of the worker

KEY (CORRECT ANSWERS)

1. C
2. C
3. A
4. D
5. D

6. B
7. A
8. C
9. A
10. B

11. A
12. B
13. B
14. D
15. D

16. C
17. D
18. B
19. C
20. C

21. C
22. A
23. A
24. B
25. C

COMMUNICATION

EXAMINATION SECTION
TEST 1

DIRECTIONS: Each question or incomplete statement is followed by several suggested answers or completions. Select the one that BEST answers the question or completes the statement. *PRINT THE LETTER OF THE CORRECT ANSWER IN THE SPACE AT THE RIGHT.*

1. In some agencies the counsel to the agency head is given the right to bypass the chain of command and issue orders directly to the staff concerning matters that involve certain specific processes and practices. 1.____
This situation MOST nearly illustrates the principle of _____ authority.
   A. the acceptance theory of
   B. multiple-linear
   C. splintered
   D. functional

2. It is commonly understood that communication is an important part of the administrative process. 2.____
Which of the following is NOT a valid principle of the communication process in administration?
   A. The channels of communication should be spontaneous.
   B. The lines of communication should be as direct and as short as possible.
   C. Communications should be authenticated.
   D. The persons serving in communications centers should be competent.

3. Of the following, the one factor which is generally considered LEAST essential to successful committee operations is 3.____
   A. stating a clear definition of the authority and scope of the committee
   B. selecting the committee chairman carefully
   C. limiting the size of the committee to four persons
   D. limiting the subject matter to that which can be handled in group discussion

4. Of the following, the failure by line managers to accept and appreciate the benefits and limitations of a new program or system VERY FREQUENTLY can be traced to the 4.____
   A. budgetary problems involved
   B. resultant need to reduce staff
   C. lack of controls it engenders
   D. failure of top management to support its implementation

5. If a manager were thinking about using a committee of subordinates to solve an operating problem, which of the following would generally NOT be an advantage of such use of the committee approach? 5.____
   A. Improved coordination
   B. Low cost
   C. Increased motivation
   D. Integrated judgment

6. Every supervisor has many occasions to lead a conference or participate in a conference of some sort. 6.____
Of the following statements that pertain to conferences and conference leadership, which is generally considered to be MOST valid?
   A. Since World War II, the trend has been toward fewer shared decisions and more conferences.
   B. The most important part of a conference leader's job is to direct discussion.
   C. In providing opportunities for group interaction, management should avoid consideration of its past management philosophy.
   D. A good administrator cannot lead a good conference if he is a poor public speaker.

7. Of the following, it is usually LEAST desirable for a conference leader to 7.____
   A. call the name of a person after asking a question
   B. summarize proceedings periodically
   C. make a practice of repeating questions
   D. ask a question without indicating who is to reply

8. Assume that, in a certain organization, a situation has developed in which there is little difference in status or authority between individuals. 8.____
Which of the following would be the MOST likely result with regard to communication in this organization?
   A. Both the accuracy and flow of communication will be improved.
   B. Both the accuracy and flow of communication will substantially decrease.
   C. Employees will seek more formal lines of communication.
   D. Neither the flow nor the accuracy of communication will be improved over the former hierarchical structure.

9. The main function of many agency administrative officers is "information management." Information that is received by an administrative officer may be classified as active or passive, depending upon whether or not it requires the recipient to take some action. 9.____
Of the following, the item received which is clearly the MOST active information is
   A. an appointment of a new staff member
   B. a payment voucher for a new desk
   C. a press release concerning a past event
   D. the minutes of a staff meeting

10. Of the following, the one LEAST considered to be a communication barrier is 10.____
   A. group feedback
   B. charged words
   C. selective perception
   D. symbolic meanings

11. Management studies support the hypothesis that, in spite of the tendency of employees to censor the information communicated to their supervisor, subordinates are more likely to communicate problem-oriented information UPWARD when they have a 11.____
   A. long period of service in the organization
   B. high degree of trust in the supervisor
   C. high educational level
   D. low status on the organizational ladder

12. Electronic data processing equipment can produce more information faster than can be generated by any other means. 12.____
In view of this, the MOST important problem faced by management at present is to
   A. keep computers fully occupied
   B. find enough computer personnel
   C. assimilate and properly evaluate the information
   D. obtain funds to establish appropriate information systems

13. A well-designed management information system essentially provides each executive and manager the information he needs for 13.____
   A. determining computer time requirements
   B. planning and measuring results
   C. drawing a new organization chart
   D. developing a new office layout

14. It is generally agreed that management policies should be periodically reappraised and restated in accordance with current conditions. 14.____
Of the following, the approach which would be MOST effective in determining whether a policy should be revised is to
   A. conduct interviews with staff members at all levels in order to ascertain the relationship between the policy and actual practice
   B. make proposed revisions in the policy and apply it to current problems
   C. make up hypothetical situations using both the old policy and a revised version in order to make comparisons
   D. call a meeting of top level staff in order to discuss ways of revising the policy

15. Your superior has asked you to notify division employees of an important change in one of the operating procedures described in the division manual. Every employee presently has a copy of this manual. 15.____
Which of the following is normally the MOST practical way to get the employees to understand such a change?
   A. Notify each employee individually of the change and answer any questions he might have
   B. Send a written notice to key personnel, directing them to inform the people under them

C. Call a general meeting, distribute a corrected page for the manual, and discuss the change
D. Send a memo to employees describing the change in general terms and asking them to make the necessary corrections in their copies of the manual

16. Assume that the work in your department involves the use of any technical terms. 16.____
In such a situation, when you are answering inquiries from the general public, it would usually be BEST to
A. use simple language and avoid the technical terms
B. employ the technical terms whenever possible
C. bandy technical terms freely, but explain each term in parentheses
D. apologize if you are forced to use a technical term

17. Suppose that you receive a telephone call from someone identifying himself as an employee in another city department who asks to be given information which your own department regards as confidential. 17.____
Which of the following is the BEST way of handling such a request?
A. Give the information requested, since your caller as official standing
B. Grant the request, provided the caller gives you a signed receipt
C. Refuse the request, because you have no way of knowing whether the caller is really who he claims to be
D. Explain that the information is confidential and inform the caller of the channels he must go through to have the information released to him

18. Studies show that office employees place high importance on the social and human aspects of the organization. What office employees like best about their jobs is the kind of people with whom they work. So strive hard to group people who are most likely to get along well together. 18.____
Based on this information, it is MOST reasonable to assume that office workers are most pleased to work in a group which
A. is congenial
B. has high productivity
C. allows individual creativity
D. is unlike other groups

19. A certain supervisor does not compliment members of his staff when they come up with good ideas. He feels that coming up with good ideas is part of the job and does not merit special attention. 19.____
This supervisor's practice is
A. *poor*, because recognition for good ideas is a good motivator
B. *poor*, because the staff will suspect that the supervisor has no good ideas of his own
C. *good*, because it is reasonable to assume that employees will tell their supervisor of ways to improve office practice
D. *good*, because the other members of the staff are not made to seem inferior by comparison

20. Some employees of a department have sent an anonymous letter containing many complaints to the department head. 20.____
Of the following, what is this MOST likely to show about the department?
   A. It is probably a good place to work.
   B. Communications are probably poor.
   C. The complaints are probably unjustified.
   D. These employees are probably untrustworthy.

21. Which of the following actions would usually be MOST appropriate for a supervisor to take after receiving an instruction sheet from his superior explaining a new procedure which is to be followed? 21.____
   A. Put the instruction sheet aside temporarily until he determines what is wrong with the old procedure.
   B. Call his superior and ask whether the procedure is one he must implement immediately.
   C. Write a memorandum to the superior asking for more details.
   D. Try the new procedure and advise the superior of any problems or possible improvements.

22. Of the following, which one is considered the PRIMARY advantage of using a committee to resolved a problem in an organization? 22.____
   A. No one person will be held accountable for the decision since a group of people was involved.
   B. People with different backgrounds give attention to the problem.
   C. The decision will take considerable time so there is unlikely to be a decision that will later be regretted.
   D. One person cannot dominate the decision-making process.

23. Employees in a certain office come to their supervisor with all their complaints about the office and the work. Almost every employee has had at least one minor complaint at some time. 23.____
The situation with respect to complaints in this office may BEST be described as probably
   A. *good*; employees who complain care about their jobs and work hard
   B. *good*; grievances brought out into the open can be corrected
   C. *bad*; only serious complaints should be discussed
   D. *bad*; it indicates the staff does not have confidence in the administration

24. The administrator who allows his staff to suggest ways to do their work will usually find that 24.____
   A. this practice contributes to high productivity
   B. the administrator's ideas produce greater output
   C. clerical employees suggest inefficient work methods
   D. subordinate employees resent performing a management function

25. The MAIN purpose for a supervisor's questioning the employees at a conference he is holding is to 25.____
    A. stress those areas of information covered but not understood by the participants
    B. encourage participants to think through the problem under discussion
    C. catch those subordinates who are not paying attention
    D. permit the more knowledgeable participants to display their grasp of the problems being discussed

KEY (CORRECT ANSWERS)

1. D
2. A
3. C
4. D
5. B

6. B
7. C
8. D
9. A
10. A

11. B
12. C
13. B
14. A
15. C

16. A
17. D
18. A
19. A
20. B

21. D
22. B
23. B
24. A
25. B

TEST 2

DIRECTIONS: Each question or incomplete statement is followed by several suggested answers or completions. Select the one that BEST answers the question or completes the statement. *PRINT THE LETTER OF THE CORRECT ANSWER IN THE SPACE AT THE RIGHT.*

1. For a superior to use *consultative supervision* with his subordinates effectively, it is ESSENTIAL that he 1.____
   A. accept the fact that his formal authority will be weakened by the procedure
   B. admit that he does not know more than all his men together and that his ideas are not always best
   C. utilize a committee system so that the procedure is orderly
   D. make sure that all subordinates are consulted so that no one feels left out

2. The *grapevine* is an informal means of communication in an organization. The attitude of a supervisor with respect to the grapevine should be to 2.____
   A. ignore it since it deals mainly with rumors and sensational information
   B. regard it as a serious danger which should be eliminated
   C. accept it as a real line of communication which should be listened to
   D. utilize it for most purposes instead of the official line of communication

3. The supervisor of an office that must deal with the public should realize that planning in this type of work situation 3.____
   A. is useless because he does not know how many people will request service or what service they will request
   B. must be done at a higher level but that he should be ready to implement the results of such planning
   C. is useful primarily for those activities that are not concerned with public contact
   D. is useful for all the activities of the office, including those that relate to public contact

4. Assume that it is your job to receive incoming telephone calls. Those calls which you cannot handle yourself have to be transferred to the appropriate office. 4.____
   If you receive an outside call for an extension line which is busy, the one of the following which you should do FIRST is to
   A. interrupt the person speaking on the extension and tell him a call is waiting
   B. tell the caller the line is busy and let him know every thirty seconds whether or not it is free
   C. leave the caller on "hold" until the extension is free
   D. tell the caller the line is busy and ask him if he wishes to wait

5. Your superior has subscribed to several publications directly related to your division's work, and he has asked you to see to it that the publications are circulated among the supervisory personnel in the division. There are eight supervisors involved. 5.____
The BEST method of insuring that all eight see these publications is to
   A. place the publication in the division's general reference library as soon as it arrives
   B. inform each supervisor whenever a publication arrives and remind all of them that they are responsible for reading it
   C. prepare a standard slip that can be stapled to each publication, listing the eight supervisors and saying, "Please read, initial your name, and pass along"
   D. send a memo to the eight supervisors saying that they may wish to purchase individual subscriptions in their own names if they are interested in seeing each issue

6. Your superior has telephoned a number of key officials in your agency to ask whether they can meet at a certain time next month. He has found that they can all make it, and he has asked you to confirm the meeting. 6.____
Which of the following is the BEST way to confirm such a meeting?
   A. Note the meeting on your superior's calendar.
   B. Post a notice of the meeting on the agency bulletin board.
   C. Call the officials on the day of the meeting to remind them of the meeting.
   D. Write a memo to each official involved, repeating the time and place of the meeting.

7. Assume that a new city regulation requires that certain kinds of private organizations file information forms with your department. You have been asked to write the short explanatory message that will be printed on the front cover of the pamphlet containing the forms and instructions. 7.____
Which of the following would be the MOST appropriate way of beginning this message?
   A. Get the readers' attention by emphasizing immediately that there are legal penalties for organizations that fail to file before a certain date.
   B. Briefly state the nature of the enclosed forms and the types of organizations that must file.
   C. Say that your department is very sorry to have to put organizations to such an inconvenience.
   D. Quote the entire regulation adopted by the city, even if it is quite long and is expressed din complicated legal language.

8. Suppose that you have been told to make up the vacation schedule for the 18 employees in a particular unit. In order for the unit to operate effectively, only a few employees can be on vacation at the same time. 8.____
Which of the following is the MOST advisable approach in making up the schedule?
   A. Draw up a schedule assigning vacations in alphabetical order
   B. Find out when the supervisors want to take their vacations, and randomly assign whatever periods are left to the non-supervisory personnel

C. Assign the most desirable times to employees of longest standing and the least desirable times to the newest employees
D. Have all employees state their own preference, and then work out any conflicts in consultation with the people involved

9. Assume that you have been asked to prepare job descriptions for various positions in your department. 9.____
Which of the following are the basic points that should be covered in a *job description*?
A. General duties and responsibilities of the position, with examples of day-to-day tasks
B. Comments on the performances of present employees
C. Estimates of the number of openings that may be available in each category during the coming year
D. Instructions for carrying out the specific tasks assigned to your department

10. Of the following, the biggest DISADVANTAGE in allowing a free flow of communications in an agency is that such a free flow 10.____
A. decreases creativity
B. increases the use of the *grapevine*
C. lengthens the chain of command
D. reduces the executive's power to direct the flow of information

11. A downward flow of authority in an organization is one example of _____ communication. 11.____
A. horizontal B. informal C. circular D. vertical

12. Of the following, the one that would MOST likely block effective communication is 12.____
A. concentration only on the issues at hand
B. lack of interest or commitment
C. use of written reports
D. use of charts and graphs

13. An ADVANTAGE of the *lecture* as a teaching tool is that it 13.____
A. enables a person to present his ideas to a large number of people
B. allows the audience to retain a maximum of the information given
C. holds the attention of the audience for the longest time
D. enables the audience member to easily recall the main points

14. An ADVANTAGE of the *small-group* discussion as a teaching tool is that 14.____
A. it always focuses attention on one person as the leader
B. it places collective responsibility on the group as a whole
C. its members gain experience by summarizing the ideas of others
D. each member of the group acts as a member of a team

15. The one of the following that is an ADVANTAGE of a *large-group* discussion, when compared to a small-group discussion, is that the large-group discussion 15.____
    A. moves along more quickly than a small-group discussion
    B. allows its participants to feel more at ease, and speak out more freely
    C. gives the whole group a chance to exchange ideas on a certain subject at the same occasion
    D. allows its members to feel a greater sense of personal responsibility

KEY (CORRECT ANSWERS)

1.	D	6.	D	11.	D
2.	C	7.	B	12.	B
3.	D	8.	D	13.	A
4.	D	9.	A	14.	D
5.	C	10.	D	15.	C

EXAMINATION SECTION
TEST 1

DIRECTIONS: Each question or incomplete statement is followed by several suggested answers or completions. Select the one that BEST answers the question or completes the statement. *PRINT THE LETTER OF THE CORRECT ANSWER IN THE SPACE AT THE RIGHT.*

1. The budget which shows the money to be spent to build and equip a new hospital is known as the _______ budget. 1.____

   A. capital B. expense C. planned D. program

2. A significant characteristic of the program budget is that it lends itself to review and analysis. 2.____
   Why?

   A. The budget has a built-in accounting system that makes close control possible.
   B. The budget includes measurable objectives.
   C. It is possible to review performance based on units of service.
   D. All of the above

3. The advantages of program budgeting over line item and performance budgeting is: 3.____
   I. Tight, administrative control
   II. Forces the administrator to think through his total operation
   III. Measurable objectives
   IV. Simplicity of development
   V. Closer estimates of future costs

   The CORRECT answer is:

   A. I, II
   B. II, III, IV
   C. II, III, V
   D. III, IV, V

4. Of the following considerations, the one which is LEAST important in preparing a department budget request is the 4.____

   A. amounts in previous budget requests
   B. cost of material
   C. cost of personnel
   D. goals of the agency

5. The type of budget which provides the MOST flexibility in the use of appropriate funds is the _______ budget. 5.____

   A. accrual B. item C. line D. program

6. A WEAKNESS of many budgetary systems today is that they 6.____

   A. are subjectively determined by those most directly involved
   B. focus on management weakness rather than management strength
   C. only show variable costs
   D. show in detail why losses are occurring

7. Standards on which budgets are developed should be based PRIMARILY on 7.____

A. a general consensus
B. agency wishes
C. analytical studies
D. historical performance

8. The income, cost, and expense goals making up a budget are aimed at achieving a predetermined objective but do not necessarily measure the lowest possible costs. This is PRIMARILY so because 8.____

A. budget committees are accounting-oriented and are not sympathetic with the supervisor's personnel problems
B. budget committees fail to recognize the difference between direct and indirect costs
C. the level of expenditures provided for in a budget by budget committees is frequently an arbitrary rather than a scientifically determined amount
D. budget committees spend considerable time evaluating data to the point that the material gathered is not representative or current

9. You, as a unit head, have been asked to submit budget estimates of staff, equipment, and supplies in terms of programs for your unit for the coming fiscal year. In addition to their use in planning, such unit budget estimates can be BEST used to 9.____

A. reveal excessive costs in operations
B. justify increases in the debt limit
C. analyze employee salary adjustments
D. predict the success of future programs

10. Which of the following is the BEST reason for budgeting a new calculating machine for an office? 10.____

A. The clerks in the office often make mistakes in adding.
B. The machine would save time and money.
C. It was budgeted last year but never received.
D. All the other offices have calculating machines.

11. As an aspect of the managerial function, a budget is described BEST as a 11.____

A. set of qualitative management controls over productivity
B. tool based on historical accounting reports
C. type of management plan expressed in quantitative terms
D. precise estimate of future quantitative and qualitative contingencies

12. Which one of the following is *generally* accepted as the MAJOR immediate advantage of installing a system of program budgeting? It 12.____

A. encourages managers to relate their decisions to the agency's long-range goals
B. is a replacement for the financial or fiscal budget
C. decreases the need for managers to make trade-offs in the decision-making process
D. helps to adjust budget figures to provide for unexpected developments

13. Of the following, the BEST means for assuring necessary responsiveness of a budgetary program to changing conditions is by 13.____

A. overestimating budgetary expenditures by 15% and assigning the excess to unforeseen problem areas
B. underestimating budgetary expenditures by at least 20% and setting aside a reserve account in the same amount
C. reviewing and revising the budget at regular intervals so that it retains its character as a current document
D. establishing *budget by exception* policies for each division in the agency

14. According to expert thought in the area of budgeting, participation in the preparation of a government agency's budget should GENERALLY involve 14.____

A. only top management
B. only lower levels of management
C. all levels of the organization
D. only a central budget office or bureau

15. Of the following, the MOST useful guide to analysis of budget estimates for the coming fiscal year is a comparison with 15.____

A. appropriations as amended for the current fiscal year
B. manpower requirements for the previous two years
C. initial appropriations for the current fiscal year
D. budget estimates for the preceding five years,

16. Line managers often request more funds for their units than are actually required to attain their current objectives. 16.____
Which one of the following is the MOST important reason for such inflated budget requests? The

A. expectation that budget examiners will exercise their prerogative of budget cutting
B. line manager's interest in improving the performance of his unit is thereby indicated to top management
C. expectation that such requests will make it easier to obtain additional funds in future years
D. opinion that it makes sense to obtain additional funds and decide later how to use them

17. Integrating budgeting with program planning and evaluation in a city agency is GENERALLY considered to be 17.____

A. *undesirable*; budgeting must focus on the fiscal year at hand, whereas planning must concern itself with developments over a period of years
B. *desirable*; budgeting facilitates the choice-making process by evaluating the financial implications of agency programs and forcing cost comparisons among them
C. *undesirable*; accountants and statisticians with the required budgetary skills have little familiarity with the substantive programs that the agency is conducting
D. *desirable*; such a partnership increases the budgetary skills of planners, thus promoting more effective use of public resources

18. In government budgeting, the problem of relating financial transactions to the fiscal year in which they are budgeted is BEST met by 18.____

A. determining the cash balance by comparing how much money has been received and how much has been paid out
B. applying net revenue to the fiscal year in which they are collected as offset by relevant expenses
C. adopting a system whereby appropriations are entered when they are received and expenditures are entered when they are paid out
D. entering expenditures on the books when the obligation to make the expenditure is made

19. If the agency's bookkeeping system records income when it is received and expenditures when the money is paid out, this system is USUALLY known as a _______ system. 19.____

A. cash
B. flow-payment
C. deferred
D. fiscal year income

20. An audit, as the term applies to budget execution, is MOST NEARLY a 20.____

A. procedure based on the budget estimates
B. control exercised by the executive on the legislature in the establishment of program priorities
C. check on the legality of expenditures and is based on the appropriations act
D. requirement which must be met before funds can be spent

21. In government budgeting, there is a procedure known as *allotment*. 21.____
Of the following statements which relate to allotment, select the one that is MOST generally considered to be correct. Allotment

A. increases the practice of budget units coming back to the legislative branch for supplemental appropriations
B. is simply an example of red tape
C. eliminates the requirement of timing of expenditures
D. is designed to prevent waste

22. In government budgeting, the establishment of the schedules of allotments is MOST generally the responsibility of the 22.____

A. budget unit and the legislature
B. budget unit and the executive
C. budget unit only
D. executive and the legislature

23. Of the following statements relating to preparation of an organization's budget request, which is the MOST generally valid precaution? 23.____

A. Give specific instructions on the format of budget requests and required supporting data.
B. Because of the complexity of preparing a budget request, avoid argumentation to support the requests
C. Put requests in whatever format is desirable.
D. Consider that final approval will be given to initial estimates.

Question 24.

DIRECTIONS: Answer Question 24 on the basis of the following information.

Sample Budget

Environmental Safety		
Air Pollution Protection		
Personal Services	$20,000,000	
Contractual Services	4,000,000	
Supplies and Materials	4,000,000	
Capital Outlay	2,000,000	
Total Air Pollution Protection		$30,000,000
Water Pollution Protection		
Personal Services	$23,000,000	
Supplies and Materials	4,500,000	
Capital Outlay	20,500,000	
Total Water Pollution Protection		$48,000,000
Total Environmental Safety		$78,000,000

24. Based on the above budget, which is the MOST valid statement? 24.____

   A. Environmental Safety, Air Pollution Protection, and Water Pollution Protection could all be considered program elements.
   B. The object listings included water pollution protection and capital outlay.
   C. Examples of the program element listings in the above are personal services and supplies and materials.
   D. Contractual Services and Environmental Safety were the program element listings.

25. Which of the following is NOT an advantage of a program budget over a line-item budget? 25.____
A program budget

   A. allows us to set up priority lists in deciding what activities we will spend our money on
   B. gives us more control over expenditures than a line-item budget
   C. is more informative in that we know the broad purposes of spending money
   D. enables us to see if one program is getting much less money than the others

26. Of the following statements which relate to the budget process in a well-organized government, select the one that is MOST NEARLY correct. 26.____

   A. The budget cycle is the step-by-step process which is repeated each and every fiscal year.
   B. Securing approval of the budget does not take place within the budget cycle.
   C. The development of a new budget and putting it into effect is a two-step process known as the budget cycle.
   D. The fiscal period, usually a fiscal year, has no relation to the budget cycle.

27. If a manager were asked what PPBS stands for, he would be right if he said 27.___

A. public planning budgeting system
B. planning programming budgeting system
C. planning projections budgeting system
D. programming procedures budgeting system

Questions 28-29

DIRECTIONS: Answer Questions 28 and 29 on the basis of the following information.

Sample Budget

	Amount
Refuse Collection	
Personal Services	$ 30,000
Contractual Services	5,000
Supplies and Materials	5,000
Capital Outlay	10,000
	$ 50,000
Residential Collections	
Dwellings—1 pickup per week	1,000
Tons of refuse collected per year	375
Cost of collections per ton	$ 8
Cost per dwelling pickup per year	$ 3
Total annual cost	$ 3,000

28. The sample budget shown is a simplified example of a ______ budget. 28.___

A. factorial
B. performance
C. qualitative
D. rational

29. The budget shown in the sample differs CHIEFLY from line-item and program budgets in that it includes 29.___

A. objects of expenditure but not activities or functions
B. only activities, functions, and controls
C. activities and functions, but not objects of expenditure
D. levels of service

30. Performance budgeting focuses PRIMARY attention upon which one of the following? The 30.___

A. things to be acquired, such as supplies and equipment
B. general character and relative importance of the work to be done or the service to be rendered
C. list of personnel to be employed, by specific title
D. separation of employee performance evaluations from employee compensation

KEY (CORRECT ANSWERS)

1. A
2. B
3. C
4. A
5. D
6. A
7. C
8. C
9. A
10. B
11. C
12. A
13. C
14. C
15. A
16. A
17. B
18. D
19. A
20. C
21. D
22. C
23. A
24. A
25. B
26. A
27. B
28. B
29. D
30. B

TEST 2

DIRECTIONS: Each question or incomplete statement is followed by several suggested answers or completions. Select the one that BEST answers the question or completes the statement. *PRINT THE LETTER OF THE CORRECT ANSWER IN THE SPACE AT THE RIGHT.*

1. Of the following, the FIRST step in the installation and operation of a performance budgeting system generally should be the 1.____

   A. identification of program costs in relationship to the accounting system and operating structure
   B. identification of the specific end results of past programs in other jurisdictions
   C. identification of work programs that are meaningful for management purposes
   D. establishment of organizational structures each containing only one work program

2. Of the following, the MOST important purpose of a system of quarterly allotments of appropriated funds generally is to enable the 2.____

   A. head of the judicial branch to determine the legality of agency requests for budget increases
   B. operating agencies of government to upgrade the quality of their services without increasing costs
   C. head of the executive branch to control the rate at which the operating agencies obligate and expend funds
   D. operating agencies of government to avoid payment for services which have not been properly rendered by employees

3. In the preparation of the agency's budget, the agency's central budget office has two responsibilities: program review and management improvement. 3.____
   Which one of the following questions concerning an operating agency's program is MOST closely related to the agency budget officer's program review responsibility?

   A. Can expenditures for supplies, materials, or equipment be reduced?
   B. Will improved work methods contribute to a more effective program?
   C. What is the relative importance of this program as compared with other programs?
   D. Will a realignment of responsibilities contribute to a higher level of program performance?

Questions 4-9.

DIRECTIONS: Questions 4 through 9 are to be answered only on the basis of the information contained in the charts below which relate to the budget allocations of City X, a small suburban community. The charts depict the annual budget allocations by Department and by Expenditures over a five-year period.

CITY X BUDGET IN MILLIONS OF DOLLARS

TABLE I. Budget Allocations by Department

Department	2017	2018	2019	2020	2021
Public Safety	30	45	50	40	50
Health and Welfare	50	75	90	60	70
Engineering	5	8	10	5	8
Human Resources	10	12	20	10	22
Conservation and Environment	10	15	20	20	15
Education and Development	15	25	35	15	15
TOTAL BUDGET	120	180	225	150	180

TABLE II. Budget Allocations by Expenditures

Category	2017	2018	2019	2020	2021
Raw Materials and Machinery	36	63	68	30	98
Capital Outlay	12	27	56	15	18
Personal Services	72	90	101	105	64
TOTAL BUDGET	120	180	225	150	160

4. The year in which the SMALLEST percentage of the total annual budget was allocated to the Department of Education and Development is 4.____

A. 2017 B. 2018 C. 2020 D. 2021

5. Assume that in 2020 the Department of Conservation and Environment divided its annual budget into the three categories of expenditures and in exactly the same proportion as the budget shown in Table II for the year 2020. The amount allocated for capital outlay in the Department of Conservation and Environment's 2020 budget was MOST NEARLY ______ million. 5.____

A. $2 B. $4 C. $6 D. $10

6. From the year 2018 to the year 2020, the sum of the annual budgets for the Departments of Public Safety and Engineering showed an overall ______ million. 6.____

A. decline of $8
B. increase of $7
C. decline of $15
D. increase of $22

7. The LARGEST dollar increase in departmental budget allocations from one year to the next was in 7.____

A. Public Safety from 2017 to 2018
B. Health and Welfare from 2017 to 2018
C. Education and Development from 2019 to 2020
D. Human Resources from 2019 to 2020

8. During the five-year period, the annual budget of the Department of Human Resources was greater than the annual budget for the Department of Conservation and Environment in ______ of the years. 8.____

A. none B. one C. two D. three

9. If the total City X budget increases at the same rate from 2021 to 2022 as it did from 2020 to 2021, the total City X budget for 2022 will be MOST NEARLY ______ million. 9.____

A. $180 B. $200 C. $210 D. $215

10. The one of the following which is LEAST important in developing a budget for the next fiscal year for project maintenance is the 10.____

A. adequacy of the current year's budget
B. changes in workload that can be anticipated
C. budget restrictions indicated in a memorandum covering budget preparations
D. staff reassignments which are expected during the next fiscal year

11. The performance budget used by the department places MOST emphasis on 11.____

A. building facilities
B. equipment costs
C. personnel costs
D. services rendered

12. The LARGEST part of the expenditures of the department is for 12.____

A. equipment
B. maintenance
C. operating materials
D. personnel services

13. The department function which requires the GREATEST expenditure of funds is 13.____

A. refuse collection
B. refuse disposal
C. snow removal
D. street cleaning

14. A FIRST step in budget preparation is *usually* 14.____

A. a realistic attempt to satisfy all unit requests
B. forecasting the amount of various kinds of work to be done during the coming budget year
C. an effort to increase work output
D. appraising the quality of work done in the previous year

15. There are various types of budgets which are used to measure different government activities. 15.____
The type of budget which *particularly* measures input of resource as compared with output of service is the ______ budget.

A. capital B. traditional C. performance D. program

16. The budget for a given cost during a given period was $100,000. The actual cost for the period was $90,000. Based upon these facts, one should say that the responsible manager has done a better than expected job in controlling the cost if the cost is 16.____

A. variable and actual production equaled budgeted production
B. a discretionary fixed cost and actual production equaled budgeted production
C. variable and actual production was 90% of budgeted production
D. variable and actual production was 80% of budgeted production

17. In most municipal budgeting systems involving capital and operating budgets, the leasing or renting of facilities is usually shown in 17.____

A. the operating budget
B. the capital budget
C. a separate schedule
D. either budget

18. New York City's budgeting procedure is unusual in that budget appropriations are considered in two parts, as follows: ______ budget and ______ budget. 18.____

A. capital; income
B. expense; income
C. revenue; expense
D. expense; capital

19. Budget planning is MOST useful when it achieves 19.____

A. cost control
B. forecast of receipts
C. performance review
D. personnel reduction

20. After a budget has been developed, it serves to 20.____

A. assist the accounting department in posting expenditures
B. measure the effectiveness of department managers
C. provide a yardstick against which actual costs are measured
D. provide the operating department with total expenditures to date

21. A budget is a plan whereby a goal is set for future operations. It affords a medium for comparing actual expenditures with planned expenditures. 21.____
The one of the following which is the MOST accurate statement on the basis of this statement is that

A. the budget serves as an accurate measure of past as well as future expenditures
B. the budget presents an estimate of expenditures to be made in the future
C. budget estimates should be based upon past budget requirements
D. planned expenditures usually fall short of actual expenditures

22. If one attempts to list the advantages of the management-by-exception principle as it is used in connection with the budgeting process, several distinct advantages could be cited. 22.____
Which of the following is NOT an advantage of this principle as it applies to the budgeting process? Management-by-exception

A. saves time
B. identifies critical problem areas
C. focuses attention and concentrates effort
D. escalates the frequency and importance of budget-related decisions

23. Of the following statements that relate to a budget, select the one that is MOST accurate. 23.____

A. A budget is made up by an organization to plan its future activities.
B. A budget specifies how much the organization to which it relates estimates it will spend over a certain period of time.
C. A budget specifies in dollars and cents how much is spent in a particular time period.
D. All plans dealing with money are budgets.

24. Of the following, the one which is NOT a contribution that a budget makes to organizational programming is that a budget 24.____

A. enables a comparison of what actually happened with what was expected
B. stresses the need to forecast specific goals and eliminates the need to focus on tasks needed to accomplish goals
C. may illustrate duplication of effort between interdependent activities
D. shows the relationship between various organizational segments

25. A line-item budget is a GOOD control budget because 25.____

A. it clearly specifies how the items being purchased will be used
B. expenditures can be shown primarily for contractual services
C. it clearly specifies what the money is buying
D. it clearly specifies the services to be provide

KEY (CORRECT ANSWERS)

1. C
2. C
3. C
4. D
5. A
6. A
7. B
8. B
9. D
10. D
11. D
12. D
13. A
14. B
15. C
16. A
17. A
18. D
19. A
20. C
21. B
22. D
23. B
24. B
25. C

EXAMINATION SECTION

TEST 1

DIRECTIONS: Each question or incomplete statement is followed by several suggested answers or completions. Select the one that BEST answers the question or completes the statement. *PRINT THE LETTER OF THE CORRECT ANSWER IN THE SPACE AT THE RIGHT.*

1. The one of the following which has had GREATEST effect upon size of the budget of large cities in the last twenty years is 1.____
   A. change in the organization of the city resulting from new charters
   B. increase in services rendered by the city
   C. development of independent authorities
   D. increase in the city's ability to borrow money
   E. increase in the size of the city

2. The one of the following services for which cities receive the LEAST amount of direct financial assistance from state governments is 2.____
   A. education B. welfare C. housing
   D. roads E. museums

3. Major problems which face most large cities, including New York, arise from the vertical sandwiching of governments in a single area and from the many independent governments that crowd the boundaries of the central city. 3.____
   Of the following methods of solving these problems, the one which has been MOST successful in the past has been to
   A. decentralize the administration of the central city
   B. create various supra-municipal authorities which tend to integrate the activities of the metropolitan area
   C. bring the metropolitan population under a single local government
   D. set up intermunicipal coordinating agencies to solve area administrative and economic problems
   E. allow each government element in the metropolitan area to work out its own solution

4. By means of the *debt limit*, the states regulate many facets of the debt of the cities. 4.____
   The one of the following factors which is NOT regulated in this manner is the
   A. purpose for which the debt is incurred
   B. amount of debt which may be incurred
   C. terms of the notes or bonds issued by the city
   D. forms of debts which may be incurred
   E. source from which the money may be borrowed

5. The one of the following which is a characteristic of NEITHER the state nor the federal governments, but which is a characteristic of the government of cities is that the latter 5.____
   A. is not sovereign but an agent
   B. does not have the power to raise taxes
   C. cannot enter into contracts
   D. may not make treaties with foreign countries
   E. may not coin money

Questions 6-8.

DIRECTIONS: Questions 6 through 8 are to be answered on the basis of the following paragraph.

The regressive uses of discipline is ubiquitous. Administrative architects who seek the optimum balance between structure and morale must accordingly look toward the identification and isolation of disciplinary elements. The whole range of disciplinary sanctions, from the reprimand to the dismissal presents opportunities for reciprocity and accommodation of institutional interests. When rightly seized upon, these opportunities may provide the moment and the means for fruitful exercise of leadership and collaboration.

6. The one of the following ways of reworking the ideas presented in this paragraph in order to be BEST suited for presentation in an in-service training course in supervision is: 6.____
   A. When one of your men does something wrong, talk it over with him. Tell him what he should have done. This is a chance for you to show the man that you are on his side and that you would welcome him on your side.
   B. It is not necessary to reprimand or to dismiss an employee because he needs disciplining. The alert foreman will lead and collaborate with his subordinates making discipline unnecessary.
   C. A good way to lead the men you supervise is to take those opportunities which present themselves to use the whole range of disciplinary sanctions from reprimand to dismissal as a means for enforcing collaboration.
   D. Chances to punish a man in your squad should be welcomed as opportunities to show that you are a "*good guy*" who does not bear a grudge.
   E. Before you talk to a man or have him report to the office for something he has done wrong, attempt to lead him and get him to work with you. Tell him that his actions were wrong, that you expect him not to repeat the same wrong act, and that you will take a firmer stand if the act is repeated.

7. Of the following, the PRINCIPAL point made in the paragraph is that 7.____
   A. discipline is frequently used improperly
   B. it is possible to isolate the factors entering into a disciplinary situation
   C. identification of the disciplinary elements is desirable

D. disciplinary situations may be used to the advantage of the organization
E. obtaining the best relationship between organizational form and spirit, depend upon the ability to label disciplinary elements

8. The MOST novel idea presented in the paragraph is that 8.____
A. discipline is rarely necessary
B. discipline may be a joint action of man and supervisor
C. there are disciplinary elements which may be identified
D. a range of disciplinary sanctions exist
E. it is desirable to seek for balance between structure and morale

9. When, in the process of developing a classification plan, it has been decided that certain positions all have distinguishing characteristics sufficiently similar to justify treating them alike in the process of selecting appointees and establishing pay rates or scales, then the kind of employment represented by such positions will be called a "class." 9.____
According to this paragraph, a group of positions is called a class if they
A. have distinguishing characteristics
B. represent a kind of employment
C. can be treated in the same manner for some functions
D. all have the same pay rates
E. are treated in the same manner in the development of a classification plan

Questions 10-12.

DIRECTIONS: Questions 10 through 12 are to be answered on the basis of the following paragraph.

The fundamental characteristic of the type of remote control which management needs to bridge the gap between itself and actual operations is the more effective use of records and reports—more specifically, the gathering and interpretation of the facts contained in records and reports. Facts, for management purposes, are those data (narrative and quantitative) which express in simple terms the current standing of the agency's program, work and resources in relation to the plans and policies formulated by management. They are those facts or measures (1) which permit management to compare current status with past performance and with its forecasts for the immediate future, and (2) which provide management with a reliable basis for long-range forecasting.

10. According to the above statement, a characteristic of a type of management control 10.____
A. is the kind of facts contained in records and reports
B. is narrative and quantitative data
C. is its remoteness from actual operations
D. is the use of records
E. which expresses in simple terms the current standing of the agency's program, provides management with a reliable basis for long-range forecasting

11. For management purposes, facts are, according to the paragraph, 11.____
    A. forecasts which can be compared to current status
    B. data which can be used for certain control purposes
    C. a fundamental characteristic of a type of remote control
    D. the data contained in records and reports
    E. data (narrative and quantitative) which describe the plans and policies formulated by management

12. An inference which can be drawn from this statement is that 12.____
    A. management which has a reliable basis for long-range forecasting has at its disposal a type of remote control which is needed to bridge the gap between itself and actual operations
    B. data which do not express in simple terms the current standing of the agency's program, work and resources in relationship to the plans and policies formulated by management, may still be facts for management purposes
    C. data which express relationships among the agency's program, work, and resources are management facts
    D. the gap between management and actual operations can only be bridged by characteristics which are fundamentally a type of remote control
    E. management compares current status with past performance in order to obtain a reliable basis for long-range forecasting

Questions 13-14.

DIRECTIONS: Questions 13 and 14 are to be answered on the basis of the following paragraph.

People must be selected to do the tasks involved and must be placed on a payroll in jobs fairly priced. Each of these people must be assigned those tasks which he can perform best: the work of each must be appraised, and good and poor work singled out appropriately. Skill in performing assigned tasks must be developed, and the total work situation must be conducive to sustained high performance. Finally, employees must be separated from the work force either voluntarily or involuntarily because of inefficient or unsatisfactory performance or because of curtailment of organizational activities.

13. A personnel function which is NOT included in the above description is 13.____
    A. classification B. training C. placement
    D. severance E. service rating

14. The underlying implied purpose of the policy enunciated in the above paragraph is 14.____
    A. to plan for the curtailment of the organizational program when it becomes necessary
    B. to single out appropriate skill in performing assigned tasks
    C. to develop and maintain a high level of performance by employees

D. that training employees in relation to the total work situation is essential if good and poor work are to be singled out
E. that equal money for equal work results in a total work situation which insures proper appraisal

15. Changes in program must be quickly and effectively translated into organizational adjustments if the administrative machinery is to be fully adapted to current operating needs. Continuous administrative planning is indispensable to the successful and expeditious accomplishment of such organization changes. 15.____
According to this statement,
A. the absence of continuous administrative planning must result in outmoded administrative machinery
B. continuous administrative planning is necessary for changes in program
C. if changes in program are quickly and effectively translated into organizational adjustments, the administrative machinery is fully adapted to current operating needs
D. continuous administrative planning results in successful and expeditious accomplishment of organization changes
E. if administrative machinery is not fully adapted to current operating needs, then continuous administrative planning is absent

16. The first-line supervisor executes policy as elsewhere formulated. He does not make policy. He is the element of the administrative structure closest to the employee group. 16.____
From this point of view, it follows that a MAJOR function of the first-line supervisor is to
A. suggest desirable changes in procedure to top management
B. prepare time schedules showing when his unit will complete a piece of work so that it will dovetail with the requirements of other units
C. humanize policy so as to respect employee needs and interests
D. report danger points to top management in order to forestall possible bottlenecks
E. discipline employees who continuously break departmental rules

17. During a supervisory staff meeting, the department head said to the first-line supervisors, "*The most important job you have is to get across to the employees in your units the desirability of achieving our department's aims and the importance of the jobs they are performing toward reaching our goals.*" 17.____
In general, adoption of this point of view would tend to result in an organization
A. in which supervisors would be faced by many disciplinary problems caused by employee reaction to the program
B. in which less supervision is required of the work of the average employee
C. having more clearly defined avenues of communication
D. lacking definition; supervisors would tend to forget their primary mission of getting the assigned work completed as efficiently as possible
E. in which most employees would be capable of taking over a supervisory position when necessary

18. A supervisor, in assigning a man to a job, generally followed the policy of fitting the man to the job. 18.____
This procedure is
   A. *undesirable*; the job should be fitted to the man
   B. *desirable*; primary emphasis should be on the work to be accomplished
   C. *undesirable*; the policy does not consider human values
   D. *desirable*; setting up a definite policy and following it permits careful analysis
   E. *undesirable*; it is not always possible to fit the available man to the job

19. Assume that one of the units under your jurisdiction has 40 typists. Their skill range from 15 to 80 words a minute. 19.____
The MOST feasible of the following methods to increase the typing output of this unit is to
   A. study the various typing jobs to determine the skill requirements for each type of work and assign to each typist tasks commensurate with her skill
   B. assign the slow typists to clerical work and hire new typists
   C. assign such tasks as typing straight copy to the slower typists
   D. reduce the skill requirements necessary to produce a satisfactory quantity of work
   E. simplify procedures and keep records, memoranda, and letters short and concise

20. In a division of a department, private secretaries were assigned to members of the technical staff since each required a secretary who was familiar with his particular field and who could handle various routine matters without referring to anyone. Other members of the staff depended for their dictation and typing work upon a small pool consisting of two stenographers and two typists. Because of turnover and the difficulty of recruiting new stenographers and typists, the pool had to be discontinued. 20.____
Of the following, the MOST satisfactory way to provide stenographic and typing service for the division is to
   A. organize the private secretaries into a decentralized pool under the direction of a supervisor to whom nontechnical staff members would send requests for stenographic and typing assistance
   B. organize the private secretaries into a central pool under the direction of a supervisor to whom all staff members would send requests for stenographic and typing assistance
   C. train clerks as typists and typists as stenographers
   D. relieve stenographers and typists of jobs that can be done by messengers or clerks
   E. conserve time by using such devices as indicating minor corrections on a final draft in such a way that they can be erased and by using duplicating machines to eliminate typing many copies

21. Even under perfect organizational conditions, the relationships between the line units and the units charged with budget planning and personnel management may be precarious at times. 21.____
The one of the following which is a MAJOR reason for this is that
   A. service units assist the head of the agency in formulating and executing policies
   B. line units frequently find lines of communication to the agency head blocked by service units
   C. there is a natural antagonism between planners and doers
   D. service units tend to become line in attitude and emphasis, and to conflict with operating units
   E. service units tend to function apart from the operating units

22. The one of the following which is the CHIEF reason for training supervisors is that 22.____
   A. untrained supervisors find it difficult to train their subordinates
   B. most persons do not start as supervisors and consequently are in need of supervisory training
   C. training permits a higher degree of decentralization of the decision-making process
   D. training permits a higher degree of centralization of the decision-making process
   E. coordinated actions on the part of many persons pre-supposes familiarity with the procedures to be employed

23. The problem of determining the type of organization which should exist is inextricably interwoven with the problem of recruitment. 23.____
In general, this statement is
   A. *correct*; since organizations are man-made, they can be changed
   B. *incorrect*; the organizational form which is most desirable is independent of the persons involved
   C. *correct*; the problem of organization cannot be considered apart from employee qualifications
   D. *incorrect*; organizational problems can be separated into many parts and recruitment is important in only few of these
   E. *correct*; a good recruitment program will reduce the problems of organization

24. The conference as an administrative tool is MOST valuable for solving problems which 24.____
   A. are simple and within a familiar frame of reference
   B. are of long standing
   C. are novel and complex
   D. are not solvable
   E. require immediate solution

25. Of the following, a recognized procedure for avoiding conflicts in the delegation of authority is to 25.____
    A. delegate authority so as to preserve control by top management
    B. provide for a workable span of control
    C. preview all assignments periodically
    D. assign all related work to the same control
    E. use the linear method of assignment

KEY (CORRECT ANSWERS)

1. B
2. E
3. C
4. E
5. A

6. A
7. D
8. B
9. C
10. D

11. B
12. A
13. A
14. C
15. A

16. C
17. B
18. B
19. A
20. A

21. D
22. C
23. C
24. C
25. D

TEST 2

DIRECTIONS: Each question or incomplete statement is followed by several suggested answers or completions. Select the one that BEST answers the question or completes the statement. *PRINT THE LETTER OF THE CORRECT ANSWER IN THE SPACE AT THE RIGHT.*

1. A danger which exists in any organization as complex as that required for administration of a large city is that each department comes to believe that it exists for its own sake. 1.____
The one of the following which has been attempted in some organizations as a cure for this condition is to
   A. build up the departmental esprit de corps
   B. expand the functions and jurisdictions of the various departments so that better integration is possible
   C. develop a body of specialists in the various subject matter fields which cut across departmental lines
   D. delegate authority to the lowest possible echelon
   E. systematically transfer administrative personnel from one department to another

2. At best, the organization chart is ordinarily and necessarily an idealized picture of the intent of top management, a reflection of hopes and aims rather than a photograph of the operating facts within an organization. 2.____
The one of the following which is the BASIC reason for this is that the organization chart
   A. does not show the flow of work within the organization
   B. speaks in terms of positions rather than of live employees
   C. frequently contains unresolved internal ambiguities
   D. is a record of past organization or of proposed future organization and never a photograph of the living organization
   E. does not label the jurisdiction assigned to each component unit

3. The drag of inadequacy is always downward. The need in administration is always for the reverse; for a department head to project his thinking to the city level, for the unit chief to try to see the problems of the department. 3.____
The inability of a city administration to recruit administrators who can satisfy this need usually results in departments characterized by
   A. disorganization
   B. poor supervision
   C. circumscribed viewpoints
   D. poor public relations
   E. a lack of programs

4. When, as a result of a shift in public sentiment, the elective officers of a city are changed, is it desirable for career administrators to shift ground without performing any illegal or dishonest act in order to conform to the policies of the new elective officers? 4.____
   A. *No*; the opinions and beliefs of the career officials are the result of long experience in administration and are more reliable than those of politicians.

B. *Yes*; only in this way can citizens, political officials, and career administrators alike have confidence in the performance of their respective functions.
C. *No*; a top career official who is so spineless as to change his views or procedures as a result of public opinion is of little value to the public service.
D. *Yes*; legal or illegal, it is necessary that a city employee carry out the orders of his superior officers
E. *No*; shifting ground with every change in administration will preclude the use of a constant overall policy.

5. Participation in developing plans which will affect levels in the organization in addition to his own, will contribute to an individual's understanding of the entire system. When possible, this should be encouraged. 5.____
This policy is, in general,
A. *desirable*; the maintenance of any organization depends upon individual understanding
B. *undesirable*; employees should participate only in those activities which affect their own level, otherwise conflicts in authority may arise
C. *desirable*; an employee's will to contribute to the maintenance of an organization depends to a great extent on the level which he occupies
D. *undesirable*; employees can be trained more efficiently and economically in an organized training program than by participating in plan development
E. *desirable*; it will enable the employee to make intelligent suggestions for adjustment of the plan in the future

6. Constant study should be made of the information contained in reports to isolate those elements of experience which are static, those which are variable and repetitive, and those which are variable and due to chance. 6.____
Knowledge of those elements of experience in his organization which are static or constant will enable the operating official to
A. fix responsibility for their supervision at a lower level
B. revise the procedure in order to make the elements variable
C. arrange for follow-up and periodic adjustment
D. bring related data together
E. provide a frame of reference within which detailed standards for measure-meant can be installed

7. A chief staff officer, serving as one of the immediate advisors to the department head, has demonstrated a special capacity for achieving internal agreements and for sound judgment. As a result he has been used more and more as a source of counsel and assistance by the department head. Other staff officers and line officials as well have discovered that it is wise for them to check with this colleague in advance on all problematical matters handed up to the department head. 7.____
Developments such as this are
A. *undesirable*; they disrupt the normal lines for flow of work in an organization

B. *desirable*; they allow an organization to make the most of its strength wherever such strength resides
C. *undesirable*; they tend to undermine the authority of the department head and put it in the hands of a staff officer who does not have the responsibility
D. *desirable*; they tend to resolve internal ambiguities in organization
E. *undesirable*; they make for bad morale by causing *cut throat* competition

8. A common difference among executives is that some are not content unless they are out in front of everything that concerns their organization, while others prefer to run things by pulling strings, by putting others out in front and by stepping into the breach only when necessary. 8.____
Generally speaking, an advantage this latter method of operation has over the former is that it
A. results in a higher level of morale over a sustained period of time
B. gets results by exhortation and direct stimulus
C. makes it necessary to calculate integrated moves
D. makes the personality of the executive felt further down the line
E. results in the executive getting the reputation for being a good fellow

9. Administrators frequently have to get facts by interviewing people. Although the interview is a legitimate fact-gathering technique, it has definite limitations which should not be overlooked. 9.____
The one of the following which is an important limitation is that
A. people who are interviewed frequently answer questions with guesses rather than admit their ignorance
B. it is a poor way to discover the general attitude and thinking of supervisors interviewed
C. people sometimes hesitate to give information during an interview which they will submit in written form
D. it is a poor way to discover how well employees understand departmental policies
E. the material obtained from the interview can usually be obtained at lower cost from existing records

10. It is desirable and advantageous to leave a maximum measure of planning responsibility to operating agencies or units, rather than to remove the responsibility to a central planning staff agency. 10.____
Adoption of the former policy (decentralized planning) would lead to
A. *less effective* planning; operating personnel do not have the time to make long-term plans
B. *more effective* planning; operating units are usually better equipped technically than any staff agency and consequently are in a better position to set up valid plans
C. *less effective* planning; a central planning agency has a more objective point of view than any operating agency can achieve
D. *more effective* planning; plans are conceived in terms of the existing situation and their execution is carried out with the will to succeed

E. *less effective* planning; there is little or no opportunity to check deviation from plans in the proposed set-up

Questions 11-15.

DIRECTIONS: The following sections appeared in a report on the work production of two bureaus of a department. Questions 10 through 12 are to be answered on the basis of the following information. Throughout the report, assume that each month has 4 weeks.

Each of the two bureaus maintains a chronological file. In Bureau A, every 9 months on the average, this material fills a standard legal size file cabinet sufficient for 12,000 work units. In Bureau B, the same type of cabinet is filled in 18 months. Each bureau maintains three complete years of information plus a current file. When the current file cabinet is filled, the cabinet containing the oldest material is emptied, the contents disposed of and the cabinet used for current material. The similarity of these operations makes it possible to consolidate these files with little effort.

Study of the practice of using typists as filing clerks for periods when there is no typing work showed (1) Bureau A has for the past 6 months completed a total of 1,500 filing work units a week using on the average 200 man-hours of trained file clerk time and 20 man-hours of typist time, (2) Bureau B has in the same period completed a total of 2,000 filing work units a week using on the average 125 man-hours of trained file clerk time and 60 hours of typist time. This includes all work in chronological files. Assuming that all clerks work at the same speed and that all typists work at the same speed, this indicates that work other than filing should be found for typists or that they should be given some training in the filing procedures used. It should be noted that Bureau A has not been producing the 1,600 units of technical (not filing) work per 30 day period required by Schedule K, but is at present 200 units behind. The Bureau should be allowed 3 working days to get on schedule.

11. What percentage (approximate) of the total number of filing work units completed in both units consists of the work involved in the maintenance of the chronological files? 11.____
    A. 5% B. 10% C. 15% D. 20% E. 25%

12. If the two chronological files are consolidated, the number of months which should be allowed for filling a cabinet is 12.____
    A. 2 B. 4 C. 6 D. 8 E. 14

13. The MAXIMUM number of file cabinets which can be released for other uses as a result of the consolidation recommended is 13.____
    A. 0
    B. 1
    C. 2
    D. 3
    E. not determinable on the basis of the data given

14. If all the filing work for both units is consolidated without any diminution in the amount to be done and all filing work is done by trained file clerks, the number of clerks required (35-hour work week) is 14.____
    A. 4 B. 5 C. 6 D. 7 E. 8

15. In order to comply with the recommendation with respect to Schedule K, the present work production of Bureau A must be increased by 15.____
    A. 50%
    B. 100%
    C. 150%
    D. 200%
    E. an amount which is not determinable on the basis of the data given

16. A certain training program during World War II resulted in training of thousands of supervisors in industry. The methods of this program were later successfully applied in various governmental agencies. The program was based upon the assumption that there is an irreducible minimum of three supervisory skills. The one of these skills among the following is 16.____
    A. to know how to perform the job at hand well
    B. to be able to deal personally with workers, especially face-to-face
    C. to be able to imbue workers with the will to perform the job well
    D. to know the kind of work that is done by one's unit and the policies and procedures of one's agency
    E. the "know-how" of administrative and supervisory processes

17. A comment made by an employee about a training course was, *We never have any idea how we are getting along in that course."* 17.____
    The fundamental error in training methods to which this criticism points is
    A. insufficient student participation
    B. failure to develop a feeling of need or active want for the material being presented
    C. the training sessions may be too long
    D. no attempt may have been made to connect the new material with what was already known
    E. no goals have been set for the students

18. Assume that you are attending a departmental conference on efficiency ratings at which it is proposed that a man-to-man rating scale be introduced. 18.____
    You should point out that, of the following, the CHIEF weakness of the man-to-man rating scale is that
    A. it involves abstract numbers rather than concrete employee characteristics
    B. judges are unable to select their own standards for comparison
    C. the standard for comparison shifts from man to man for each person rated
    D. not every person rated is given the opportunity to serve as a standard for comparison
    E. standards for comparison will vary from judge to judge

19. Assume that you are conferring with a supervisor who has assigned to his subordinates efficiency ratings which you believe to be generally too low. The supervisor argues that his ratings are generally low because his subordinates are generally inferior. 19.____
Of the following, the evidence MOST relevant to the point at issue can be secured by comparing efficiency ratings assigned by this supervisor
   A. with ratings assigned by other supervisors in the same agency
   B. this year with ratings assigned by him in previous years
   C. to men recently transferred to his unit with ratings previously earned by these men
   D. with the general city average of ratings assigned by all supervisors to all employees
   E. with the relative order of merit of his employees as determined independently by promotion test marks

20. The one of the following which is NOT among the most common of the compensable factors used in wage evaluation studies is 20.____
   A. initiative and ingenuity required
   B. physical demand
   C. responsibility for the safety of others
   D. working conditions
   E. presence of avoidable hazards

21. If independent functions are separated, there is an immediate gain in conserving special skills. If we are to make optimum use of the abilities of our employees, these skills must be conserved. 21.____
Assuming the correctness of this statement, it follows that
   A. if we are not making optimum use of employee abilities, independent functions have not been separated
   B. we are making optimum use of employee abilities if we conserve special skills
   C. we are making optimum use of employee abilities if independent functions have been separated
   D. we are not making optimum use of employee abilities if we do not conserve special skills
   E. if special skills are being conserved, independent functions need not be separated

22. A reorganization of the bureau to provide for a stenographic pool instead of individual unit stenographer will result in more stenographic help being available too each unit when it is required, and consequently will result in greater productivity for each unit. An analysis of the space requirements shows that setting up a stenographic pool will require a minimum of 400 square feet of good space. In order to obtain this space, it will be necessary to reduce the space available for technical personnel, resulting in lesser productivity for each unit. 22.____
On the basis of the above discussion, it can be stated that in order to obtain greater productivity for each unit,

A. a stenographic pool should be set up
B. further analysis of the space requirement should be made
C. it is not certain as to whether or not a stenographic pool should be set up
D. the space available for each technician should be increased in order to compensate for the absence of a stenographic pool
E. a stenographic pool should not be set up

23. The adoption of a single consolidated form will mean that most of the form will not be used in any one operation. This would create waste and confusion. This conclusion is based upon the unstated hypothesis that 23.____
A. if waste and confusion are to be avoided, a single consolidated form should be used
B. if a single consolidated form is constructed, most of it can be used in each operation
C. if waste and confusion are to be avoided, most of the form employed should be used
D. most of a single consolidated form is not used
E. a single consolidated form should not be used

24. Assume that you are studying the results of mechanizing several hand operations. 24.____
The type of data which would be MOST useful in proving that an increase in mechanization is followed by a lower cost of operation is data which show that in
A. some cases a lower cost of operation was not preceded by an increase in mechanization
B. no case was a higher cost of operation preceded by a decrease in mechanization
C. some cases a lower cost of operation was preceded by a decrease in mechanization
D no case was a higher cost of operation preceded by an increase in mechanization
E. some cases an increase in mechanization was followed by a decrease in cost of operation

25. The type of data which would be MOST useful in determining if an increase in the length of rest periods is followed by an increased rate of production is data which would indicate that _____ in the length of the rest period. 25.____

A. *decrease* in the total production never follows an increase in
B. *increase* in the total production never follows an increase
C. *increase* in the rate of production never follows a decrease
D. *decrease* in the total production may follow a decrease
E. *increase* in the total production sometimes follows an increase

KEY (CORRECT ANSWERS)

1. E
2. B
3. C
4. B
5. E

6. A
7. B
8. A
9. A
10. D

11. C
12. C
13. B
14. D
15. E

16. B
17. E
18. E
19. C
20. E

21. D
22. C
23. C
24. D
25. A

TEST 3

DIRECTIONS: Each question or incomplete statement is followed by several suggested answers or completions. Select the one that BEST answers the question or completes the statement. *PRINT THE LETTER OF THE CORRECT ANSWER IN THE SPACE AT THE RIGHT.*

1. You have been asked to answer a request from a citizen of the city. After giving the request careful consideration, you find that it cannot be granted. In answering the letter, you should begin by 1.____
   A. saying that the request cannot be granted
   B. discussing in detail the consideration you have to the request
   C. quoting the laws relating to the request
   D. explaining in detail why the request cannot be granted
   E. indicating an alternative method of achieving the end desired

2. Reports submitted to the department head should be complete to the last detail. A far as possible, summaries should be avoided. 2.____
   This statement is, in general,
   A. *correct*; only on the basis of complete information can a proper decision be reached
   B. *incorrect*; if all reports submitted were of this character, a department head would never complete his work
   C. *correct*; the decision as to what is important and what is not can only be made by the person who is responsible for the action
   D. *incorrect*; preliminary reports, obviously, cannot be complete to the last detail
   E. *correct*; summaries tend to conceal the actual state of affairs and to encourage generalizations which would not be made if the details were known; consequently, they should be avoided if possible

3. The supervisor of a large bureau, who was required in the course of business to answer a large number of letters from the public, completely formalized his responses, that is, the form and vocabulary of every letter he prepared were the same as far as possible. 3.____
   This method of solving the problem of how to handle correspondence is, in general
   A. *good*; it reduces the time and thought necessary for a response
   B. *bad*; the time required to develop a satisfactory standard form and vocabulary is usually not available in an active organization
   C. *good*; the use of standard forms causes similar requests to be answered in a similar way
   D. *bad*; the use of standard forms and vocabulary to the extent indicated results in letters in *officialese* hindering unambiguous explanation and clear understanding
   E. *good*; if this method were applied to an entire department, the answering of letters could be left to clerks and the administrators would be free for more constructive work

4. Of the following systems of designating the pages in a looseleaf manual subject to constant revision and addition, the MOST practicable one is to use _____ for main divisions and _____ for subdivisions. 4.____
   A. decimals; integers
   B. integers; letters
   C. integers; decimals
   D. letters; integers
   E. integers; integers

5. A subordinate submits a proposed draft of a form which is being revised to facilitate filling in the form on a typewriter. The draft shows that the captions for each space will be printed below the space to be filled in. 5.____
   This proposal is
   A. *undesirable*; it decreases visibility
   B. *desirable*; it makes the form easy to understand
   C. *undesirable*; it makes the form more difficult to understand
   D. *desirable*; it increases visibility
   E. *undesirable*; it is less compact than other layouts

6. The one of the following which is NOT an essential element of an integrated reporting system for work-measurement is a 6.____
   A. uniform record form for accumulating data and instructions for its maintenance
   B. procedure for routing reports upward through the organization and routing summaries downward
   C. standard report form for summarizing basic records and instructions for its preparation
   D. method for summarizing, analyzing and presenting data from several reports
   E. looseleaf revisable manual which contains all procedural materials that are reasonably permanent and have a substantial reference value

7. Forms control only accomplishes the elimination, consolidation, and simplification of forms. It contributes little to the elimination, consolidation, and simplification of procedures. 7.____
   This statement is
   A. *correct*; the form is static while the procedure is dynamic; consequently, control of one does not necessarily result in control of the other
   B. *incorrect*; forms frequently dictate the way work is laid out; consequently, control of one frequently results in control of the other
   C. *correct*; the procedure is primary and the form secondary; consequently, control of procedure will also control form
   D. *incorrect*; the form and procedure are identical from the viewpoint of work control; consequently, control of one means control of the other
   E. *correct*; the assurance that forms are produced and distributed economically has little relationship to the consolidation and simplification of procedures

8. Governmental agencies frequently attempt to avoid special interest group pressures by referring them to the predetermined legislative policy, or to the necessity for rules and regulations applying generally to all groups and situations. 8.____
Of the following, the MOST important weakness of this formally correct position is that
   A. it is not tenable in the face of determined opposition
   B. it tends to legalize and formalize the informal relationships between citizen groups and the government
   C. the achievement of an agency's aims is in large measure dependent upon its ability to secure the cooperation and support of special interest groups
   D. independent groups which participate in the formulation of policy in their sphere of interest tend to criticize openly and to press for changes in the direction of their policy
   E. agencies following this policy find it difficult to decentralize their public relation activities as subdivisions can only refer to the agency's overall policy

9. One of the primary purposes of the performance budget is to improve the ability to examine budgetary requirement by groups who have not been engaged in the construction of the budget. 9.____
This is accomplished by
   A. making line by line appropriations
   B. making lump sum appropriations by department
   C. enumerating authorization for all expenditures
   D. standardizing the language used and the kinds of authorizations permitted
   E. permitting examination on the level of accomplishment

10. When engaged in budget construction or budget analysis, there is no point in trying to determine the total or average benefits to be obtained from total expenditures for a particular commodity or function. 10.____
The validity of this argument is USUALLY based upon the
   A. viewpoint that it is not possible to construct a functional budget
   B. theory (or phenomenon) of diminishing utility
   C. hypothesis that as governmental budgets provide in theory for minimum requirements, there is no need to determine total benefits
   D. assumption that such determinations are not possible
   E. false hypothesis that a comparison between expected and achieved results does not aid in budget construction

Questions 11-12.

DIRECTIONS: Questions 11 and 12 are to be answered on the basis of the following paragraph.

Production planning is mainly a process of synthesis. As a basis for the positive act of bringing complex production elements properly together, however, analysis is necessary, especially if improvement is to be made in an existing organization. The necessary analysis requires customary means of orientation and preliminary fact gathering with emphasis, however, on the recognition of administrative goals and of the relationship among work steps.

11. The entire process described is PRIMARILY one of 11.____
    A. taking apart, examining, and recombining
    B. deciding what changes are necessary, making the changes and checking on their value
    C. fact finding so as to provide the necessary orientation
    D. discovering just where the emphasis in production should be placed and then modifying the existing procedure so that it is placed properly
    E. recognizing administrative goals and the relationship among work steps

12. In production planning according to the above paragraph, analysis is used PRIMARILY as 12.____
    A. a means of making important changes in an organization
    B. the customary means of orientation and preliminary fact finding
    C. a development of the relationship among work steps
    D. a means for holding the entire process intact by providing a logical basis
    E. a method to obtain the facts upon which a theory can be built

Questions 13-15.

DIRECTIONS: Questions 13 through 15 are to be answered on the basis of the following paragraph.

Public administration is policy-making. But it is not autonomous, exclusive or isolated policy-making. It is policy-making on a field where mighty forces contend, forces engendered in and by society. It is policy-making subject to still other and various policy makers. Public administration is one of a number of basic political processes by which these people achieves and controls government.

13. From the point of view expressed in the above paragraph, public administration is 13.____
    A. becoming a technical field with completely objective processes
    B. the primary force in modern society
    C. a technical field which should be divorced from the actual decision-making function
    D. basically anti-democratic
    E. intimately related to politics

14. According to the above paragraph, public administration is NOT entirely 14.____
    A. a force generated in and by society
    B. subject at times to controlling influences
    C. a social process
    D. policy-making relating to administrative practices
    E. related to policy-making at lower levels

15. The above paragraph asserts that public administration 15.____
    A. develops the basic and controlling policies
    B. is the result of policies made by many different forces
    C. should attempt to break through its isolated policy-making and engage on a broader field
    D. is a means of directing government
    E. is subject to the political processes by which acts are controlled

Questions 16-18.

DIRECTIONS: Questions 16 through 18 are to be answered on the basis of the following chart.

In order to understand completely the source of an employee's insecurity on his job, it is necessary to understand how he came to be, who he is and what kind of person he is away from his job. This would necessitate an understanding of those personal assets and liabilities which the employee brings to the job situation. These arise from his individual characteristics and his past experiences and established patterns of interpersonal relations. This whole area is of tremendous scope, encompassing everything included within the study of psychiatry and interpersonal relations. Therefore, it has been impracticable to consider it in detail. Attention has been focused on the relatively circumscribed area of the actual occupational situation. The factors considered those which the employee brings to the job situation and which arise from his individual characteristics and his past experience and established patterns of interpersonal relations are: intellectual-level or capacity, specific aptitudes, education, work experience, health, social and economic background, patterns of interpersonal relations and resultant personality characteristics.

16. According to the above paragraph, the one of the following fields of study which would be of LEAST importance in the study of the problem is the 16.____
    A. relationships existing among employees
    B. causes of employee insecurity in the job situation
    C. conflict, if it exists, between intellectual level and work experience
    D. distribution of intellectual achievement
    E. relationship between employee characteristics and the established pattern of interpersonal relations in the work situation

17. According to the above paragraph, in order to make a thoroughgoing and comprehensive study of the sources of employee insecurity, the field of study should include 17.____
    A. only such circumscribed areas as are involved in extra-occupational situations
    B. a study of the dominant mores of the period
    C. all branches of the science of psychology
    D. a determination of the characteristics, such as intellectual capacity, which an employee should bring to the job situation
    E. employee personality characteristics arising from previous relationships with other people

18. It is implied by this paragraph that it would be of GREATEST advantage to bring to this problem a comprehensive knowledge of 18.____
    A. all established patterns of interpersonal relations
    B. the milieu in which the employee group is located
    C. what assets and liabilities are presented in the job situation
    D. methods of focusing attention on relatively circumscribed regions
    E. the sources of an employee's insecurity on his job

Questions 19-20.

DIRECTIONS: Questions 19 and 20 are to be answered on the basis of the following paragraph.

If, during a study, some hundreds of values of a variable (such as annual number of latenesses for each employee in a department) have been noted merely in the arbitrary order in which they happen to occur, the mind cannot properly grasp the significance of the record, the observations must be ranked or classified in some way before the characteristics of the series can be comprehended, and those comparisons, on which arguments as to causation depend, can be made with other series. A dichotomous classification is too crude; if the values are merely classified according to whether they exceed or fall short of some fixed value, a large part of the information given by the original record is lost. Numerical measurements lend themselves with peculiar readiness to a manifold classification.

19. According to the above paragraph, if the values of a variable which are gathered during a study are classified in a few subdivisions, the MOST likely result will be 19.____
    A. an inability to grasp the signification of the record
    B. an inability to relate the series with other series
    C. a loss of much of the information in the original data
    D. a loss of the readiness with which numerical measurements lend themselves to a manifold classification
    E. that the order in which they happen to occur will be arbitrary

20. The above paragraph advocates, with respect to numerical data, the use of 20.____
    A. arbitrary order
    B. comparisons with other series
    C. a two-value classification
    D. a many value classification
    E. all values of a variable

Questions 21-25.

DIRECTIONS: Questions 21 through 25 are to be answered on the basis of the following chart.

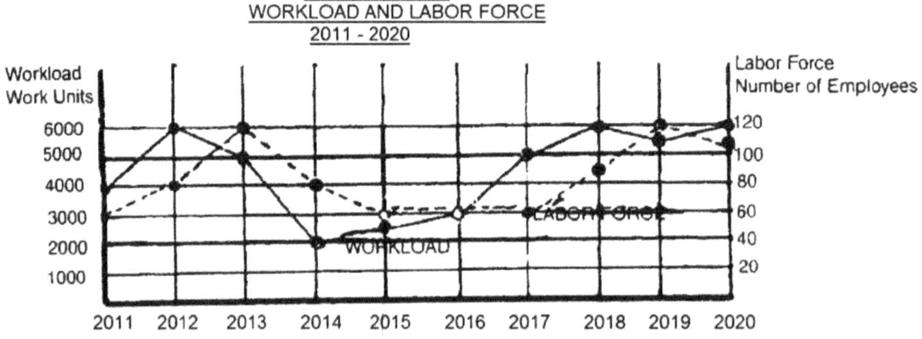

21. The one of the following years for which average employee production was LOWEST was 21.____
A. 2012 B. 2014 C. 2016 D. 2018 E. 2020

22. The average annual employee production for the ten-year period was, in terms of work units, MOST NEARLY 22.____
A. 30 B. 50 C. 70 D. 80 E. 90

23. On the basis of the chart, it can be deduced that personnel needs for the coming year are budgeted on the basis of 23.____
A. workload for the current year
B. expected workload for the coming year
C. no set plan
D. average workload over the five years immediately preceding the period
E. expected workload for the five coming years

24. The chart indicates that the operation is carefully programmed and that the labor force has been used properly. 24.____
This opinion is
A. *supported* by the chart; the organization has been able to meet emergency situations requiring much additional work without commensurate increase in staff
B. *not supported* by the chart; the irregular workload shows a complete absence of planning
C. *supported* by the chart; the similar shapes of the workload and labor force curves show that these important factors are closely related
D. *not supported* by the chart; poor planning with respect to labor requirements is obvious from the chart
E. *supported* by the chart; the average number of units of work performed in any 5-year period during the 10 years shows sufficient regularity to indicate a definite trend

25. The chart indicates that the department may be organized in such a way as to require a permanent minimum staff which is too large for the type of operation indicated. 25.____
This opinion is
A. *supported* by the chart; there is indication that the operation calls for an irreducible minimum number of employees and application of the most favorable work production records shows this to be too high for normal operation
B. *not supported* by the chart; the absence of any sort of regularity makes it impossible to express any opinion with any degree of certainty
C. *supported* by the chart; the expected close relationship between workload and labor force is displaced somewhat, a phenomenon which usually occurs as a result of a fixed minimum requirement
D. *not supported* by the chart; the violent movement of the labor force curve makes it evident that no minimum requirements are in effect

E. *supported* by the chart; calculation shows that the average number of employees was 84 with an average variation of 17.8, thus indicating that the minimum number of 60 persons was too high for efficient operation

---

KEY (CORRECT ANSWERS)

1.	A	11.	A
2.	B	12.	E
3.	D	13.	E
4.	C	14.	D
5.	A	15.	D
6.	E	16.	D
7.	B	17.	E
8.	C	18.	B
9.	E	19.	C
10.	B	20.	D

21.	B
22.	B
23.	A
24.	D
25.	A

SUPERVISION, ADMINISTRATION, MANAGEMENT, AND ORGANIZATION

EXAMINATION SECTION

TEST 1

DIRECTIONS: Each question or incomplete statement is followed by several suggested answers or completions. Select the one that BEST answers the question or completes the statement. *PRINT THE LETTER OF THE CORRECT ANSWER IN THE SPACE AT THE RIGHT.*

1. In coaching a subordinate on the nature of decision-making, an executive would be right if he stated that the one of the following which is general the BEST definition of decision-making is: 1.____
   A. Choosing between alternatives
   B. Making diagnoses of feasible ends
   C. Making diagnoses of feasible means
   D. Comparing alternatives

2. Of the following, which one would be LEAST valid as a purpose of an organizational policy statement? 2.____
   To
   A. keep personnel from performing improper actions and functions on routine matters
   B. prevent the mishandling of non-routine matters
   C. provide management personnel with a tool that precludes the need for their use of judgment
   D. provide standard decisions and approaches in handling problems of a recurrent nature

3. Much has been written criticizing bureaucratic organizations. Current thinking on the subject is GENERALLY that 3.____
   A. bureaucracy is on the way out
   B. bureaucracy, though not perfect, is unlikely to be replaced
   C. bureaucratic organizations are most effective in dealing with constant change
   D. bureaucratic organizations are most effective when dealing with sophisticated customers or clients

4. The development of alternate plans as a major step in planning will normally result in the planner having several possible courses of action available. 4.____
   GENERALLY, this is
   A. *desirable*, since such development helps to determine the most suitable alternative and to provide for the unexpected
   B. *desirable*, since such development makes the use of planning premises and constraints unnecessary

C. *undesirable*, since the planners should formulate only one way of achieving given goals at a given time
D. *undesirable*, since such action restricts efforts to modify the planning to take advantage of opportunities

5. The technique of departmentation by task force includes the assigning of a team or task force to a definite project or block of work which extends from the beginning to the completing of a wanted and definite type and quantity of work. Of the following, the MOST important actor aiding the successful use of this technique *normally* is 5.____
   A. having the task force relatively large, at least one hundred members
   B. having a definite project termination date established
   C. telling each task force member what his next assignment will be only after the current project ends
   D. utilizing it only for projects that are regularly recurring

6. With respect to communication in small group settings such as may occur in business, government, and the military, it is generally TRUE that people usually derive more satisfaction and are usually more productive under conditions which 6.____
   A. permit communication only with superiors
   B. permit the minimum intragroup communication possible
   C. are generally restricted by management
   D. allow open communication among all group members

7. If an executive were asked to list some outstanding features of decentralization, which one of the following would NOT be such a feature? 7.____
   Decentralization
   A. provides decision-making experience for lower level managers
   B. promotes uniformity of policy
   C. is a relatively new concept in management
   D. is similar to the belief in encouragement of free enterprise

8. Modern management experts have emphasized the importance of the informal organization in motivating employees to increase productivity. 8.____
   Of the following, the characteristic which would have the MOST direct influence on employee motivation is the tendency of members of the informal organization to
   A. resist change
   B. establish their own norms
   C. have similar outside interests
   D. set substantially higher goals than those of management

9. According to leading management experts, the decision-making process contains separate and distinct steps that must be taken in an orderly sequence. 9.____
   Of the following arrangements, which one is in CORRECT order?

A. I. Search for alternatives; II. diagnosis; III. comparison; IV. choice
B. I. Diagnose; II. comparison; III. search for alternatives; IV. choice
C. I. Diagnose; II. search for alternatives; III. comparison; IV. choice
D. I. Diagnose; II. search for alternatives; III. choice; IV. comparison

10. Of the following, the growth of professionalism in large organizations can PRIMARILY be expected to result in 10.____
A. greater equalization of power
B. increased authoritarianism
C. greater organizational disloyalty
D. increased promotion opportunities

11. Assume an executive carries out his responsibilities to his staff according to what is now known about managerial leadership. 11.____
Which of the following statements would MOST accurately reflect his assumptions about proper management?
A. Efficiency in operations results from allowing the human element to participate in a minimal way.
B. Efficient operation result from balancing work considerations with personnel considerations.
C. Efficient operation results from a workforce committed to its self-interest.
D. Efficient operation results from staff relationships that produce a friendly work climate.

12. Assume that an executive is called upon to conduct a management audit. To do this properly, he would have to take certain steps in a specific sequence. 12.____
Of the following steps, which step should this manager take FIRST?
A. Managerial performance must be surveyed.
B. A method of reporting must be established.
C. Management auditing procedures and documentation must be developed.
D. Criteria for the audit must be considered.

13. If a manager is required to conduct a scientific investigation of an organizational problem, the FIRST step he should take is to 13.____
A. state his assumptions about the problem
B. carry out a search for background information
C. choose the right approach to investigate the validity of his assumptions
D. define and state the problem

14. An executive would be right to assert that the principle of delegation states that decisions should be made PRIMARILY 14.____
A. by persons in an executive capacity qualified to make them
B. by persons in a non-executive capacity
C. at as low an organization level of authority as practicable
D. by the next lower level of authority

15. Of the following, which one is NOT regarded by management authorities as a FUNDAMENTAL characteristic of an *ideal* bureaucracy? 15.____
    A. Division of labor and specialization
    B. An established hierarchy
    C. Decentralization of authority
    D. A set of operating rules and regulations

16. As the number of subordinates in a manager's span of control increases, the ACTUAL number of possible relationships 16.____
    A. increases disproportionately to the number of subordinates
    B. increases in equal number to the number of subordinates
    C. reaches a stable level
    D. will first increase then slowly decrease

17. An executive's approach to controlling the activities of his subordinates concentrated on ends rather than means, and was diagnostic rather than punitive. 17.____
    This manager may MOST properly be characterized as using the managerial technique of management-by-
    A. exception B. objectives C. crisis D. default

18. In conducting a training session on the administrative control process, which of the following statements would be LEAST valid for an executive to make? 18.____
    Controlling
    A. requires checking upon assignments to see what is being done
    B. involves comparing what is being done to what ought to be done
    C. requires corrective action when what is being done does not meet expectations
    D. occurs after all the other managerial processes have been performed

19. The "brainstorming" technique for creative solutions of management problems MOST generally consists of 19.____
    A. bringing staff together in an exchange of a quantity of freewheeling ideas
    B. isolating individual staff members to encourage thought
    C. developing improved office procedures
    D. preparation of written reports on complex problems

20. Computer systems hardware MOST often operates in relation to which one of the following steps in solving a data-processing problem? 20.____
    A. Determining the problem
    B. Defining and stating the problem
    C. Implementing the programmed solution
    D. Completing the documentation of every unexplored solution

21. There is a tendency in management to upgrade objectives. 21.____
    This trend is generally regarded as
    A. *desirable*; the urge to improve is demonstrated by adopting objectives that have been adjusted to provide improved service

B. *undesirable*; the typical manager searches for problems which obstruct his objectives
C. *desirable*; it is common for a manager to find that the details of an immediate operation have occupied so much of his time that he has lost sight of the basic overall objective
D. *undesirable*; efforts are wasted when they are expended on a mass of uncertain objectives, since the primary need of most organizations is a single target or several major ones

22. Of the following, it is generally LEAST effective for an executive to delegate authority where working conditions involve 22.____
A. rules establishing normal operating procedures
B. consistent methods of operation
C. rapidly changing work standards
D. complex technology

23. If an executive was explaining the difficulty of making decisions under *risk* conditions, he would be MOST accurate if he said that such decisions would be difficult to make when the decision maker has _____ information and experience and can expect _____ outcomes for each action. 23.____
A. limited; many
B. much; many
C. much; few
D. limited; few

24. If an executive were asked to list some outstanding features of centralized organization, which one of the following would be INCORRECT? 24.____
Centralized organization
A. lessens risks of errors by unskilled subordinates
B. utilizes the skills of specialized experts at a central location
C. produces uniformity of policy and non-uniformity of action
D. enables closer control of operations than a decentralized set-up

25. It is possible for an organization's management to test whether or not the organization has a sound structure. 25.____
Of the following, which one is NOT a test of soundness in an organization's structure?
The
A. ability to replace key personnel with minimum loss of effectiveness
B. ability of information and decisions to flow more freely through the *grapevine* than through formal channels
C. provision for orderly organizational growth with the ability to handle change as the need arises.

KEY (CORRECT ANSWERS)

1.	A	11.	B
2.	C	12.	D
3.	B	13.	D
4.	A	14.	C
5.	B	15.	C
6.	D	16.	A
7.	B	17.	B
8.	B	18.	D
9.	C	19.	A
10.	A	20.	C
21.	A		
22.	C		
23.	A		
24.	C		
25.	B		

TEST 2

DIRECTIONS: Each question or incomplete statement is followed by several suggested answers or completions. Select the one that BEST answers the question or completes the statement. *PRINT THE LETTER OF THE CORRECT ANSWER IN THE SPACE AT THE RIGHT.*

1. Management experts generally believe that computer-based management information systems (MIS) have greater potential for improving the process of management than any other development in recent decades. 1.____
The one of the following which MOST accurately describes the objectives of MIS is to
   A. provide information for decision-making on planning, initiating, and controlling the operations of the various units of the organization
   B. establish mechanization of routine functions such as clerical records, payroll, inventory, and accounts receivable in order to promote economy and efficiency
   C. computerize decision-making on planning, initiative, organizing, and controlling the operations of an organization
   D. provide accurate facts and figures on the various programs of the organization to be used for purposes of planning and research

2. The one of the following which is the BEST application on the *management-by-exception* principle is that this principle 2.____
   A. stimulates communication and aids in management of crisis situations, thus reducing the frequency of decision-making
   B. saves time and reserves top-management decisions only for crisis situations, thus reducing the frequency of decision-making
   C. stimulates communication, saves time, and reduces the frequency of decision-making
   D. is limited to crisis-management situations

3. It is generally recognized that each organization is dependent upon availability of qualified personnel. 3.____
Of the following, the MOST important factor affecting the availability of qualified people to each organization is
   A. innovations in technology and science
   B. the general decline in the educational levels of our population
   C. the rise of sentiment against racial discrimination
   D. pressure by organized community groups

4. A fundamental responsibility of all managers is to decide what physical facilities and equipment are needed to help attain basic goals. 4.____
Good planning for the purchase and use of equipment is seldom easy to do and is complicated MOST by the fact that
   A. organizations rarely have stable sources of supply
   B. nearly all managers tend to be better at personnel planning than at equipment planning

C. decisions concerning physical resources are made too often on a *crash basis* rather than under carefully prepared policies
D. legal rulings relative to depreciation fluctuate very frequently

5. In attempting to reconcile managerial objectives and an individual employee's goals, it is generally LEAST desirable for management to 5.____
A. recognize the capacity of the individual to contribute toward realization of managerial goals
B. encourage self-development of the employee to exceed minimum job performance
C. consider an individual employee's work separately from other employees
D. demonstrate that an employee advances only to the extent that he contributes directly to the accomplishment of stated goals

6. As a management tool for discovering individual training needs a job analysis would generally be of LEAST assistance in determining 6.____
A. the performance requirements of individual jobs
B. actual employee performance on the job
C. acceptable standards of performance
D. training needs for individual jobs

7. One of the major concerns of organizational managers today is how the spread of automation will affect them and the status of their positions. Realistically speaking, one can say that the MOST likely effect of our newer forms of highly automated technology on managers will be to 7.____
A. make most top-level positions superfluous or obsolete
B. reduce the importance of managerial work in general
C. replace the work of managers with the work of technicians
D. increase the importance of and demand for top managerial personnel

8. Which one of the following is LEAST likely to be an area or cause of trouble in the use of staff people (e.g., assistants to the administrator)? 8.____
A. Misunderstanding of the role the staff people are supposed to play, as a result of vagueness of definition of their duties and authority
B. Tendency of staff personnel almost always to be older than line personnel at comparable salary levels with who they must deal
C. Selection of staff personnel who fail to have simultaneously both competence in their specialties and skill in staff work
D. The staff person fails to understand mixed staff and operating duties

9. The one of the following which is the BEST measure of decentralization in an agency is the 9.____
A. amount of checking required on decisions made at lower levels in the chain of command
B. amount of checking required on decisions made at lower levels of the chain of command and the number of functions affected thereby
C. number of functions affected by decisions made at higher levels
D. number of functions affected by middle echelon decision-making

10. Which of the following is generally NOT a valid statement with respect to the supervisory process? 10.____
    A. General supervision is more effective than close supervision.
    B. Employee-centered supervisors lead more effectively than do production-centered supervisors.
    C. Employee satisfaction is directly related to productivity.
    D. Low-producing supervisors use techniques that are different from high-producing supervisors.

11. The one of the following which is the MOST essential element for proper evaluation of the performance of subordinate supervisors is a 11.____
    A. careful definition of each supervisor's specific job responsibilities and of his progress in meeting mutually agreed upon work goals
    B. system of rewards and penalties based on each supervisor's progress in meeting clearly defined performance standards
    C. definition of personality traits, such as industry, initiative, dependability, and cooperativeness, required for effective job performance
    D. breakdown of each supervisor's job into separate components and a rating of his performance on each individual task

12. The one of the following which is the PRINCIPAL advantage of specialization for the operating efficiency of a public service agency is that specialization 12.____
    A. reduces the amount of red tape in coordinating the activities of mutually dependent departments
    B. simplifies the problem of developing adequate job controls
    C. provides employees with a clear understanding of the relationship of their activities to the overall objectives of the agency
    D. reduces destructive competition for power between departments

13. Of the following, the group which generally benefits MOST from supervisory training programs in public service agencies are those supervisors who have 13.____
    A. accumulated a long period of total service to the agency
    B. responsibility for a large number of subordinate personnel
    C. been in the supervisory ranks for a long period of time
    D. a high level of formalized academic training

14. A list of conditions which encourages good morale inside a work group would NOT include a 14.____
    A. high rate of agreement among group members on values and objectives
    B. tight control system to minimize the risk of individual error
    C. good possibility that joint action will accomplish goals
    D. past history of successful group accomplishment

15. Of the following, the MOST important factor to be considered in selecting a training strategy or program is the 15.____
    A. requirements of the job to be performed by the trainees
    B. educational level or prior training of the trainees
    C. size of the training group
    D. quality and competence of available training specialists

16. Of the following, the one which is considered to be LEAST characteristic of the higher ranks of management is 16.____
    A. that higher levels of management benefit from modern technology
    B. that success is measured by the extent to which objectives are achieved
    C. the number of subordinates that directly report to an executive
    D. the de-emphasis of individual and specialized performance

17. Assume that an executive is preparing a training syllabus to be used in training members of his staff. 17.____
    Which of the following would NOT be a valid principle of the learning process for this manager to keep in mind in the preparation of the training syllabus?
    A. When a person has thoroughly learned a task, it takes a lot of effort to create a little more improvement.
    B. In complicated learning situations, there is a period in which an additional period of practice produces an equal amount of improvement in learning.
    C. The less a person knows about the task, the slower the initial progress.
    D. The more the person knows about the risk, the slower the initial progress.

18. Of the following, which statement BEST illustrates when collective bargaining agreements are working well? 18.____
    A. Executives strongly support subordinate managers.
    B. The management rights clause in the contract is clear and enforced.
    C. Contract provisions are competently interpreted.
    D. The provisions of the agreement are properly interpreted, communicated, and observed.

19. An executive who wishes to encourage subordinates to communicate freely with him about a job-related problem should FIRST 19.____
    A. state his own position on the problem before listening to the subordinates' ideas
    B. invite subordinates to give their own opinions on the problem
    C. ask subordinates for their reactions to his own ideas about the problem
    D. guard the confidentiality of management information about the problem

20. The ability to deal constructively with intra-organizational conflict is an essential attribute of the successful manager. 20.____
    The one of the following types of conflict which would be LEAST difficult to handle constructively is a situation in which there is
    A. agreement on objectives, but disagreement as to the probable results of adopting the various alternatives
    B. agreement on objectives, disagreement on alternative courses of action, and relative certainty as to the outcome of one of the alternatives
    C. disagreement on objectives and on alternate courses of action, but relative certainty as to the outcome of the alternatives
    D. disagreement on objectives and on alternative course of action, but uncertainty as to the outcome of the alternatives

21. Which of the following statements is LEAST accurate in describing formal job evaluation and wage and salary classification plans? 21.____
    A. Parties that disagree on wage matters can examine an established system rather than unsupported opinions.
    B. The use of such plans tends to overlook the effect of age and seniority of employees on job values in the plan.
    C. Such plans can eliminate salary controversies in organizations designing and using them properly.
    D. These plans are not particularly useful in checking on executive compensation.

22. In carrying out disciplinary action, the MOST important procedure for all managers to follow is to 22.____
    A. sell all levels of management on the need for discipline from the organization's viewpoint
    B. follow up on a disciplinary action and not assume that the action has been effective
    C. convince all executives that proper discipline is a legitimate tool for their use
    D. convince all executives that they need to display confidence in the organization's rules

Questions 23-25.

DIRECTIONS: Questions 23 through 25 are to be answered on the basis of the following situation. Richard Ford, a top administrator, is responsible for output in his organization. Because productivity had been lagging for two periods in a row, Ford decided to establish a committee of his subordinate managers to investigate the reasons for the poor performance and to make recommendations for improvements. After two meetings, the committee came to the conclusions and made the recommendations that follow:

Output forecasts had been handed down from the top without prior consultation with middle management and first level supervision. Lines of authority and responsibility had been unclear. The planning and control process should be decentralized.

After receiving the committee's recommendations, Ford proceeded to take the following actions:

Ford decided he would retain final authority to establish quotas but would delegate to the middle managers the responsibility for meeting quotas.

After receiving Ford's decision, the middle managers proceeded to delegate to the first-line supervisors the authority to establish their own quotas. The middle managers eventually received and combined the first-line supervisors' quotas so that these conformed with Ford's.

23. Ford's decision to delegate responsibility for meeting quotas to the middle managers is INCONSISTENT with sound management principles because of which one of the following? 23.____
    A. Ford shouldn't have involved himself in the first place.
    B. Middle managers do not have the necessary skills.

C. Quotas should be established by the chief executive.
D. Responsibility should not be delegated.

24. The principle of co-extensiveness of responsibility and authority bears on Ford's decision. 24.____
In this case, it IMPLIES that
A. authority should exceed responsibility
B. authority should be delegated to match the degree of responsibility
C. both authority and responsibility should be retained and not delegated
D. responsibility should be delegated but authority should be retained

25. The middle manager's decision to delegate to the first-line supervisors the authority to establish quotas was INCORRECTLY reasoned because 25.____
A. delegation and control must go together
B. first-line supervisors are in no position to establish quotas
C. one cannot delegate authority that one does not possess
D. the meeting of quotas should not be delegated

KEY (CORRECT ANSWERS)

1.	A	11.	A
2.	C	12.	B
3.	A	13.	D
4.	C	14.	B
5.	C	15.	A
6.	B	16.	C
7.	D	17.	D
8.	B	18.	D
9.	B	19.	B
10.	C	20.	B

21.	C
22.	B
23.	D
24.	B
25.	C

TEST 3

DIRECTIONS: Each question or incomplete statement is followed by several suggested answers or completions. Select the one that BEST answers the question or completes the statement. *PRINT THE LETTER OF THE CORRECT ANSWER IN THE SPACE AT THE RIGHT.*

1. A danger which exists in any organization as complex as that required for administration of a large public agency is that each department comes to believe that it exists for its own sake. 1.____
The one of the following which has been attempted in some organizations as a cure for this condition is to
   A. build up the departmental esprit de corps
   B. expand the functions and jurisdictions of the various departments so that better integration is possible
   C. develop a body of specialists in the various subject matter fields which cut across departmental lines
   D. delegate authority to the lowest possible echelon
   E. systematically transfer administrative personnel from one department to another

2. At best, the organization chart is ordinarily and necessarily an idealized picture of the intent of top management, a reflection of hopes and aims rather than a photograph of the operating facts within the organization. 2.____
The one of the following which is the basic reason for this is that the organization chart
   A. does not show the flow of work within the organization
   B. speaks in terms of positions rather than of live employees
   C. frequently contains unresolved internal ambiguities
   D. is a record of past organization or proposed future organization and never a photograph of the living organization
   E. does not label the jurisdiction assigned to each component unit

3. The drag of inadequacy is always downward. The need in administration is always for the reverse; for a department head to project his thinking to the city level, for the unit chief to try to see the problems of the department. 3.____
The inability of a city administration to recruit administrators who can satisfy this need usually results in departments characterized by
   A. disorganization
   B. poor supervision
   C. circumscribed viewpoints
   D. poor public relations
   E. a lack of programs

4. When, as a result of a shift in public sentiment, the elective officers of a city are changed, is it desirable for career administrators to shift ground without performing any illegal or dishonest act in order to conform to the policies of the new elective officers? 4.____
   A. *No*; the opinions and beliefs of the career officials are the result of long experience in administration and are more reliable than those of politicians

B. *Yes*; only in this way can citizens, political officials, and career administrators alike have confidence in the performance of their respective functions
C. *No*; a top career official who is so spineless as to change his views or procedures as a result of public opinion is of little value to the public service
D. *Yes*; legal or illegal, it is necessary that a city employee carry out the orders of his superior officers
E. *No*; shifting ground with every change in administration will preclude the use of a constant overall policy

5. Participation in developing plans which will affect levels in the organization in addition to his own, will contribute to an individual's understanding of the entire system. When possible, this should be encouraged. 5.____
This policy is, in general,
A. *desirable*; the maintenance of any organization depends upon individual understanding
B. *undesirable*; employees should participate only in these activities which affect their own level, otherwise conflicts in authority may arise
C. *desirable*; an employee's will to contribute to the maintenance of an organization depends to a great extent on the level which he occupies
D. *undesirable*; employees can be trained more efficiently and economically in an organized training program than by participating in plan development
E. *desirable*; it will enable the employee to make intelligent suggestions for adjustment of the plan in the future

6. Constant study should be made of the information contained in reports to isolate those elements of experience which are static, those which are variable and repetitive, and those which are variable and due to chance. 6.____
Knowledge of those elements of experience in his organization which are static or constant will enable the operating official to
A. fix responsibility for their supervisor at a lower level
B. revise the procedure in order to make the elements variable
C. arrange for follow-up and periodic adjustment
D. bring related data together
E. provide a frame of reference within which detailed standards for measurement can be installed

7. A chief staff officer, serving as one of the immediate advisors to the department head, has demonstrated a special capacity for achieving internal agreements and for sound judgment. As a result he has been used more and more as a source of counsel and assistance by the department head. Other staff officers and line officials as well have discovered that it is wise for them to check with this colleague in advance on all problematical matters handed up to the department head. 7.____

Developments such as this are
- A. *undesirable*; they disrupt the normal lines for flow of work in an organization
- B. *desirable*; they allow an organization to make the most of its strength wherever such strength resides
- C. *undesirable*; they tend to undermine the authority of the department head and put it in the hands of a staff officer who does not have the responsibility
- D. *desirable*; they tend to resolve internal ambiguities in organization
- E. *undesirable*; they make for bad morale by causing *cutthroat* competition

8. A common difference among executives is that some are not content unless they are out in front of everything that concerns their organization, while others prefer to run things by pulling strings, by putting others out in front and by stepping into the breach only when necessary. 8.____
Generally speaking, an advantage this latter method of operation has over the former is that it
- A. results in a higher level of morale over a sustained period of time
- B. gets results by exhortation and direct stimulus
- C. makes it unnecessary to calculate integrated moves
- D. makes the personality of the executive felt further down the line
- E. results in the executive getting the reputation for being a good fellow

9. Administrators frequently have to get facts by interviewing people. Although the interview is a legitimate fact gathering technique, it has definite limitations which should not be overlooked. 9.____
The one of the following which is an important limitation is that
- A. people who are interviewed frequently answer questions with guesses rather than admit their ignorance
- B. it is a poor way to discover the general attitude and thinking of supervisors interviewed
- C. people sometimes hesitate to give information during an interview which they will submit in written form
- D. it is a poor way to discover how well employees understand departmental policies
- E. the material obtained from the interview can usually be obtained at lower cost from existing records

10. It is desirable and advantageous to leave a maximum measure of planning responsibility to operating agencies or units, rather than to remove the responsibility to a central planning staff agency. 10.____
Adoption of the former policy (decentralized planning) would lead to
- A. *less effective planning*; operating personnel do not have the time to make long-term plans
- B. *more effective planning*; operating units are usually better equipped technically than any staff agency and consequently are in a better position to set up valid plans
- C. *less effective planning*; a central planning agency has a more objective point of view than any operating agency can achieve

D. *more effective planning*; plans are conceived in terms of the existing situation and their execution is carried out with the will to succeed
E. *less effective planning*; there is little or no opportunity to check deviation from plans in the proposed set-up

Questions 11-15.

DIRECTIONS: The following sections appeared in a report on the work production of two bureaus of a department. Base your answers to Questions 11 through 15 on this information. Throughout the report, assume that each month has 4 weeks.

Each of the two bureaus maintains a chronological file. In Bureau A, every 9 months on the average, this material fills a standard legal size cabinet sufficient for 12,000 work units. In Bureau B the same type of cabinet is filled in 18 months. Each bureau maintains three complete years of information plus a current file. When the current file cabinet is filled, the cabinet containing the oldest material is emptied, the contents disposed of, and the cabinet used for current material. The similarity of these operations makes it possible to consolidate these files with little effort.

Study of the practice of using typists as filing clerks for periods when there is no typing work showed: (1) Bureau A has for the past 6 months completed a total of 1,500 filing work units a week using on the average 100 man-hours of trained file clerk time and 20 man-hours of typist time; (2) Bureau B has in the same period completed a total of 2,000 filing work units a week using on the average 125 man-hours of trained file clerk time and 60 hours of typist time. This includes all work in chronological files. Assuming that all clerks work at the same speed and that all typists work at the same speed, this indicates that work other than filing should be found for typists or that they should be given some training in the filing procedures used. It should be noted that Bureau A has not been producing the 1,600 units of technical (not filing) work per 30-day period required by Schedule K, but is at present 200 units behind. The Bureau should be allowed 3 working days to get on schedule.

11. What percentage (approximate) of the total number of filing work units completed in both units consists of the work involved in the maintenance of the chronological files? 11.____
A. 5% B. 10% C. 15% D. 20% E. 25%

12. If the two chronological files are consolidated, the number of months which should be allowed for filling a cabinet is 12.____
A. 2 B. 4 C. 6 D. 8 E. 14

13. The MAXIMUM number of file cabinets which can be released for other uses as a result of the consolidation recommended is 13.____
A. 0
B. 1
C. 2
D. 3
E. not determinable on the basis of the data given

14. If all the filing work for both units is consolidated without diminution in the amount to be done and all filing work is done by trained file clerks, the number of clerks required (35-hour work week) is 14.____
   A. 4 B. 5 C. 6 D. 7 E. 8

15. In order to comply with the recommendation with respect to Schedule K, the present work production of Bureau A must be increased by 15.____
   A. 50%
   B. 100%
   C. 150%
   D. 200%
   E. an amount which is not determinable

16. A certain training program during World War II resulted in the training of thousands of supervisors in industry. The methods of this program were later successfully applied in various government agencies. The program was based upon the assumption that there is an irreducible minimum of three supervisory skills. 16.____
   The one of these skills among the following is
   A. to know how to perform the job at hand well
   B. to be able to deal personally with workers, especially face-to-face
   C. to be able to imbue workers with the will to perform the job well
   D. to know the kind of work that is done by one's unit and the policies and procedures of one's agency
   E. the *know-how* of administrative and supervisory processes

17. A comment made by an employee about a training course was, "*We never have any idea how we ae getting along in that course.*" 17.____
   The fundamental error in training methods to which this criticism points is
   A. insufficient student participation
   B. failure to develop a feeling of need or active want for the material being presented
   C. the training sessions may be too long
   D. no attempt may have been made to connect the new material with what was already known
   E. no goals have been set for the students

18. Assume that you are attending a departmental conference on efficiency ratings at which it is proposed that a man-to-man rating scale be introduced. 18.____
   You should point out that, of the following, the CHIEF weakness of the man-to-man rating scale is that
   A. it involves abstract numbers rather than concrete employee characteristics
   B. judges are unable to select their own standards for comparison
   C. the standard for comparison shifts from man-to-man for each person rated
   D. not every person rated is given the opportunity to serve as a standard for comparison
   E. standards for comparison will vary from judge to judge

19. Assume that you are conferring with a supervisor who has assigned to his subordinates efficiency ratings which you believe to be generally too low. The supervisor argues that his ratings are generally low because his subordinates are generally inferior. 19.____
Of the following, the evidence MOST relevant to the point at issue can be secured by comparing efficiency ratings assigned by the supervisor
   A. with ratings assigned by other supervisors in the same agency
   B. this year with ratings assigned by him in previous years
   C. to men recently transferred to his unit with ratings previously earned by these men
   D. with the general city average of ratings assigned by all supervisors to all employees
   E. with the relative order of merit of his employees as determined independently by promotion test marks

20. The one of the following which is NOT among the most common of the compensable factors used in wage evaluation studies is 20.____
   A. initiative and ingenuity required
   B. physical demand
   C. responsibility for the safety of others
   D. working conditions
   E. presence of avoidable hazards

21. If independent functions are separated, there is an immediate gain in conserving special skills. If we are to make optimum use of the abilities of our employees, these skills must be conserved. 21.____
Assuming the correctness of this statement, it follows that
   A. if we are not making optimum use of employee abilities, independent functions have not been separated
   B. we are making optimum uses of employee abilities if we conserve special skills
   C. we are making optimum use of employee abilities if independent functions have been separated
   D. we are not making optimum use of employee abilities if we do not conserve special skills
   E. if special skills are being conserved, independent functions need not be separated

22. A reorganization of the bureau to provide for a stenographic pool instead of individual unit stenographers will result in more stenographic help being available to each unit when it is required, and consequently will result in greater productivity for each unit. An analysis of the space requirements shows that setting up a stenographic pool will require a minimum of 400 square feet of good space. In order to obtain this space, it will be necessary to reduce the space available for technical personnel, resulting in lesser productivity for each unit. 22.____

On the basis of the above discussion, it can be stated that, in order to obtain greater productivity for each unit,
A. a stenographic pool should be set up
B. further analysis of the space requirement should be made
C. it is not certain as to whether or not a stenographic pool should be set up
D. the space available for each technician should be increased in order to compensate for the absence of a stenographic pool
E. a stenographic pool should not be set up

23. The adoption of single consolidated form will mean that most of the form will not be used in any one operation. This would create waste and confusion. This conclusion is based upon the unstated hypothesis that 23.____
A. if waste and confusion are to be avoided, a single consolidated form should be used
B. if a single consolidated form is constructed, most of it can be used in each operation
C. if waste and confusion are to be avoided, most of the form employed should be used
D. most of a single consolidation form is not used
E. a single consolidated form should not be used

KEY (CORRECT ANSWERS)

1.	E	11.	C
2.	B	12.	C
3.	C	13.	B
4.	B	14.	D
5.	E	15.	E
6.	A	16.	B
7.	B	17.	E
8.	A	18.	E
9.	A	19.	C
10.	D	20.	E

21. D
22. C
23. C

EXAMINATION SECTION

TEST 1

DIRECTIONS: Each question or incomplete statement is followed by several suggested answers or completions. Select the one that BEST answers the question or completes the statement. *PRINT THE LETTER OF THE CORRECT ANSWER IN THE SPACE AT THE RIGHT.*

1. The MAJOR responsibility of a director is to 1.____
   A. make certain that his line supervisors keep proper control of staff activity
   B. see that training is given to his staff according to individual needs
   C. insure that his total organization is coordinated toward agency goals and objectives
   D. work constructively with groups so that programs will reflect their needs

2. A good organizational chart of a department is an IMPORTANT instrument because it can 2.____
   A. make it easier to understand the mission of the department
   B. help new employees become acquainted with department personnel
   C. clarify relationships and responsibilities of the various department components
   D. simplify the task of *going to the top*

3. Unnecessary and obsolete forms can be eliminated MOST effectively by 3.____
   A. appointing a representative committee to review and evaluate all forms in relation to operating procedures
   B. discarding all forms which have not been used during the past year
   C. assembling all forms and destroying those which are duplicates or obsolete
   D. directing office managers to review the forms to determine which should be revised or abolished

4. The director must adopt methods and techniques to insure that his budgeted allowances are properly spent and that organizational objectives are being reached. 4.____
   These responsibilities can be fulfilled BEST by
   A. controlling operations with electronic data processing equipment
   B. shifting caseload controls from caseworkers to clerical staff
   C. installing a work simplification program and establishing controls for crucial areas of operation
   D. assigning employees with special skills and training to perform the more important and specialized jobs

5. The MOST appropriate technique for making the staff thoroughly familiar with department policies would be to 5.____
   A. maintain an up-to-date loose-leaf binder of written policies in a central point in the office
   B. issue copies of all policy directives to the unit supervisors
   C. distribute copies of policy directives to the entire staff and arrange for follow-up discussion on a unit basis
   D. discuss all major policy directives at an office-wide staff meeting

6. When a proposed change in a departmental procedure is being evaluated, the factor which should be considered MOST important in reaching the decision is the 6.____
   A. extent of resistance anticipated from members of the staff
   B. personnel needed to execute the proposed change
   C. time required for training staff in the revised procedure
   D. degree of organizational dislocation compared with gains expected from the change

7. A director anticipates that certain aspects of a new departmental procedure will be distasteful to many staff members. 7.____
   Assuming that the procedure is basically sound in spite of this drawback, the BEST approach for the director to take with his staff is to
   A. advise them to accept the procedure since it has the support of the highest authorities in the department
   B. point out that other procedures which were resisted initially have come to be accepted in time
   C. challenge staff members to suggest another procedure which will accomplish the same purpose better
   D. ask the staff members to discuss the *pros* and *cons* of the procedure and suggest how it can be improved

8. At a staff meeting at which a basic change in departmental procedure is to be announced, a director begins the discussion by asking the participants for criticisms of the existing procedure. He then describes the new procedure to be employed and explains the improvements that are anticipated. 8.____
   The director's method of introducing the change is
   A. *good*, mainly because the participants would be more receptive to the new procedure is they understood the inadequacies of the old one
   B. *good*, mainly because the participants' comments on the old procedure will provide the basis for evaluation of the feasibility of the new one
   C. *bad*, mainly because the participants will realize that the decision for change has been made before the meeting, without consideration of the participants' comments
   D. *bad*, mainly because the discussion is focused on the old procedure, rather than on the procedure being introduced

9. Assume that you are conducting a staff conference to discuss the development of a procedure implementing a change in state policy. There are twelve participants whose office titles range from unit supervisor to senior supervisor, each of whom has responsibility for some aspect of the program affected by the policy change. 9.____
After some introductory remarks, the BEST procedure for you to follow is to call upon the participants in the order of their
   A. titles, with the highest titles first because they are likely to have the most experience and knowledge of the subject
   B. titles, with the lower titles first because they are likely to be less inhibited if they are permitted to give their views before the senior participants speak
   C. places around the table, to promote informality and democratic procedure
   D. specialized knowledge of the subject so that those with the most knowledge and competence may lead the discussion

10. A staff member has suggested a way of reducing the time required to prepare a monthly report by combining several items of information, separating one item into two part, and generally revising definitions of terms. 10.____
The CHIEF disadvantage of such a revision is that
   A. comparison of present with past periods will be more difficult
   B. subordinates who prepare the report will require retraining
   C. forms currently in use will have to be discarded
   D. employees using the records will be confused by the changes

11. Assume that a director happens to be present at a regular staff conference conducted by a senior supervisor. During the course of the conference, the director frequently takes over the discussion in order to amplify remarks made by the supervisor, to impart information about departmental policies, and to modify or correct possible misinterpretations of the supervisor's remarks. 11.____
The director's actions in this situation are
   A. *proper*, mainly because the conference members were given the latest and most accurate information concerning departmental policies
   B. *proper*, mainly because the director has an obligation to assist and support the supervisor
   C. *improper*, mainly because the director did not completely take over the conference
   D. *improper*, mainly because the supervisor was put in a difficult position in the presence of his staff

12. A center has a serious staff morale problem because of rumors that it will probably be abolished. To handle this situation, the direct adopts a policy of promptly corroborating rumors that he knows to be true and denying false ones. 12.____
Although this method of dealing with the situation should have some good results, its CHIEF weakness is that
   A. it chases the rumors instead of forestalling them by giving correct information concerning the center's future

B. the director may not have the necessary information at hand
C. status is given to the rumors as a result of the attention paid to them
D. the director may inadvertently divulge confidential information

13. Realizing the importance of harmonious staff relationships, one of your supervisors makes a practice of unobtrusively intervening in any conflict situation among staff members. Whenever friction seems to be developing, he attempts to soothe ruffled feelings and remove the source of difficulty by such methods as rescheduling, reassigning personnel, etc. His efforts are always behind the scenes and unknown to the personnel involved. 13.____
This practice may produce some good results, but the CHIEF drawback is that it
A. permits staff to engage in unacceptable practices without correction
B. violates the principle of chain of command
C. involves the supervisor in personal relationships which are not properly his concern
D. requires confidential sources of information about personal relationships within the center

14. Assume that the department adopts a policy of transferring administrative personnel from one center to another after stated periods of service in a center, or in a central office. 14.____
Of the following, the MAIN advantage of such a policy is that it helps
A. prevent the formation of cliques among staff members
B. key staff members keep abreast of new developments
C. effect a greater utilization of staff members' special talents
D. develop a broader outlook and loyalty to the department as a whole, rather than to one center

15. A delegation of union members meets with you in your role as director to discuss obtaining assistance for a group of strikers who live in the neighborhood covered by the center. In the course of discussion, you learn that the strike has been called by the local union against the explicit directive of the national union's leadership. 15.____
The MOST appropriate course of action for you to take in this instance is to advise the union committee
A. of your sympathy and assure them that individual applications from the strikers for assistance will receive priority
B. that if the strikers are in need, they will be able to receive assistance as long as they are on strike
C. that since the strike is illegal, none of the workers will be eligible for assistance
D. that there is no bar to an of the strikers receiving assistance provided they are in need and are ready and willing to accept other employment if offered

16. The quality control system is a management tool used to test the validity of the eligibility caseload. 16.____
This system can be helpful to a director in the following ways, with the EXCEPTION of
    A. obtaining objective data to use in evaluating the performance of specific staff members
    B. identifying the need for policy changes
    C. sorting out the source of errors in determining eligibility
    D. setting up training objectives for his staff

17. As director, you observe that there has been a sharp rise in the number of fair hearings. The increase seems to coincide with the intensified activities of the local recipients' organization. 17.____
The MOST appropriate action under the circumstances is to
    A. determine whether the fair hearing requests result from weaknesses in the center's operation, and remedy the causes, if feasible
    B. disregard the matter for the time being because complaints have been stirred up by an organized client group
    C. emphasize to your staff the importance of meeting client needs promptly in order to avoid fair hearing requests
    D. resolve the grievances with the leaders of the recipients' organization

18. As director, you receive notice of a fair hearing decision from the State Commissioner ordering you to restore assistance to a family. You are appalled by the order because the facts cited by the hearing officer are at complete variance with what actually occurred, according to your personal knowledge of the case. 18.____
Of the following, the MOST appropriate course of action for you to take FIRST is to
    A. point out to central office that the decision should be reconsidered and appropriately modified
    B. comply with the decision under protest because it is patently wrong
    C. recommend to central office that it consider court action through an Article 78 proceeding to correct the erroneous decision
    D. comply with the decision, although an order of the State Commissioner has no force and effect of law

19. In your capacity as director, you have received a copy of the monthly statistical report issued by the department. In reviewing the report, you note that your center is showing a rise in caseload which is substantially higher than the average rise throughout the city. 19.____
Which of the alternatives listed below would be MOST appropriate in order to deal with this situation?
    A. Make plans to discuss the situation with central office so that appropriate corrective action can be taken on the basis of your consultation
    B. Collect necessary information and data about the operations of your center and the area it serves to determine the cause of the trend, and plan appropriate action on the basis of your findings

C. Call a meeting of your unit supervisors in order to impress upon them the importance of more diligent efforts to assist clients
D. Assume that the rise in caseload is an inevitable result of the substantial increase in unemployment, and take no immediate action

20. Of the following phases of a training program for administrative personnel, the one which is usually the MOST difficult to formulate is the 20.____
A. selection of training methods for the program
B. obtaining of frank opinions of the participants as to the usefulness of the program
C. chief executive officer's judgment as to the need for such a program
D. evaluation of the effectiveness of the program

21. Assume that you are conducting a conference dealing with problems of the center of which you are the director. The problem being discussed is one with which you have had no experience. However, two of the participants, who have had considerable experience with it, carry on an extended discussion, showing that they understand the problem thoroughly. The others are very much interested in the discussion and are taking notes on the material presented. 21.____
To permit the two staff members to continue for the length of time allowed for discussion of the problem is
A. *desirable*, chiefly because introduction of the material by the two participants themselves may encourage others to contribute their work experience
B. *desirable*, chiefly because their discussion may be more meaningful to the others than a discussion which is not based on work experience
C. *undesirable*, chiefly because they are discussing material only in light of their own experience rather than in general terms
D. *undesirable*, chiefly because it would reveal your own lack of experience with the problem and undermine your authority with the staff

22. In dealing with staff members, it is a commonly accepted principle that individual differences exist, suggesting that employees should be treated in an unlike manner in order to achieve maximum results from their work assignments. 22.____
This statement means MOST NEARLY that
A. supervisors should be aware of the personal problems of their subordinates and make allowances for poor performance because of such problems
B. standardized work rules are ineffective because of the different capabilities of employees to maintain such work rules
C. employees' individual needs should be considered by their supervisors to the greatest extent possible, within the practical limitations of the work situation
D. knowledge of general principles of human behavior is generally of little use to a supervisor in assisting him to supervise his subordinates effectively

23. A supervisor under your jurisdiction reports to you that one of his subordinates has been taking unusually long lunch hours, has been absent from work frequently, and has been doing poorer work than previously. 23.____
The BEST procedure for you to follow FIRST is to advise the supervisor to
   A. prefer charges against the employee
   B. arrange for a psychological consultation for the employee
   C. ascertain whether the employee is ill and, if so, arrange a medical examination for him
   D. have a private conversation with the employee to obtain more information about the reasons for his behavior

24. If the term *executive development* is defined as the continuous, ongoing, on-the-job process of constructing plans to improve individuals in specific positions, both for the purpose of present improvement as well as for any future advancement which is envisaged for the employee, it follows that the emphasis in an executive development program should 24.____
   A. provide learning experiences through formal or informal classes, seminars, or conferences, for which the focus is on the function of the position
   B. be oriented to the individual participant and may include a host of planned activities, such as appraisal, coaching, counseling, and job rotation
   C. attempt to create needs, to awaken, enlarge, and stimulate the individual so as to broaden his outlook and potentialities as a human being
   D. insure that the individual is able to plan, organize, direct, and control operations in the bureau, division, or agency

25. Most psychologists agree that employees have a need for recognition for the work they perform. 25.____
Therefore, it can be concluded that
   A. employees should be praised every time they complete a job satisfactorily
   B. praise is a more effective incentive to good performance than is punishment
   C. administrative personnel should be aware that subordinates do not have needs similar to their own
   D. a formalized system of rewards and punishment is better than no system at all, as long as there is a built-in consistency in its administration

KEY (CORRECT ANSWERS)

1.	C	11.	D
2.	C	12.	A
3.	A	13.	A
4.	C	14.	D
5.	C	15.	D
6.	D	16.	A
7.	D	17.	A
8.	C	18.	A
9.	D	19.	B
10.	A	20.	D

21.	B
22.	C
23.	D
24.	B
25.	B

TEST 2

DIRECTIONS: Each question or incomplete statement is followed by several suggested answers or completions. Select the one that BEST answers the question or completes the statement. *PRINT THE LETTER OF THE CORRECT ANSWER IN THE SPACE AT THE RIGHT.*

1. Studies have shown that the MOST effective kind of safety training program is one in which the 1.____
   A. training is conducted by consultants who are expert in the nature of the work performed
   B. lectures are given by the top executives in an agency
   C. employees participate in all phases of the program
   D. supervisors are responsible for the safety training

2. Of the following, the MOST effective method of selecting potential top executives would be 2.____
   A. situational testing which simulates actual conditions
   B. a written test which covers the knowledge required to perform the job
   C. an oral test which requires candidate to discuss significant aspects of the job
   D. a confidential interview with his former employee

3. With regard to staff morale, MOST evidence shows that 3.____
   A. employees with positive job attitudes always outproduce those with negative job attitudes
   B. morale always relates to the employee's attitude toward his working conditions and his job
   C. low morale always results in poor job performance
   D. high morale has a direct relationship to effective union leadership

4. Of the following groups of factors, the group which has been shown to be related to the incidence of job accidents is 4.____
   A. personality characteristics, intelligence, defective vision
   B. experience, fatigue, motor and perceptual speed
   C. coordination, fatigue, intelligence
   D. defective vision, motor and perceptual speed, intelligence

5. Executives who have difficulty making decisions when faced with a number of choices USUALLY 5.____
   A. have domestic problems which interfere with the decision-making process
   B. can be trained to improve their ability to make decisions
   C. are production-oriented rather than employee-centered
   D. do not know their jobs well enough to act decisively

6. Studies of disciplinary dismissals of workers reveal that 6.____
   A. the majority of employees were dismissed because of lack of technical competence
   B. the supervisors were unusually demanding of employee competence
   C. most employees were dismissed because of inability to work with their co-workers
   D. the chief executive set unrealistic standards of performance

7. One philosophy of assigning workers to a specific job is that the worker and his job are an integral unit. 7.____
   This means MOST NEARLY that the
   A. employee and the job may both require adjustment
   B. employee must meet all the specifications of the job as a prerequisite for employment
   C. employee's morale will be affected by his salary
   D. employee's job satisfaction has a direct effect on his emotional health

8. The statement that the supervisor and the administrator are the *primary personnel men* means MOST NEARLY that 8.____
   A. supervisors and administrators are more skilled in personnel techniques than are professional personnel technicians
   B. they are in the best position to implement personnel policies and procedures
   C. employees have more confidence in their supervisors and administrators than in the professional personnel administrator
   D. personnel administration is most effective when it combines both centralized and decentralized approaches

9. Administrators frequently have to interview people in order to obtain information. Although the interview is a legitimate fact-gathering technique, it has limitations which should not be overlooked. 9.____
   The one of the following which is an IMPORTANT limitation is that
   A. individuals generally hesitate to give information orally which they would usually answer in writing
   B. the material derived from the interview can usually be obtained at lower cost from existing records
   C. the emotional attitudes of individuals during an interview often affect the accuracy of the information given
   D. the interview is a poor technique for discovering how well clients understand departmental policies

10. Leadership styles have frequently been categorized as authoritarian, laissez-faire, and democratic. 10.____
    In general, management's reliance on leadership to produce desired results would be MOST effectively implemented through
    A. the laissez-faire approach when group results are desired
    B. the authoritarian approach in a benevolent manner when quick decisions are required

C. the democratic approach, when quick decisions are unimportant
D. all three approaches, depending upon circumstances

11. As director, you are responsible for enforcing a recently established regulation which has aroused antagonism among many clients. 11.____
You should deal with this situation by
A. explaining to the clients that you are not responsible for making regulations
B. enforcing the regulation but reporting to your superior the number and kind of complaints against it
C. carrying out your duty of enforcing the regulation as well as you can without comment
D. suggesting to your clients that you may overlook violations of the regulation

12. One of the observations made in a recent psychological study of leadership is that the behavior of a new employee in a leadership position can be predicted more accurately on the basis of the behavior of the previous incumbent in the post than on the behavior of the new employee in his previous job. 12.____
The BEST explanation for this observation is that there is a tendency
A. for a newly appointed executive to avoid making basic changes in operational procedures
B. to choose similar types of personalities to fill the same type of position
C. for a given organizational structure and set of duties and responsibilities to produce similar patterns of behavior
D. for executives to develop more mature patterns of behavior as a result of increased responsibility

13. A director finds that reports submitted by him to his subordinates tend to emphasize the favorable and minimize the unfavorable aspects of situations. 13.____
The MOST valid reason for this is that
A. subordinates usually hesitate to give their supervisors an honest picture of a situation
B. the director may not have been sufficiently critical of previous reports submitted by his subordinates
C. subordinates have a normal tendency to represent themselves and their actions in the best possible light
D. many subordinates in the field have developed a tendency to understatement in the depiction of unfavorable situations

14. Effective delegation of authority and responsibility to subordinates is essential for the proper administration of a center. However, the director should retain some activities under his direct control. 14.____
Of the following activities, the one for which there is LEAST justification for delegation by the director to a subordinate is one involving
A. relationships with client groups
B. physical danger to clients
C. policies which are unpopular with staff
D. matters for which there are no established policies

15. According to the principle of *span of control*, there should be a limited number of subordinates reporting to one supervisor. 15.____
Of the following, the CHIEF disadvantage which may result from the application of this principle is a reduction in the
   A. contact between lower ranking staff members and higher ranking administrative personnel
   B. freedom of action of subordinates
   C. authority and responsibility of subordinates
   D. number of organizational levels through which a matter must pass before action is taken

16. The CHIEF objection to a practice of decentralizing the preparation and distribution of memoranda by bureaus, rather than controlling distribution through central office is that it is LIKELY to result in 16.____
   A. overloading bureaus with a multiplicity of communications
   B. limited and specialized rather than broad and general viewpoints in the memoranda
   C. violation of the principle of unit of command
   D. unimportant information being communicated to all bureaus

17. A report has been completed by members of your staff. As director, you have reviewed the report and feel that the information revealed could be damaging to the department. You find yourself in conflict in your multiple role as director, as a professional, and as a citizen. 17.____
The one of the following actions which would be MOST desirable for you to take FIRST would be to
   A. send a copy of the report to your supervisor and request an immediate conference with him
   B. instruct staff to re-check the report and defer issuance of the report until the findings are confirmed
   C. immediately share the report with your supervisors and your advisory committee
   D. file the report until your advisory committee makes a request for it

18. In order for employees to function effectively, they should have a feeling of being treated fairly by management. 18.____
Which of the following general policies is MOST likely to give employees such a feeling?
   A. An employee publication should be mailed directly to the home of each employee.
   B. Employee attitude surveys should be conducted at regular intervals.
   C. Employees should be consulted and kept informed on all matters that affect them.
   D. Employees should be informed when the press publishes statements of policy.

19. In order to give employees greater job satisfaction, some management experts advocate a policy of job enrichment. 19.____
The one of the following which would be the BEST example of job enrichment is to
   A. allow an aide to decide which portion of his normal duties and responsibilities he prefers
   B. increase the fringe benefits currently available to paraprofessional employees
   C. add variety to the duties of an employee
   D. permit more flexible working schedules for professional employees

20. Management of large organizations has often emphasized high salaries and fringe benefits as the most important means of motivating employees. 20.____
The one of the following which is NOT an argument used to support this approach is
   A. most people endure work mainly in order to collect the rewards and to have the opportunity to enjoy them
   B. material incentives have proved to be the best means of stimulating creative capacity and the will to work
   C. the majority of employees place little emphasis on work-centered motivation to perform
   D. numerous research studies have shown that pay ranks first on a scale of factors motivating employees in government and industry in the United States

21. Some organizations provide psychologists or other professionally trained persons with whom employees can consult on a confidential basis regarding personal problems. 21.____
Of the following, which is MOST likely to be a benefit management can derive from such a practice?
   A. Increase in the authority of management
   B. Disclosure of the corrupt practices of those handling money
   C. Receipt of new ideas and approaches to organizational problems
   D. Obtaining tighter control on employees' private behavior

22. Authorities agree that it is generally most desirable for an employee experiencing mental health problems to seek competent professional help without being required or forced to do so by another person. 22.____
They view self-referral as a most desirable action PRIMARILY because
   A. it shows that the employee probably is more aware of the problem and more highly motivated to solve his problems
   B. the employee's right to privacy in his personal affairs is maintained
   C. another person cannot be blamed in the event the outcome of the referral is not successful
   D. the employee knows best his problems and will do what is necessary to serve his own best interests

Questions 23-25.

DIRECTIONS: Questions 23 through 25 consist of three excerpts each. Consider an excerpt correct if all the statements in the excerpt are correct. Mark your answer as follows:
A. if only excerpts I and II are correct
B. if only excerpts II and III are correct
C. if only excerpt I is correct
D. if only excerpt II is correct

23. I. Many executive decisions are based on assumptions. They may be assumptions supported by sketchy data about future needs for services; assumptions about the attitudes and future behavior of employees, perhaps based on reports of staff members or hearsay evidence; or assumptions about agency values that are as much a reflection of personal desires as of agency goals. 23.____
II. A good pattern of well-conceived plans is only a first step in administration. The administrator must also create an organization to formulate and carry out such plans. Resources must be assembled; supervision of actual operations is necessary; and before the executive's task is completed, he must exercise control.
III. When a problem is well defined, good alternatives identified, and the likely consequences of each alternative forecast as best we can, one can assume that the final choice of action to be taken would be easy, if not obvious.

24. I. Principles of motivation are not difficult to establish because human behavior is not complex and is easily understood; individual differences in human beings are substantial; and people are continuously learning and changing. 24.____
II. What gives employees satisfaction or dissatisfaction indicates the nature of the motivation problem and provides positive guidance to the administrator who faces the problem of trying to get people to carry out a set of plans.
III. The administrator's job of motivation can be described as that of creating a situation in which actions that provide net satisfaction to individual members of the enterprise are at the same time actions that make appropriate contributions toward the objectives of the enterprise.

25. I. Administrative organization is primarily concerned with legal, technical, or ultimate authority; the operational authority relationships that may be created by organization are of major significance. 25.____
II. Accountability is not removed by delegation. Appraisal of results should be tempered by the extent to which an administrator must rely on subordinates.
III. In delegations to operating subordinate, authority to plan exceeds authority to do, inasmuch as the executive typically reserves some of the planning for himself.

KEY (CORRECT ANSWERS)

1. C
2. A
3. B
4. B
5. B

6. C
7. A
8. B
9. C
10. D

11. B
12. C
13. C
14. D
15. A

16. A
17. B
18. C
19. C
20. D

21. C
22. A
23. A
24. B
25. D

READING COMPREHENSION UNDERSTANDING AND INTERPRETING WRITTEN MATERIAL

EXAMINATION SECTION

TEST 1

DIRECTIONS: Each question or incomplete statement is followed by several suggested answers or completions. Select the one that BEST answers the question or completes the statement. *PRINT THE LETTER OF THE CORRECT ANSWER IN THE SPACE AT THE RIGHT.*

In its current application to art, the term *"primitive"* is as vague and unspecific as the term "heathen" is in its application to religion. A heathen sect is simply one which is not affiliated with one or another of three or four organized systems of theology. Similarly, a primitive art is one which flourishes outside the small number of cultures which we have chosen to designate as civilizations. Such arts differ vastly and it is correspondingly difficult to generalize about them. Any statements which will hold true for such diverse aesthetic experiences as the pictographs of the Australians, the woven designs of the Peruvians, and the abstract sculptures of the African tribes must be of the broadest and simplest sort. Moreover, the problem is complicated by the meaning attached to the term "primitive" in its other uses. It stands for something simple, undeveloped, and, by implication, ancestral to more evolved forms. Its application to arts and cultures other than our own is an unfortunate heritage from the nineteenth-century scientists who laid the foundations of anthropology. Elated by the newly enunciated doctrines of evolution, these students saw all cultures as stages in a single line of development and assigned them to places in this series on the simple basis of the degree to which they differed from European culture, which was blandly assumed to be the final and perfect flower of the evolutionary process. This idea has long since been abandoned by anthropologists, but before its demise it diffused to other social sciences and became a part of the general body of popular misinformation. It still tinges a great deal of the thought and writing about the arts of non-European peoples and has been responsible for many misunderstandings.

1. The MAIN purpose of the passage is to 1.____
   A. explain the various definitions of the term "primitive"
   B. show that the term "primitive" can be applied validly to art
   C. compare the use of the term "primitive" to the use of the term "heathen"
   D. deprecate the use of the term "primitive" as applied to art
   E. show that "primitive" arts vary greatly among themselves

2. The nineteenth-century scientists believed that the theory of evolution 2.____
   A. could be applied to the development of culture
   B. was demonstrated in all social sciences
   C. was substantiated by the diversity of "primitive" art
   D. could be applied only to European culture
   E. disproved the idea that some arts are more "primitive" than others

3. With which of the following would the author agree? 3.____
   A. The term "primitive" is used only by the misinformed.
   B. "Primitive" arts may be as highly developed as "civilized" arts.
   C. The arts of a culture often indicated how advanced that culture was.
   D. Australian, Peruvian, and African tribal arts are much like the ancestral forms from which European art evolved.
   E. A simple culture is likely to have a simple art.

4. According to the author, many misunderstandings have been caused by the belief that 4.____
   A. most cultures are fundamentally different
   B. inferior works of art in any culture are "primitive" art
   C. "primitive" arts are diverse
   D. non-European arts are diverse
   E. European civilization is the final product of the evolutionary process

KEY (CORRECT ANSWERS)

1. D
2. A
3. B
4. E

TEST 2

DIRECTIONS: Each question or incomplete statement is followed by several suggested answers or completions. Select the one that BEST answers the question or completes the statement. *PRINT THE LETTER OF THE CORRECT ANSWER IN THE SPACE AT THE RIGHT.*

One of the ways the intellectual *avant-garde* affects the technical intelligentsia is through the medium of art, and art is, if only implicitly, a critique of experience. The turning upon itself of modern culture in the forms of the new visual art, the utilization of the detritus of daily experience to mock that experience, constitutes a mode of social criticism. Pop art, it is true, does not go beyond the surface of the visual and tactile experience of an industrial (and a commercialized) culture. Dwelling on the surface, it allows its consumers to mock the elements of their daily life, without abandoning it. Indeed, the consumption of art in the organized market for leisure serves at times to encapsulate the social criticism of the *avant-garde*. However, the recent engagement of writers, artists, and theater people in contemporary issues suggests that this sort of containment may have begun to reach its limits.

In an atmosphere in which the intellectually dominant group insists on the contradictions inherent in daily experience, the technical intelligentsia will find it difficult to remain unconscious of those contradictions. The technical intelligentsia have until now avoided contradictions by accepting large rewards for their expertise. As expertise becomes increasingly difficult to distinguish from ordinary service on the one hand, and merges on the other with the change of the social environment, the technical intelligentsia's psychic security may be jeopardized. Rendering of labor services casts it back into spiritual proletarianization; a challenge to the social control exercised by elites, who use the technical intelligentsia's labor power, pushes it forward to social criticism and revolutionary politics. That these are matters, for the moment, of primarily spiritual import does not diminish their ultimate political significance. A psychological precondition for radical action is usually far more important than an "objectively" revolutionary situation—whatever that may be.

The chances for a radicalization of the technical intelligentsia, thus extending the student revolt cannot be even approximated. I believe I have shown there is a chance.

1. It may be *inferred* that the technical intelligentsia are 1.____
   I. The executives and employers in society
   II. Critics of *avant-garde* art
   III. Highly skilled technical workers

   The CORRECT answer is:
   A. I only B. I and III C. I, II, and III
   D. III only E. I and II

2. The engagement of the intellectual *avant-garde* in contemporary issues 2.____
   A. indicates that people tire of questioning the contradictions inherent in day-to-day living
   B. indicates that the technical intelligentsia are close to the point where they will rebel against the *avant-garde*
   C. could cause a challenge to the social control of the elites
   D. could cause the public to become more leisure-oriented
   E. could cause an increase in the consumption of art in the organized market for leisure services

3. The *possible* effect of the intellectual *avant-garde* on the technical intelligentsia is that 3.____
   A. the intellectual *avant-garde* makes the technical intelligentsia conscious of society's contradictions
   B. rapid curtailment of large rewards for expertise will result
   C. it may cause a strong likelihood of a radicalization of the technical intelligentsia
   D. the *avant-garde* will replace the employment of the technical intelligentsia in contemporary issues
   E. the rendering of labor services will be eliminated

4. If it is assumed that the technical intelligentsia becomes fully aware of the contradictions of modern life, it is the author's position that 4.____
   A. revolution will result
   B. the technical intelligentsia may refuse to perform manual labor
   C. the technical intelligentsia will be pushed forward to social criticism and revolutionary politics
   D. the technical intelligentsia will experience some psychic dislocation
   E. ordinary service will replace technical expertise

5. According to the author, 5.____
   A. the state of mind of a particular group may have more influence on its action than the effect of environmental factors
   B. the influence of art will often cause social upheaval
   C. matters of primarily spiritual import necessarily lack political significance
   D. the detritus of day-to-day living should be mocked by the intellectual *avant-garde*
   E. the technical intelligentsia can only protect their psychic security by self-expression through art

6. With which of the following would the author agree? 6.____
   I. As contradictions are less contained, the psychic security of all members of the working class would be jeopardized.
   II. The expertise of the technical intelligentsia evolved from the ownership and management of property.
   III. The technical intelligentsia is not accustomed to rendering labor services.

   The CORRECT answer is:
   A. I only B. III only C. I and III
   D. II only E. None of the above

7. The MAIN purpose of the passage is to 7.____
   A. discuss the influence of the *avant-garde* art form on the expertise of the technical intelligentsia
   B. discuss the effect of the intellectual *avant-garde* on the working classes
   C. discuss the social significance of the technical intelligentsia
   D. discuss the possible effects of the de-encapsulation of *avant-garde* social criticism
   E. point out that before a change psychological preconditions are first established

KEY (CORRECT ANSWERS)

1.	D	5.	A
2.	C	6.	B
3.	A	7.	D
4.	D		

TEST 3

DIRECTIONS: Each question or incomplete statement is followed by several suggested answers or completions. Select the one that BEST answers the question or completes the statement. *PRINT THE LETTER OF THE CORRECT ANSWER IN THE SPACE AT THE RIGHT.*

Turbulent flow over a boundary is a complex phenomenon for which there is no really complete theory even in simple laboratory cases. Nevertheless, a great deal of experimental data has been collected on flows over solid surfaces, both in the laboratory and in nature, so that, from an engineering point of view at least, the situation is fairly well understood. The force exerted on a surface varies with the roughness of that surface and approximately with the square of the wind speed at some fixed height above it. A wind of 10 meters per second (about 20 knots, or 22 miles per hour) measured at a height of 10 meters will produce a force of some 30 tons per square kilometer on a field of mown grass or of about 70 tons per square kilometer on a ripe wheat field. On a really smooth surface, such as glass, the force is only about 10 tons per square kilometer.

When the wind blows over water, the whole thing is much more complicated. The roughness of the water is not a given characteristic of the surface but depends on the wind itself. Not only that, the elements that constitute the roughness—the waves—themselves move more or less in the direction of the wind. Recent evidence indicates that a large portion of the momentum transferred from the air into the water goes into waves rather than directly into making currents in the water; only as the waves break, or otherwise lose energy, does their momentum become available to generate currents, or produce Ekman layers. Waves carry a substantial amount of both energy and momentum (typically about as much as is carried by the wind in a layer about one wavelength thick), and so the wave-generation process is far from negligible. A violently wavy surface belies its appearance by acting, as far as the wind is concerned, as though it were very smooth. At 10 meters per second, recent measurements seem to agree, the force on the surface is quite a lot less than the force over mown grass and scarcely more than it is over glass; some observations in light winds of two or three meters per second indicate that the force on the wavy surface is less than it is on a surface as smooth as glass. In some way the motion of the waves seems to modify the airflow so that air slips over the surface even more freely than it would without the waves. This seems not to be the case at higher wind speeds, above about five meters per second, but the force remains strikingly low compared with that over other natural surfaces.

One serious deficiency is the fact that there are no direct observations at all in those important cases in which the wind speed is greater than about 12 meters per second and has had time and fetch (the distance over water) enough to raise substantial waves. The few indirect studies indicate that the apparent roughness of the surface increases somewhat under high-wind conditions, so that the force on the surface increases rather more rapidly than as the square of the wind speed.

Assuming that the force increases at least as the square of the wind speed, it is evident that high-wind conditions produce effects far more important than their frequency of occurrence would suggest. Five hours of 60-knot storm winds will put more momentum into the water than a week of 10-knot breezes. If it should be shown that, for high winds, the force on the surface increases appreciably more rapidly than as the square of the wind speed, then the transfer of momentum to the ocean will turn out to be dominated by what happens during the occasional storm rather than by the long-term average winds.

1. According to the passage, several hours of storm winds (60 miles per hour) over the ocean would 1.____
   A. be similar to the force exerted by light winds for several hours over glass
   B. create an ocean roughness which reduces the force exerted by the high winds
   C. have proved to be more significant in creating ocean momentum than light winds
   D. create a force not greater than 6 times the force of a 10-mile-per-hour wind
   E. eventually affect ocean current

2. According to the passage, a rough-like ocean surface 2.____
   A. is independent of the force of the wind
   B. has the same force exerted against it by high and light winds
   C. is more likely to have been caused by a storm than by continuous light winds
   D. nearly always allows airflow to be modified so as to cause the force of the wind to be less than on glass
   E. is a condition under which the approximate square of wind speed can never be an accurate figure in measuring the wind force

3. The author indicates that, where a hurricane is followed by light winds of 10 meters per second or less, 3.____
   I. ocean current will be unaffected by the light winds
   II. ocean current will be more affected by the hurricane winds than the following light winds
   III. the force of the light winds on the ocean would be less than that exerted on a wheat field.

   The CORRECT combination is:
   A. I only B. III only C. II and III D. I and III E. II only

4. The MAIN purpose of the passage is to discuss 4.____
   A. oceanic momentum and current
   B. turbulent flow of wind over water
   C. wind blowing over water as related to causing tidal flow
   D. the significance of high wind conditions on ocean momentum
   E. experiments in wind force

5. The author would be incorrect in concluding that the transfer of momentum to the ocean is dominated by the occasional storm if 5.____
   A. air momentum went directly into making ocean current
   B. high speed winds slipped over waves as easily as low speed winds
   C. waves did not move in the direction of wind
   D. the force exerted on a wheat field was the same as on mown grass
   E. the force of wind under normal conditions increased as the square of wind speed

6. A wind of 10 meters per second measured at a height of 10 meters will produce a force close to 30 tons per square mile on which of the following? 6.____
   A. Unmown grass
   B. Mown grass
   C. Glass
   D. Water
   E. A football field

KEY (CORRECT ANSWERS)

1. E
2. C
3. C
4. B
5. B
6. A

TEST 4

DIRECTIONS: Each question or incomplete statement is followed by several suggested answers or completions. Select the one that BEST answers the question or completes the statement. *PRINT THE LETTER OF THE CORRECT ANSWER IN THE SPACE AT THE RIGHT.*

Political scientists, as practitioners of a negligibly formalized discipline, tend to be accommodating to formulations and suggested techniques developed in related behavioral sciences. They even tend, on occasion, to speak of psychology, sociology, and anthropology as "hard core sciences." Such a characterization seems hardly justified. The disposition to uncritically adopt into political science non-indigenous sociological and general systems concepts tends, at times, to involve little more than the adoption of a specific, and sometimes barbarous, academic vocabulary which is used to redescribe reasonably well-confirmed or intuitively-grasped low-order empirical generalizations.

At its worst, what results in such instances is a runic explanation, a redescription in a singular language style, i.e., no explanation at all. At their best, functional accounts as they are found in the contemporary literature provide explanation sketches, the type of elliptical explanation characteristic of historical and psychoanalytic accounts. For each such account there is an indeterminate number of equally plausible ones, the consequence of either the complexity of the subject matter, differing perspectives, conceptual vagueness, the variety of sometimes mutually exclusive empirical or quasi-empirical generalizations employed, or syntactical obscurity, or all of them together.

Functional explanations have been most reliable in biology and physiology (where they originated) and in the analysis of servo mechanical and cybernetic systems (to which they have been effectively extended). In these areas we possess a well-standardized body of lawlike generalizations. Neither sociology nor political science has as yet the same resource of well-confirmed lawlike statements. Certainly sociology has few more than political science. What passes for functional explanation in sociology is all too frequently parasitic upon suggestive analogy and metaphor, trafficking on our familiarity with goal-directed systems.

What is advanced as "theory" in sociology is frequently a non-theoretic effort at classification or "codification," the search for an analytic conceptual schema which provides a typology or a classificatory system serviceable for convenient storage and ready retrieval of independently established empirical regularities. That such a schema takes on a hierarchic and deductive character, imparting to the collection of propositions a *prima facie* theoretical appearance, may mean no more than that the terms employed in the high-order propositions are so vague that they can accommodate almost any inference and consequently can be made to any conceivable state of affairs.

1. The author *implies* that, when the political scientist is at his best, his explanations 1.____
   A. are essentially a retelling of events
   B. only then form the basis of an organized discipline
   C. plausibly account for past occurrences
   D. are prophetic of future events
   E. are confirmed principles forming part of the political scientist's theory

2. With which of the following would the author probably agree? 2.____
   I. Because of an abundance of reasonable explanations for past conduct, there is the possibility of contending schools within the field of political science developing.
   II. Political science is largely devoid of predictive power.
   III. Political science has very few verified axioms.
   The CORRECT answer is:
   A. III only B. I and III C. I and II D. I, II, III E. I only

3. The passage *implies* that many sociological theories 3.____
   A. are capable of being widely applied to various situations
   B. do not even appear to be superficially theoretical in appearance
   C. contrast with those of political science in that there are many more confirmed lawlike statements
   D. are derived from deep analysis and exhaustive research
   E. appear theoretical but are really very well proved

4. The author's thesis would be UNSUPPORTABLE if 4.____
   A. the theories of the political scientist possessed predictive power
   B. political science did not consist of redescription
   C. political scientists were not restricted to "hard core sciences"
   D. political science consisted of a body of theories capable of application to any situation
   E. none of the above

5. The author believe that sociology as a "hard core science," contains reliable and functional explanations 5.____
   A. is never more than a compilation of conceptual schema
   B. is in nearly every respect unlike political science
   C. is a discipline which allows for varied inferences to be drawn from its general propositions
   D. is a science indigenous *prima facie* theoretical appearance containing very little codification posing as theory

KEY (CORRECT ANSWERS)

1. C
2. D
3. A
4. A
5. D

TEST 5

DIRECTIONS: Each question or incomplete statement is followed by several suggested answers or completions. Select the one that BEST answers the question or completes the statement. *PRINT THE LETTER OF THE CORRECT ANSWER IN THE SPACE AT THE RIGHT.*

James' own prefaces to his works were devoted to structural composition and analytics and his approach in those prefaces has only recently begun to be understood. One of his contemporary critics, with the purest intention to blame, wrote what might be recognized today as sophisticated praise when he spoke of the later James as "an impassioned geometer" and remarked that "what interested him was not the figures but their relations, the relations which alone make pawns significant." James's explanations of his works often are so bereft of interpretation as to make some of our own austere defenses against interpretation seem almost embarrassingly rich with psychological meanings. They offer, with a kind of brazen unselfconsciousness, an astonishingly artificial, even mechanical view of novelistic invention. It's not merely that James asserts the importance of technique; more radically, he tends to discuss character and situation almost entirely as functions of technical ingenuities. The very elements in a Jamesian story which may strike us as requiring the most explanation are presented by James either as a *solution* to a problem of compositional harmony or else as the *donnee* about which it would be irrelevant to ask any questions at all.

James should constantly be referred to as a model of structuralist criticism. He consistently redirects our attention from the referential aspect of a work of art (its extensions into "reality") to its own structural coherence as the principal source of inspiration.

What is most interesting about James's structurally functional view of character is that a certain devaluation of what we ordinarily think of as psychological interest is perfectly consistent with an attempt to portray reality. It's as if he came to feel that a kind of autonomous geometric pattern, in which the parts appeal for their value to nothing but their contributive place in the essentially abstract pattern, is the artist's most successful representation of life. Thus, he could perhaps even think that verisimilitude—a word he liked—has less to do with the probability of the events the novelist describes than with those processes, deeply characteristic of life, by which he creates sense and coherence from any event. The only faithful picture of life in art is not in the choice of a significant subject (James always argues against the pseudo realistic prejudice), but rather in the illustration of sense- or design-making processes. James proves the novel's connection with life by deprecating its derivation from life; and it's when he is most abstractly articulating the growth of a structure that James is almost most successfully defending the mimetic function of art (and of criticism). His deceptively banal position that only execution matters means most profoundly that verisimilitude, properly considered, is the grace and the truth of a formal unity.

1. The author suggests that James, in explanations of his own art, 1.____
   A. was not bound by formalistic strictures but concentrated on verisimilitude
   B. was deeply psychological and concentrated on personal insight
   C. felt that his art had a one-to-one connection with reality
   D. was basically mechanical and concentrated on geometrical form
   E. was event-and-character-oriented rather than technique-oriented

2. The passage indicates that James's method of approaching reality was 2.____
   A. that objective reality did not exist and was patterned only by the mind
   B. that formalism and pattern were excellent means of approaching reality
   C. not to concentrate on specific events but rather on character development
   D. that the only objective reality is the psychological processes of the mind
   E. that in reality events occur which are not structured but rather as random occurrences

3. The MAIN purpose of the paragraph is to 3.____
   A. indicate that James's own approach to his work is only now beginning to be understood
   B. deprecate the geometrical approach towards the novel
   C. question whether James's novels were related to reality
   D. indicate that James felt that society itself could be seen as a geometric structure
   E. discuss James's explanation of his works

4. In discussing his own works, James 4.____
   I. talks of people and events as a function of technique to the exclusion of all else
   II. is quick to emphasize the referential aspect of the work
   III. felt that verisimilitude could be derived not from character but rather from the ordering of event

   The CORRECT answer is:
   A. I only B. II only C. III only D. I and III E. I and II

5. The author 5.____
   A. *approves* of James's explanations of his work but *disapproves* his lack of discussion into the psychological makings of his characters
   B. *disapproves* of James's explanation of his own work and his lack of discussion into the psychological makings of his characters
   C. *approves* of James's explanations of his works in terms of structure as being well-rated to life
   D. *disapproves* of James's explanation of his works in terms of structure as lacking verisimilitude
   E. *approves* of James's explanation of his works because of the significance of the subjects chosen

6. The following is NOT true of James's explanation of his own works: He 6.____
   A. did not explain intriguing elements of a story except as part of a geometric whole
   B. felt the artist could represent life by its patterns rather than its events
   C. defended the imitative function of art by detailing the growth of a structure
   D. attempted to give the reader insight into the psychology of his characters by insuring that his explanation followed a strict geometrical pattern
   E. was able to devalue psychological interest and yet be consistent with an attempt to truly represent life

7. James believed it to be *essential* to 7.____
   A. carefully choose a subject which would lend itself to processes by which sense and cohesion is achieved
   B. defend the mimetic function of art by emphasizing verisimilitude
   C. emphasize the manner in which different facets of a story could fit together
   D. explain character in order to achieve literary harmony
   E. be artificial and unconcerned with representing life

KEY (CORRECT ANSWERS)

1.	D	5.	C
2.	B	6.	D
3.	E	7.	C
4.	C		

TEST 6

DIRECTIONS: Each question or incomplete statement is followed by several suggested answers or completions. Select the one that BEST answers the question or completes the statement. *PRINT THE LETTER OF THE CORRECT ANSWER IN THE SPACE AT THE RIGHT.*

The popular image of the city as it is now is a place of decay, crime, of fouled streets, and of people who are poor or foreign or odd. But what is the image of the city of the future? In the plans for the huge redevelopment projects to come, we are being shown a new image of the city. Gone are the dirt and the noise—and the variety and the excitement and the spirit. That it is an ideal makes it all the worse; these bleak new utopias are not bleak because they have to be; they are the concrete manifestation—and how literally—of a deep, and at times arrogant, misunderstanding of the function of the city.

Being made up of human beings, the city is, of course, a wonderfully resilient institution. Already it has reasserted itself as an industrial and business center. Not so many years ago, there was much talk of decentralizing to campus-like offices, and a wholesale exodus of business to the countryside seemed imminent. But a business pastoral is something of a contradiction in terms, and for the simple reason that the city is the center of things because it is a center, the suburban heresy never came off. Many industrial campuses have been built, but the overwhelming proportion of new office building has been taking place in the big cities. But the rebuilding of downtown is not enough; a city deserted at night by its leading citizens is only half a city. If it is to continue as the dominant cultural force in American life, the city must have a core of people to support its theatres and museums, its shops and its restaurants—even a Bohemia of sorts can be of help. For it is the people who like living in the city who make it an attraction to the visitors who don't. It is the city dwellers who support its style; without them there is nothing to come downtown to.

The cities have a magnificent opportunity. There are definite signs of a small but significant move back from suburbia. There is also evidence that many people who will be moving to suburbia would prefer to stay in the city—and it would not take too much more in amenities to make them stay. But the cities seem on the verge of muffing their opportunity and muffing it for generations to come. In a striking failure to apply marketing principles and an even more striking failure of aesthetics, the cities are freezing on a design for living ideally calculated to keep everybody in suburbia. These vast, barracks-like superblocks are not designed for people who like cities, but for people who have no other choice. A few imaginative architects and planners have shown that redeveloped blocks don't have to be repellent to make money, but so far their ideas have had little effect. The institutional approach is dominant, and, unless the assumptions embalmed in it are re-examined, the city is going to be turned into a gigantic bore.

1. The author would NOT be pleased with 1.____
   A. a crowded, varied, stimulating city
   B. the dedication of new funds to the reconstruction of the cities
   C. a more detailed understanding of the poor
   D. the elimination of assumptions which do not reflect the function of the city
   E. the adoption of a laissez-faire attitude by those in charge of redevelopment

2. "The rebuilding of downtown" (1st sentence, 3rd paragraph) refers to 2.____
   A. huge redevelopment projects to come
   B. the application of marketing and aesthetic principles to rejuvenating the city
   C. keeping the city as the center of business
   D. attracting a core of people to support the city's functions
   E. the doing away with barracks-like structures

3. According to the author the city, in order to better itself, *must* 3.____
   A. increase its downtown population
   B. attract an interested core of people to support its cultural institutions
   C. adhere to an institutional approach rather than be satisfied with the status quo
   D. erect campus-like business complexes
   E. establish an ideal for orderly future growth

4. The MAIN purpose of the passage is to 4.____
   A. show that the present people inhabiting the city do not make the city viable
   B. discuss the types of construction which should and should not take place in the city's future
   C. indicate that imaginative architects and planners have shown that redeveloped areas don't have to be ugly to make money
   D. discuss the human element in the city
   E. point out the lack of understanding by many city planners of the city's functions

5. The author's thesis would be LESS supportable if 5.____
   I. city planners presently understood that stereotyped reconstruction is doomed to ultimate failure
   II. the institutional approach referred to in the passage was based upon assumptions which took into account the function of the city
   III. there were signs that a shift back to the city from suburbia were occurring
   The CORRECT answer is:
   A. II only B. II and III C. I and II D. I only E. III only

KEY (CORRECT ANSWERS)

1. D
2. C
3. B
4. E
5. C

TEST 7

DIRECTIONS: Each question or incomplete statement is followed by several suggested answers or completions. Select the one that BEST answers the question or completes the statement. *PRINT THE LETTER OF THE CORRECT ANSWER IN THE SPACE AT THE RIGHT.*

In estimating the child's conceptions of the world, the first question is to decide whether external reality is as external and objective for the child as it is for adults. In other words, can the child distinguish the self from the external world? So long as the child supposes that everyone necessarily thinks like himself, he will not spontaneously seek to convince others, nor to accept common truths, nor, above all, to prove or test his opinions. If his logic lacks exactitude and objectivity, it is because the social impulses of mature years are counteracted by an innate egocentricity. In studying the child's thought, not in this case in relation to others but to things, one is faced at the outset with the analogous problem of the child's capacity to dissociate thought from self in order to form an objective conception of reality.

The child, like the uncultured adult, appears exclusively concerned with things. He is indifferent to the life of thought and the originality of individual points of view escape him. His earliest interests, his first games, his drawings are all concerned solely with the imitation of what is. In short, the child's thought has every appearance of being exclusively realistic.

But realism is of two types, or, rather, objectivity must be distinguished from realism. Objectivity consists in so fully realizing the countless intrusions of the self in everyday thought and the countless illusions which result—illusions of sense, language, point of view, value, etc.—that the preliminary step to every judgment is the effort to exclude the intrusive self. Realism, on the contrary, consists in ignoring the existence of self and thence regarding one's own perspective as immediately objective and absolute. Realism is thus anthropocentric illusion, finality—in short, all those illusions which teem in the history of science. So long as thought has not become conscious of self, it is a prey to perpetual confusions between objective and subjective, between the real and the ostensible; it values the entire content of consciousness on a single lane in which ostensible realities and the unconscious interventions of the self are inextricably mixed. It is thus not futile, but, on the contrary, indispensable to establish clearly and before all else the boundary the child draws between the self and the external world.

1. The result of a child's not learning that others think differently than he does is that 1.____
   A. the child will not be able to function as an adult
   B. when the child has matured, he will be innately egocentric
   C. when the child has matured, his reasoning will be poor
   D. upon maturity, the child will not be able to distinguish thought from objects
   E. upon maturity, the child will not be able to make non-ego-influenced value

2. Objectivity is the ability to 2.____
   A. distinguish ego from the external world
   B. dissociate oneself from others
   C. realize that others have a different point of view
   D. dissociate ego from thought

3. When thought is not conscious of self, 3.____
   A. one is able to draw the correct conclusions from his perceptions
   B. the apparent may not be distinguishable from the actual
   C. conscious thought may not be distinguishable from the unconscious
   D. the ego may influence the actual
   E. ontogeny recapitulates phylogony

4. The MAIN purpose of the passage is to 4.____
   A. argue that the child should be made to realize that others may not think like he does
   B. estimate the child's conception of the world
   C. explain the importance of distinguishing the mind from external objects
   D. emphasize the importance of non-ego-influenced perspective
   E. show how the child establishes the boundary between himself and the external world

5. The author *implies* that, if an adult is to think logically, 5.____
   A. his reasoning, as he matures, must be tempered by other viewpoints
   B. he must be able to distinguish one physical object from another
   C. he must be exclusively concerned with thought instead of things
   D. he must be able to perceive reality without the intrusions of the self
   E. he must not value the content of consciousness on a single plain

6. Realism, according to the passage, is 6.____
   A. the realization of the countless intrusions of the self
   B. final and complete objectivity
   C. a desire to be truly objective and absolute
   D. the ability to be perceptive and discerning
   E. none of the above

7. The child who is exclusively concerned with things 7.____
   A. thinks only objectivity
   B. is concerned with imitating the things he sees
   C. must learn to distinguish between realism and anthropomorphism
   D. has no innate ability
   E. will, through interaction with others, often prove his opinions

KEY (CORRECT ANSWERS)

1.	C	5.	A
2.	E	6.	E
3.	B	7.	B
4.	D		

TEST 8

DIRECTIONS: Each question or incomplete statement is followed by several suggested answers or completions. Select the one that BEST answers the question or completes the statement. *PRINT THE LETTER OF THE CORRECT ANSWER IN THE SPACE AT THE RIGHT.*

Democracy is not logically antipathetic to most doctrines of natural rights, fundamental or higher law, individual rights, or any similar ideals—but merely asks citizens to take note of the fact that the preservation of these rights rests with the majority, in political processes, and does not depend upon a legal or constitutional Maginot line. Democracy may, then, be supported by believers in individual rights providing they believe that rights—or any transcendental ends—are likely to be better safeguarded under such a system. Support for democracy on such instrumental ground may, of course, lead to the dilemma of loyalty to the system vs. loyalty to a natural right—but the same kind of dilemma may arise for anyone, over any prized value, and in any political system, and is insoluble in advance.

There is unanimous agreement that—as a matter of fact and law, not of conjecture—no single right can be realized, except at the expense of other rights and claims. For that reason their absolute status, in some philosophic sense, is of little political relevance. Political policies involve much more than very generable principles or rights. The main error of the older natural rights school was not that it had an absolute right, but that it had too many absolute rights. There must be compromise, and, as any compromise destroys the claim to absoluteness, the natural outcome of experience was the repudiation of all of them. And now the name of "natural right" can only creep into sight with the reassuring placard, "changing content guaranteed." Nor is it at all easy to see how many doctrine of inalienable, natural, individual rights can be reconciled with a political doctrine of common consent—except in an anarchist society, or one of saints. Every natural right ever put forward, and the lists are elusive and capricious, is every day invaded by governments, in the public interest and with widespread public approval.

To talk of relatively attainable justice or rights in politics is not to plump for a moral relativism—in the sense that all values are equally good. But while values may be objective, the specific value judgments and policies are inevitably relative to a context, and is only when a judgment divorces context from general principle that it looks like moral relativism. Neither, of course, does the fact of moral diversity invalidate all moral rules.

Any political system, then, deals only with relatively attainable rights, as with relative justice and freedoms. Hence, we may differ in given instances on specific policies, despite agreement on broad basic principles such as a right or a moral "ought"; and, per contra, we may agree on specific policies while differing on fundamental principles or long-range objectives or natural rights. Politics and through politics, law and policies, give these rights—and moral principles—their substance and limits. There is no getting away from the political nature of this or any other prescriptive ideal in a free society.

1. With which of the following would the author *agree*? 1.____
   A. Natural and individual rights can exist at all only under a democracy.
   B. While natural rights may exist, they are only relatively attainable.
   C. Civil disobedience has no place in a democracy where natural rights have no philosophic relevance.
   D. Utilitarianism, which draws its criteria from the happiness and welfare of individuals, cannot logically be a goal of a democratic state.
   E. Some natural rights should never be compromised for the sake of political policy.

2. It can be *inferred* that a democratic form of government 2.____
   A. can be supported by natural rightists as the best pragmatic method of achieving their aims
   B. is a form of government wherein fundamental or higher law is irrelevant
   C. will inn time repudiate all inalienable rights
   D. forces a rejection of moral absolutism
   E. will soon exist in undeveloped areas of the world

3. The MAIN purpose of the passage is to 3.____
   A. discuss natural rights doctrine
   B. compare and contrast democracy to individual rights
   C. discuss the reconciliation of a doctrine of inalienable natural rights with a political system
   D. discuss the safeguarding of natural rights in a democratic society
   E. indicate that moral relativism is antipathetic to democracy

4. The author indicates that natural rights 4.____
   I. are sometimes difficult to define
   II. are easily definable but at times unreconcilable with a system of government predicated upon majority rule
   III. form a basis for moral relativism
   The CORRECT answer is:
   A. I only B. II only C. I and II D. III only E. II and III

5. The fact that any political system deals with relatively attainable rights 5.____
   A. shows that all values are equally good or bad
   B. is cause for divorcing political reality from moral rules
   C. shows that the list of natural rights is elusive and capricious
   D. is inconsistent with the author's thesis
   E. does not necessarily mean that natural rights do not exist

6. The passage indicates that an important conflict which can exist in a democracy is the rights of competing groups, i.e., labor versus management 6.____
   A. adherence to the democratic process versus non-democratic actions by government
   B. difficulty in choosing between two effective compromises
   C. adherence to the democratic process versus the desire to support a specific right
   D. difficulty in reconciling conflict by natural rights

KEY (CORRECT ANSWERS)

1.	B	4.	A
2.	A	5.	E
3.	C	6.	D

READING COMPREHENSION
UNDERSTANDING AND INTERPRETING WRITTEN MATERIAL

EXAMINATION SECTION

TEST 1

DIRECTIONS: Each question or incomplete statement is followed by several suggested answers or completions. Select the one that BEST answers the question or completes the statement. *PRINT THE LETTER OF THE CORRECT ANSWER IN THE SPACE AT THE RIGHT.*

1. Most managers make the mistake of using absolutes as signals of trouble or its absence. A quality problem emerges—that means trouble; a test is passed—we have no problems. Outside of routine organizations, there are always going to be such signals of trouble or success, but they are not very meaningful. Many times everything looks good, but the roof is about to cave in because something no one thought about and for which there is no rule, procedure, or test has been neglected. The specifics of such problems cannot be predicted, but they are often signaled in advance by changes in the organizational system: Managers spend less time on the project; minor problems proliferate; friction in the relationships between adjacent work groups or departments increases; verbal progress reports become overly glib, or overly reticent; change occur in the rate at which certain events happen, not in whether or not they happen. And they are monitored by random probes into the organization—seeing how things are going. 1.____
According to the above paragraph,
   A. managers do not spend enough time managing
   B. managers have a tendency to become overly glib when writing reports
   C. managers should be aware that problems that exist in the organization may not exhibit predictable signals of trouble
   D. managers should attempt to alleviate friction in the relationship between adjacent work groups by monitoring random probes into the organization's problems

2. *Lack of challenge* and *excessive zeal* are opposite villains. You cannot do your best on a problem unless you are motivated. Professional problem solvers learn to be motivated somewhat by money and future work that may come their way if they succeed. However, challenge must be present for at least some of the time, or the process ceases to be rewarding. On the other hand, an excessive motivation to succeed, especially to succeed quickly, can inhibit the creative process. The tortoise-and-the-hare phenomenon is often apparent in problem solving. The person who thinks up the simple elegant solution, although he or she may take longer in doing so, often wins. As in the race, the tortoise depends upon an inconsistent performance from the rabbit. And if the rabbit spends so little time on conceptualization that the rabbit merely chooses the first answers that occur, such inconsistency is almost guaranteed. 2.____

According to the above paragraph,
A. excessive motivation to succeed can be harmful in problem solving
B. it is best to spend a long time on solving problems
C. motivation is the most important component in problem solving
D. choosing the first solution that occurs is a valid method of problem solving

3. Virginia Woolf's approach to the question of women and fiction, about which she wrote extensively, polemically, and in a profoundly feminist way, was grounded in a general theory of literature. She argued that the writer was the product of her or his historical circumstances and that material conditions were of crucial importance. Secondly, she claimed that these material circumstances had a profound effect on the psychological aspects of writing, and that they could be seen to influence the nature of the creative work itself. 3.____
According to this paragraph,
A. the material conditions and historical circumstances in which male and female writers find themselves greatly influence their work
B. a woman must have an independent income to succeed as a writer
C. Virginia Woolf preferred the writings of female authors, as their experiences more clearly reflected hers
D. male writers are less likely than women writers to be influenced by material circumstances

4. A young person's first manager is likely to be the most influential person in his or her career. If this manager is unable or unwilling to develop the skills the young employee needs to perform effectively, the latter will set lower personal standards than he or she is capable of achieving, that person's self-image will be impaired, and he or she will develop negative attitudes toward the job, the employer—in all probability—his or her career. Since the chances of building a successful career with the employer will decline rapidly, he or she will leave, if that person has high aspirations, in hope of finding a better opportunity. If, on the other hand, the manager helps the employee to achieve maximum potential, he or she will build a foundation for a successful career. 4.____
According to the above paragraph,
A. If an employee has negative attitudes towards his or her job, the manager is to blame
B. managers of young people often have a great influence upon their careers
C. good employees will leave a job they like if they are not given a chance to develop their skills
D. managers should develop the full potential of their young employees

5. The reason for these difference is not that the Greeks had a superior sense of form or an inferior imagination or joy in life, but that they thought differently. Perhaps an illustration will make this clear. With the historical plays of Shakespeare in mind, let the reader contemplate the only extant Greek play on a historical subject, the Persians of Aeschylus, a play written less than ten years after the event which it deals with, and performed before the Athenian people who had played so notable a part in the struggle—incidentally, 5.____

immediately below the Acropolis which the Persians had sacked and defiled. Any Elizabethan dramatist would have given us a panorama of the whole war, its moments of despair, hope, and triumph; we should see on the stage the leaders who planned and some of the soldiers who won the victory. In the Persians we see nothing of the sort. The scene is laid in the Persian capital, one action is seen only through Persian eyes, the course of the war is simplified so much that the naval battle of Artemisium is not mentioned, nor even the heroic defense of Thermopylae, and not a single Greek is mentioned by name. The contrast could hardly be more complete.
Which sentence is BEST supported by the above paragraph?

A. Greek plays are more interesting than Elizabethan plays.
B. Elizabethan dramatists were more talented than Greek dramatists.
C. If early Greek dramatists had the same historical material as Shakespeare had, the final form the Greek work would take would be very different from the Elizabethan work.
D. Greeks were historically more inaccurate than Elizabethans.

6. The problem with present planning systems, public or private, is that accountability is weak. Private planning systems in the global corporations operate on a set of narrow incentives that frustrate sensible public policies such as full employment, environmental protection, and price stability. Public planning is Olympian and confused because there is neither a clear consensus on social values nor political priorities. To accomplish anything, explicit choices must be made, but these choices can be made effectively only with the active participation of the people most directly involved. This, not nostalgia for small-town times gone forever, is the reason that devolution of political power to local communities is a political necessity. The power to plan locally is a precondition for sensible integration of cities, regions, and countries into the world economy. 6.____
According to the author,

A. people most directly affected by issues should participate in deciding those issues
B. private planning systems are preferable to public planning systems
C. there is no good system of government
D. county governments are more effective than state governments

Questions 7-11.

DIRECTIONS: Questions 7 through 11 are to be answered SOLELY on the basis of the following passage.

The ideal relationship for the interview is one of mutual confidence. To try to pretend, to put on a front of cordiality and friendship is extremely unwise for the interviewer because he will certainly convey, by subtle means, his real feelings. It is the interviewer's responsibility to take the lead in establishing a relationship of mutual confidence.

As the interviewer, you should help the interviewee to feel at ease and ready to talk. One of the best ways to do this is to be at ease yourself. If you are, it will probably be evident; if you are not, it will almost certainly be apparent to the interviewee. Begin the interview with topics for discussion which are easy to talk about and non-menacing. This interchange can be like the conversation of people when they are waiting for a bus, at the ballgame, or discussing the weather. However, do not prolong this warm-up too long since the interviewee knows as well as you do that these are not the things he came to discuss. Delaying too long in betting down too business may suggest to him that you are reluctant to deal with the topic.

Once you get onto the main topics, do all that you can to get the interviewee to talk freely with a little prodding from you as possible. This will probably require that you give him some idea of the area and of ways of looking at it. Avoid, however, prejudicing or coloring his remarks by what you say; especially, do not in any way indicate that there are certain things you want to hear, others which you do not want to hear. It is essential that he feel free to express his own ideas unhampered by your ideas, your values and preconceptions.

Do not appear to dominate the interview, nor have even the suggestion of a patronizing attitude. Ask some questions which will enable the interviewee to take pride in his knowledge. Take the attitude that the interviewee sincerely wants the interview to achieve its purpose. This creates a warm, permissive atmosphere that is most important in all interviews.

7. Of the following, the BEST title for the above passage is 7.____
   A. PERMISSIVENESS IN INTERVIEWING
   B. INTERVIEW TECHNIQUES
   C. THE FACTOR OF PRETENSE IN THE INTERVIEW
   D. THE CORDIAL INTERVIEW

8. Which of the following recommendations on the conduct of an interview is made by the above passage? 8.____
   A. Conduct the interview as if it were an interchange between people discussing the weather.
   B. The interview should be conducted in a highly impersonal manner.
   C. Allow enough time for the interview so that the interviewee does not feel rushed.
   D. Start the interview with topics which are not threatening to the interviewee.

9. The above passage indicates that the interviewer should 9.____
   A. feel free to express his opinions
   B. patronize the interviewee and display a permissive attitude
   C. permit the interviewee to give the needed information in his own fashion
   D. provide for privacy when conducting the interview

10. The meaning of the word *unhampered*, as it is used in the last sentence of the fourth paragraph of the above passage, is MOST NEARLY 10.____
   A. unheeded B. unobstructed C. hindered D. aided

11. It can be INFERRED from the above passage that 11.____
   A. interviewers, while generally mature, lack confidence
   B. certain methods in interviewing are more successful than others in obtaining information
   C. there is usually a reluctance on the part of interviewers to deal with unpleasant topics
   D. it is best for the interviewer not to waiver from the use of hard and fast rules when dealing with clients

Questions 12-19.

DIRECTIONS: Questions 12 through 19 are to be answered SOLELY on the basis of the following passage.

Disabled cars pose a great danger to bridge traffic at any time, but during rush hours it is especially important that such vehicles be promptly detected and removed. The term *disable car* is an all-inclusive label referring to cars stalled due to a flat tire, mechanical failure, an accident, or locked bumpers. Flat tires are the most common reason why cars become disabled. The presence of disabled vehicles caused 68% of all traffic accidents last year. Of these, 75% were serious enough to require hospitalization of at least one of the vehicle's occupants.

The basic problem in the removal of disabled vehicles is detection of the car. Several methods have been proposed to aid detection. At a 1980 meeting of traffic experts and engineers, the idea of sinking electronic eyes into roadways was first suggested. Such *eyes* let officers know when traffic falls below normal speed and becomes congested. The basic argument against this approach is the high cost of installation of these eyes. One Midwestern state has, since 1978, employed closed circuit television to detect the existence and locations of stalled vehicles. When stalled vehicles are seen on the closed circuit television screen, the information is immediately communicated by radio to units stationed along the roadway, thus enabling the prompt removal of these obstructions to traffic. However, many cities lack the necessary manpower and equipment to use this approach. For the past five years, several east-coast cities have used the method known as *safety chains*, consisting of mobile units which represent the links at the *safety chain*. These mobile units are stationed as posts one or two miles apart along roadways to detect disabled cars. Standard procedure is for the units in the *safety chain* to have roof blinker lights turned on to full rotation. The officer, upon spotting a disabled car, at once assumes a post that gives him the most control in directing traffic around the obstruction. Only after gaining such control does he investigate and decide what action should be taken.

12. From the above passage, The PERCENTAGE of accidents caused by disabled cars in which hospitalization was required by at least one of the occupants of a vehicle last year was 12.____
    A. 17% B. 51% C. 68% D. 75%

13. According to the above passage, vehicles are MOST frequently disabled because of 13.____
    A. flat tires
    B. locked bumpers
    C. brake failure
    D. overheated motors

14. According to the above passage, in the electronic eye method of detection, the *eyes* are placed 14.____
    A. on lights along the roadway
    B. on patrol cars stationed along the roadway
    C. in booths spaced two miles apart
    D. into the roadway

15. According to the above passage, the factor COMMON to both the *safety chain* method and the *closed circuit television* method of detecting disabled vehicles is that both 15.____
   A. require the use of *electronic eyes*
   B. may be used where there is a shortage of officers
   C. employ units that are stationed along the highway
   D. require the use of trucks to move the heavy equipment used

16. The one of the following which is NOT discussed in the above passage as a method that may be used to detect disabled vehicles is 16.____
   A. closed circuit television
   B. radar
   C. electronic eyes
   D. safety chains

17. One DRAWBACK mentioned by the above passage to the use of the closed circuit television method for detection of disabled cars is that this technique 17.____
   A. cannot be used during bad weather
   B. does not provide for actual removal of the cars
   C. must be operated by a highly skilled staff of traffic engineers
   D. requires a large amount of manpower and equipment

18. The NEWEST of the methods discussed in the above passage for detection of disabled vehicles is 18.____
   A. electronic eyes
   B. the mobile unit
   C. the safety chain
   D. closed circuit television

19. When the *safety chain* method is being used, an officer who spots a disabled vehicle should FIRST 19.____
   A. turn off his roof blinker lights
   B. direct traffic around the disabled vehicle
   C. send a ratio message to the nearest mobile unit
   D. conduct an investigation

20. The universe is 15 billion years old, and the geological underpinnings of the earth were formed long before the first sea creature slithered out of the slime. But it is only in the last 6,000 years or so that men have descended into mines to chop and scratch at the earth's crust. Human history is, as Carl Sagan has put it, the equivalent of a few seconds in the 15 billion year life of the earth. What alarms those who keep track of the earth's crust is that since 1950 human beings have managed to consume more minerals than were mined in all previous history, a splurge of a millisecond in geologic time that cannot be long repeated without using up the finite riches of the earth. 20.____
   Of the following, the MAIN idea of this paragraph is:
   A. There is true cause for concern at the escalating consumption of the earth's minerals in recent years.
   B. Human history is the equivalent of a few seconds in the 15 billion year life of the earth
   C. The earth will soon run out of vital mineral resources

21. The authors of the Economic Report of the President are collectively aware, despite their vision of the asset-rich household, of the real economy in which millions of Americans live. There are glimpses, throughout the Report, of the underworld in which about 23 million people do not have public or private health insurance; in which the number of people receiving unemployment compensation was 41 percent of the total unemployed, in which the average dole for the compensated unemployed is about one-half of take-home pay. The authors understand, for example, that a worker may become physically disabled and that individuals generally do not like the risk of losing their ability to earn income. But such realities justify no more than the most limited interference in the (imperfect) market for disability insurance. There is only, as far as I can tell, one moment of genuine emotion in the entire Report when the authors' passions are stirred beyond market principles. They are discussing the leasing provisions of the 1981 Tax Act (conditions which so reduce tax revenues that they are apparently opposed in their present form by the Business Roundtable, the American Business Conference, and the National Association of Manufacturers). 21.____
In the dark days before the 1981 ACT, according to the Report, (*firms with temporary tax losses* (a condition especially characteristic of new enterprises) were often unable to take advantage of investment tax incentives. The reason was that temporarily unprofitable companies had no taxable income against which to apply the investment tax deduction. It was a piteous contingency for the truly needy entrepreneur. But all was made right with the Tax Act. Social Security for the disabled incompetent corporation: the compassionate soul of Reagan's new economy.
According to the above passage,
   A. the National Association of Manufacturers and those companies that are temporarily unprofitable oppose the leasing provisions of the 1981 Tax Act
   B. the authors of the Report are willing to ignore market principles in order to assist corporations unable to take advantage of tax incentives
   C. the authors of the Report feel the National Association of Manufacturers and the Business Roundtable are wrong in opposing the leasing provisions of the 1981 Tax Act
   D. the authors of the Report have more compassion for incompetent corporations than for disabled workers

22. Much of the lore of management in the West regards ambiguity as a symptom of a variety of organizational ills whose cure is larger doses of rationality, specificity, and decisiveness. But is ambiguity sometimes desirable? Ambiguity may be thought of as a shroud of the unknown surrounding certain events. The Japanese have a word for it, *ma*, for which there is no English translation. The word is valuable because it gives an explicit place to the unknowable aspect of things. In English, we may refer to an empty space between the chair and the table; the Japanese don't say the space is empty but *full of nothing*. However amusing the illustration, it goes to the core of the issue. Westerners speak of what is unknown primarily in reference to what is known (like the space between the chair and the table, while most eastern languages give honor to the unknown in its own right. 22.____

Of course, there are many situations that a manager finds himself in where being explicit and decisive is not only helpful but necessary. There is considerable advantage, however, in having a dual frame of reference—recognizing the value of both the clear and the ambiguous. The point to bear in mind is that in certain situations, ambiguity may serve better than absolute clarity.

Which sentence is BEST supported by the above passage?

A. We should cultivate the art of being ambiguous.
B. Ambiguity may sometimes be an effective managerial tool,
C. Westerners do not have a dual frame of reference.
D. It is important to recognize the ambiguous aspects of all situations.

23. Everyone ought to accustom himself to grasp in his thought at the same time facts that are at once so few and so simple, that he shall never believe that he has knowledge of anything which he does not mentally behold with a distinctiveness equal to that of the objects which he knows most distinctly of all. It is true that some people are born with a much greater aptitude for such discernment than others, but the mind can be made much more expert at such work by art and exercise. But there is one fact which I should here emphasize above all others; and that is everyone should firmly persuade himself that none of the sciences, however abstruse, is to be deduced from lofty and obscure matters, but that they all proceed only from what is easy and more readily understood. 23.____

According to the author,

A. people should concentrate primarily on simple facts
B. intellectually gifted people have a great advantage over others
C. even difficult material and theories proceed from what is readily understood
D. if a scientist cannot grasp a simple theory, he or she is destined to fail

24. Goethe's casual observations about language contain a profound truth. Every word in every language is a part of a system of thinking unlike any other. Speakers of different languages live in different worlds; or rather, they live in the same world but can't help looking at it in different ways. Words stand for patterns of experience. As one generation hand its language down to the next, it also hands down a fixed pattern of thinking, seeing, and feeling. When we go from one language to another, nothing stays put; different peoples carry different nerve patterns in their brains, and there's no point where they fully match. 24.____

According to the above passage,

A. language differences and their ramifications are a major cause of tensions between nations
B. it is not a good use of one's time to read novels that have been translated from another language because of the tremendous differences in interpretation
C. differences in languages reflect the different experiences of people the world over
D. language students should be especially careful to retain awareness of the subtleties of their native language

Questions 25-27.

DIRECTIONS: Questions 25 through 27 are to be answered SOLELY on the basis of the following passage.

The context of all education is twofold—individual and social. Its business is to make us more and more ourselves, too cultivate in each of us our own distinctive genius, however modest it may be, while showing us how this genius may be reconciled with the needs and claims of the society of which we are a part. Thought it is not education's aim to cultivate eccentrics, that society is richest, most flexible, and most humane that best uses and most tolerates eccentricity. Conformity beyond a point breeds sterile minds and, therefore, a sterile society.

The function of secondary—and still more of higher education is to affect the environment. Teachers are not, and should not be, social reformers. But they should be the catalytic agents by means of which young minds are influenced to desire and execute reform. To aspire to better things is a logical and desirable part of mental and spiritual growth.

25. Of the following, the MOST suitable title for the above passage is 25.____
   A. EDUCATION'S FUNCTION IN CREATING INDIVIDUAL DIFFERENCES
   B. THE NEED FOR EDUCATION TO ACQUAINT US WITH OUR SOCIAL ENVIRONMENT
   C. THE RESPONSIBILITY OF EDUCATION TOWARD THE INDIVIDUAL AND SOCIETY
   D. THE ROLE OF EDUCATION IN EXPLAINIING THE NEEDS OF SOCIETY

26. On the basis of the above passage, it may be inferred that 26.____
   A. conformity is one of the forerunners of totalitarianism
   B. education should be designed to create at least a modest amount of genius in everyone
   C. tolerance of individual differences tends to give society opportunities for improvement
   D. reforms are usually initiated by people who are somewhat eccentric

27. On the basis of the above passage, it may be inferred that 27.____
   A. genius is likely to be accompanied by a desire for social reform
   B. nonconformity is an indication of the inquiring mind
   C. people who are not high school or college graduates are not able to affect the environment
   D. teachers may or may not be social reformers

Questions 28-30.

DIRECTIONS: Questions 28 through 30 are to be answered SOLELY on the basis of the following passage.

Disregard for odds and complete confidence in one's self have produced many of our great successes. But every young man who wants to go into business for himself should appraise himself as a candidate for the one percent to survive. What has he to offer that is new or better? Has he special talents, special know-how, a new invention or service, or more capital than the average competitor? Has he the most important qualification of all, a willingness to work harder than anyone else? A man who is working for himself without limitation of hours or personal sacrifice can run circles around any operation that relies on paid help. But he must forget the eight-hour day, the forty-hour week, and the annual vacation. When he stops work, his income stops unless he hires a substitute. Most small operations have their busiest day on Saturday, and the owner uses Sunday to catch up on his correspondence, bookkeeping, inventorying, and maintenance chores. The successful self-employed man invariably works harder and worries more than the man on a salary. His wife and children make corresponding sacrifices of family unity and continuity; they never know whether their man will be home or in a mood to enjoy family activities.

28. The title that BEST expresses the ideas of the above passage is 28.____
   A. OVERCOMING OBSTACLES
   B. RUNNING ONE'S OWN BUSINESS
   C. HOW TO BECOME A SUCCESS
   D. WHY SMALL BUSINESSES FAIL

29. The above passage suggests that 29.____
   A. small businesses are the ones that last
   B. salaried workers are untrustworthy
   C. a willingness to work will overcome loss of income
   D. working for one's self may lead to success

30. The author of the above passage would MOST likely believe in 30.____
   A. individual initiative
   B. socialism
   C. corporations
   D. government aid to small business

KEY (CORRECT ANSWERS)

1.	C	11.	B	21.	D
2.	A	12.	B	22.	B
3.	A	13.	A	23.	C
4.	B	14.	D	24.	C
5.	C	15.	C	25.	C
6.	A	16.	B	26.	D
7.	B	17.	D	27.	D
8.	D	18.	A	28.	B
9.	C	19.	B	29.	D
10.	B	20.	A	30.	A

READING COMPREHENSION
UNDERSTANDING AND INTERPRETING WRITTEN MATERIAL

EXAMINATION SECTION

TEST 1

DIRECTIONS: Each question or incomplete statement is followed by several suggested answers or completions. Select the one that BEST answers the question or completes the statement. *PRINT THE LETTER OF THE CORRECT ANSWER IN THE SPACE AT THE RIGHT.*

1. The question *Who shall now teach Hegel?* is shorthand for the question *Who is going to teach this genre—all the so-called Continental philosophers?* The obvious answer to this question is *Whoever cares to study them.* This is also the right answer, but we can only accept it whole heartedly if we clear away a set of factitious questions. On such question is: *Are these Continental philosophers really philosophers?* Analytic philosophers, because they identify philosophical ability with argumentative skill and notice that there is nothing they would consider an argument in the bulk of Heidegger or Foucault, suggest that these must be people who tried to be philosophers and failed-incompetent philosophers. This is as silly as saying that Plato was an incompetent sophist, or that a hedgehog is an incompetent fox. Hegel knew what he thought about philosophers who imitated the method and style of mathematics. He thought they were incompetent. These reciprocal charges of incompetence do nobody any good. We should just drop the questions of what philosophy really is or who really counts as a philosopher. 1.____
Which sentence is BEST supported by the above paragraph?
   A. The study of Hegel's philosophy is less popular now than in the past.
   B. Philosophers must stop questioning the competence of other philosophers.
   C. Philosophers should try to be as tolerant as Foucault and Heidegger.
   D. Analytic philosophers tend to be more argumentative than other philosophers.

2. It is an interesting question: the ease with which organizations of different kinds at different stages in their history can continue to function with ineffectual leadership at the top, or even function without a clear system of authority. Certainly, the success of some experiments in worker self-management shows that bosses are not always necessary, as some contemporary Marxists argue. Indeed, sometimes the function of those at the top is merely to symbolize organizational accountability, especially in dealing with outside authorities, but not to guide the actions of those within the organization. A vice president of a large insurance company remarked to us that *Presidents are powerless; no one needs them. They should all be sent off to do public relations for the company.* While this is clearly a self-serving statement from someone next in line to command, it does give meaning to the expression being kicked upstairs. 2.____
According to the author,

A. organizations function very smoothly without bosses
B. the function of those at the top is sometimes only to symbolize organizational accountability
C. company presidents are often inept at guiding the actions of those within the organization
D. presidents of companies have less power than one might assume they have

3. The goal of a problem is a terminal expression one wishes to cause to exist in the world of the problem. There are two types of goals: specified goal expressions in proof problems and incompletely specified goal expressions in find problems. For example, consider the problem of finding the value of X, given the expression 4X+5 = 17. In this problem, one can regard the goal expression as being of the form X = _____, the goal expression. The goal expression in a find problem of this type is incompletely specified. If the goal expression were specified completely—for example, X = 3—then the problem would be a proof problem, with only the sequence of operations to be determined in order to solve the problem. Of course, if one were not guaranteed that the goal expression X = 3 was true, then the terminal goal expression should really be considered to be incompletely specified—something like the statement X = 3 (true or false). 3._____
According to the preceding paragraph,
A. the goal of the equation 4X+5 = 17 is true, not false
B. if the goal expression was specified as being equal to 3, the problem 4X+5 = 17 would be a proof problem
C. if the sequence of operations of the problem given in the paragraph is predetermined, the goal of the problem becomes one of terminal expression, or the number 17
D. X cannot be found unless X is converted into a proof problem

4. We have human psychology and animal psychology, but no plant psychology. Why? Because we believe that plants have no perceptions or intentions. Some plants exhibit *behavior* and have been credited with *habits*. If you stroke the midrib of the compound leaf of a sensitive plant, the leaflets close. The sunflower changes with the diurnal changes in the source of light. The lowest animals have not much more complicated forms of behavior. The sea anemone traps and digests the small creatures that the water brings to it; the pitcher plant does the same thing and even more, for it presents a cup of liquid that attracts insects, instead of letting the surrounding medium drift them into its trap. Here as everywhere in nature where the great, general classes of living things diverge, the lines between them are not perfectly clear. A sponge is an animal; the pitcher plant is a flowering plant, but it comes nearer to *feeding itself* than the animal. Yet the fact is that we credit all animals, and only the animals, with some degree of feeling. 4._____
Of the following, the MAIN idea expressed in the above paragraph is:
A. The classification of plants has been based on beliefs about their capacity to perceive and feel
B. Many plants are more evolved than species considered animals

C. The lines that divide the classes of living things are never clear.
D. The abilities and qualities of plants are undervalued.

5. Quantitative indexes are not necessarily adequate measures of true economic significance or influence. But even the raw quantitative data speak loudly of the importance of the new transnationalized economy. The United Nations estimated value added in this new sector of the world economy at $500 billion in 2001, mounting to one-fifth of total GNP of the non-socialist world and exceeding the GNP of any one other country except the United States. Furthermore, all observers agree that the share of this sector in the world economy is growing rapidly. At least since 1980, its annual rate of growth has been high and remarkably steady at 10 percent compared to 4 percent for noninternationalized output in the Western developed countries. 5.____
One spokesman for the new system franklin envisages that within a generation some 400 to 500 multinational corporations will own close to two-thirds of the world's fixed assets.
According to the author, all of the following are true EXCEPT
A. Quantitative indexes are not necessarily adequate measures of actual economic influence.
B. The transnational sector of the world economy is growing rapidly.
C. Since 1980, the rate of growth of transnationals has been 10% compared to 4% for internationalized output in the Western developed countries.
D. Continued growth for multinational corporations is likely.

6. A bill may be sent to the Governor when it has passed both houses. During the session, he is given ten days to act on bills that reach his desk. Bills sent to him within ten days of the end of the session must be acted on within 30 days after the last day of the session. If the Governor takes no action on a ten day bill, it automatically becomes a law. If he disapproves or vetoes a ten day bill, it can become law only if it is re-passed by two-thirds vote in each house. If he fails to act on a 30 day bill, the bill is said to have received a *pocket veto.* It is customary for the Governor to act, however, on all bills submitted to him, and give his reason in writing for approving or disapproving important legislation. 6.____
According to the above paragraph, all of the following are true EXCEPT:
A. Bills sent to the Governor in the last ten days of the session must be acted on within thirty days after the last day of the session,
B. If the Governor takes no action on a 10 day bill, it is said to have received a *pocket veto.*
C. It is customary for the Governor to act on all bills submitted to him.
D. If the Governor vetoes a ten day bill, it can become law only if passed by a two-thirds vote of the Legislature.

7. It is particularly when I see a child going through the mechanical process of manipulating numbers without any intuitive sense of what it is all about that I recall the lines of Lewis Carroll: *Reeling and Writhing, of course, to begin with...and then the different branches of Arithmetic-Ambition, Distraction, Uglification, and Derision.* Or, as Max Beberman has put it, much more gently: *Somewhat related to the notion of discovery in teaching is our insistence that* 7.____

the student become aware of a concept before a name has been assigned to the concept. I am quite aware that the issue of intuitive understanding is a very live one among teachers of mathematics, and even a casual reading of the yearbook of the National Council of Teachers of Mathematics makes it clear that they are also very mindful of the gap that exists between proclaiming the importance of such understanding and actually producing it in the classroom.
The MAIN idea expressed in the above paragraph is:

A. Math teachers are concerned about the difficulties inherent in producing an understanding of mathematics in their students.
B. It is important that an intuitive sense in approaching math problems be developed, rather than relying on rote, mechanical learning.
C. Mathematics, by its very nature, encourages rote, mechanical learning.
D. Lewis Carroll was absolutely correct in his assessment of the true nature of mathematics.

8. Heisenberg's *Principle of Uncertainty*, which states that events at the atomic level cannot be observed with certainty, can be compared to this: In the world of everyday experience, we can observe any phenomenon and measure its properties without influencing the phenomenon in question to any significant extent. To be sure, if we try to measure the temperature of a demitasse with a bathtub thermometer, the instrument will absorb so much heat from the coffee that it will change the coffee's temperature substantially. But with a small chemical thermometer, we may get a sufficiently accurate reading. We can measure the temperature of a living cell with a miniature thermometer, which has almost negligible heat capacity. But in the atomic world, we can never overlook the disturbance caused by the introduction of the measuring apparatus. 8.____
Which sentence is BEST supported by the above paragraph?

A. There is little we do not alter by the mere act of observation.
B. It is always a good idea to use the smallest measuring device possible.
C. Chemical thermometers are more accurate than bathtub thermometers.
D. It is not possible to observe events at the atomic level and be sure that the same events would occur if we were not observing them.

9. It is a myth that American workers are pricing themselves out of the market, relative to workers in other industrialized countries of the world. The wages of American manufacturing workers increased at a slower rate in the 1990s than those of workers in other major western countries. In terms of American dollars, between 1990 and 2000, hourly compensation increased 489 percent in Japan and 464 percent in Germany, compared to 128 percent in the United States. Even though these countries experienced faster productivity growth, their unit labor costs still rose faster than in the United States, according to the Bureau of Labor Statistics. During the 1990s, unit labor costs rose 192 percent in Japan, 252 percent in Germany, and only 78 percent in the United States. 9.____
According to the above passage,

A. unit labor costs in the 1990s were higher in Japan than they were in Germany or the United States
B. the wages of American workers need to be increased to be consistent with other countries

C. American worker are more productive than Japanese or German workers
D. the wages of American workers in manufacturing increased at a slower rate in the 1990s than the wages of workers in Japan or Germany

10. No people have invented more ways to enjoy life than the Chinese, perhaps to balance floods, famines, warlords, and other ills of fate. The clang of gongs, clashing cymbals, and beating of drums sound through their long history. No month is without fairs and theatricals when streets are hung with fantasies of painted lanterns and crowded with *carriages that flow like water, horses like roaming dragons.* Night skies are illumined by firecrackers—a Chinese invention—bursting in the form of flowerpots, peonies, fiery devils. The ways of pleasure are myriad. Music plays in the air through bamboo whistles of different pitch tied to the wings of circling pigeons. To skim a frozen lake in an ice sleigh with a group of friends on a day when the sun is warm is rapture, like *moving in a cup of jade.* What more delightful than the ancient festival called *Half an Immortal*, when everyone from palace officials to the common man took a ride on a swing? When high in the air, one felt like an Immortal, when back to earth once again human—no more than to be for an instant a god. 10.____
According to the above passage,
A. if the Chinese hadn't had so many misfortunes, they wouldn't have created so many pleasurable past times
B. the Chinese invented flowerpots
C. every month the Chinese have fairs and theatricals
D. pigeons are required to play the game *Half an Immortal*

11. In our century, instead, poor Diphilus is lost in the crowd of his peers. We flood one another. No one recognizes him as he loads his basket in the supermarket. What grevious fits of melancholy have I not suffered in one of our larger urban bookstores, gazing at the hundreds, thousands, tens of thousands of books on shelve and tables? And what are they to the hundreds of thousands, the millions that stand in our research libraries? More books than Noah saw raindrops. How many readers will read a given one of them—mine, yours—in their lifetimes? And how will it be in the distant future? Incomprehensible masses of books, Pelion upon Ossa, hordes of books, each piteously calling for attention, respect, love, in competition with the vast disgorgements of the past and with one another in the present. Neither is it at all helpful that books can even now be reduced to the size of a postage stamp. Avanti! Place the Bible on a pinhead! Crowding more books into small spaces does not cram more books into our heads. Here I come to the sticking point that unnerves the modern Diphilus. The number of books a person can read in a given time is, roughly speaking, a historical constant. It does not change significantly even when the number of books available for reading does. Constants are pitted against variables to confound both writer and reader. 11.____
Of the following, the MAIN idea in this passage is:
A. It is difficult to attain immortality because so many books are being published.
B. Too many books are being published, so fewer people are reading them.

C. Because so many books are being published, the quality of the writing is poorer.
D. Because so many books are available, but only a fixed amount of time to read them, frustration results for both the reader and the writer.

12. Until recently, consciousness of sexual harassment has been low. But workers have become aware of it as more women have arrived at levels of authority in the workplace, feminist groups have focused attention on rape and other violence against women, and students have felt freer to report perceived abuse by professors. In the last 5 years, studies have shown that sexual misconduct at the workplace is a big problem. For example, in a recently published survey of federal employees, 42% of 694,000 women and 15% of 1,168,000 men said they had experienced some form of harassment. According to the author, 12.____
A. the awareness of sexual harassment at the workplace is increasing
B. the incidence of harassment is higher in universities than workplaces
C. sexual harassment is much more commonly experienced by women than men
D. it is rare for men to experience sexual harassment

Questions 13-17.

DIRECTIONS: Questions 13 through 17 are to be answered SOLELY on the basis of the following paragraph.

Since discounts are in common use in the commercial world and apply to purchases made by government agencies as well as business firms, it is essential that individuals in both public and private employment who prepare bills, check invoices, prepare payment vouchers, or write checks to pay bills have an understanding of the terms used. These include cash or time discount, trade discount, and discount series. A cash or time discount offers a reduction in price to the buyer for the prompt payment of the bill and is usually expressed as a percentage with a time requirement, stated in days, within which the bill must be paid in order to earn the discount. An example would be 3/10, meaning a 3% discount may be applied to the bill if the payment is forwarded to the vendor within 10 days. On an invoice, the cash discount terms are usually followed by the net terms, which is the time in days allowed for ordinary payment of the bill. Thus, 3/10, Net 30 means that full payment is expected in thirty days if the cash discount of 3% is not taken for having paid the bill within ten days. When the expression Terms Net Cash is listed on a bill, it means that no deduction for early payment is allowed. A trade discount is normally applied to list prices by a manufacturer to show the actual price to retailers so that they may know their cost and determine markups that will allow them to operate competitively and at a profit. A trade discount is applied by the seller to the list price and is independent of a cash or time discount. Discounts may also be used by manufacturers to adjust prices charged to retailers without changing list prices. This is usually done by series discounting and is expressed as a series of percentages. To compute a series discount, such as 40%, 20%, 10%, first apply the 40% discount to the list price, then apply the 20% discount to the remainder, and finally apply the 10% discount to the second remainder.

13. According to the above paragraph, trade discounts are 13.____
    A. applied by the buyer
    B. independent of cash discounts
    C. restricted to cash sales
    D. used to secure rapid payment of bills

14. According to the above paragraph, if the sales terms 5/10, Net 60 appear on a bill in the amount of $100 dated December 5 and the buyer submits his payment on December 15, his PROPER payment should be 14.____
    A. $60 B. $90 C. $95 D. $100

15. According to the above paragraph, if a manufacturer gives a trade discount of 40% for an item with a list price of $250 and the terms are Net Cash, the price a retail merchant is required to pay for this item is 15.____
    A. $250 B. $210 C. $150 D. $100

16. According to the above paragraph, a series discount of 25%, 20%, 10% applied to a list price of $200 results in an ACTUAL price to the buyer of 16.____
    A. $88 B. $90 C. $108 D. $110

17. According to the above paragraph, if a manufacturer gives a trade discount of 50% and the terms are 6/10, Net 30, the cost to a retail merchant of an item with a list price of $500 and for which he takes the time discount, is 17.____
    A. $220 B. $235 C. $240 D. $250

Questions 18-22.

DIRECTIONS: Questions 18 through 22 are to be answered SOLELY on the basis of the following paragraph.

The city may issue its own bonds or it may purchase bonds as an investment. Bonds may be issued in various denominations, and the face value of the bond is its par value. Before purchasing a bond, the investor desires to know the rate of income that the investment will yield. In computing the yield on a bond, it is assumed that the investor will keep the bond until the date of maturity, except for callable bonds which are not considered in this paragraph. To compute exact yield is a complicated mathematical problem, and scientifically prepared tables are generally used to avoid such computation. However, the approximate yield can be computed much more easily. In computing approximate yield, the accrued interest on the date of purchase should be ignored, because the buyer who pays accrued interest to the seller receives it again at the next interest date. Bonds bought at a premium (which cost more) yield a lower rate of income than the same bonds bought at par (face value), and bonds bought at a discount (which cost less) yield a higher rate of income than the same bonds bought at par.

18. An investor bought a $10,000 city bond paying 6% interest. Which of the following purchase prices would indicate that the bond was bought at a PREMIUM? 18.____
    A. $9,000 B. $9,400 C. $10,000 D. $10,600

19. During the year, a particular $10,000 bond paying 74% sold at fluctuating prices. 19.____
Which of the following prices would indicate that the bond was bought at a DISCOUNT?
A. $9,800 B. $10,000 C. $10,200 D. $10,750

20. A certain group of bonds was sold in denominations of $5,000, $10,000, $20,000 and $50,000. 20.____
In the following list of four purchase prices, which one is MOST likely to represent a bond sold at par value?
A. $10,500 B. $20,000 C. $22,000 D. $49,000

21. When computing the approximate yield on a bond, it is DESIRABLE to 21.____
A. assume the bond was purchased at par
B. consult scientifically prepared tables
C. ignore accrued interest on the date of purchase
D. wait until the bond reaches maturity

22. Which of the following is MOST likely to be an exception to the information provided in the above paragraph? Bonds 22.____
A. purchased at a premium
B. sold at par
C. sold before maturity
D. which are callable

Questions 23-25

DIRECTIONS: Questions 23 through 25 are to be answered SOLELY on the basis of the following paragraph.

There is one bad habit of drivers that often causes chain collisions at traffic lights. It is the habit of keeping one foot poised over the accelerator pedal, ready to step on the gas the instant the light turns green. A driver who is watching the light, instead of watching the cars in front of him, may *jump the gun* and bump the car in front of him, and this car in turn may bump the next car. If a driver is resting his foot on the accelerator, his foot will be slammed down when he bumps into the car ahead. This makes the collision worse and makes it very likely that cars further ahead in the line are going to get involved in a series of violent bumps.

23. Which of the following conclusions can MOST reasonably drawn from the information given in the above paragraph? 23.____
A. American drivers have a great many bad driving habits.
B. Drivers should step on the gas as soon as the light turns green.
C. A driver with poor driving habits should be arrested and fined.
D. A driver should not rest his foot on the accelerator when the car is stopped for a traffic light.

24. From the information given in the above paragraph, a reader should be able to tell that a chain collision may be defined as a collision 24.____
A. caused by bad driving habits at traffic lights
B. in which one car hits another, this second car hits a third car, and so on

C. caused by drivers who fail to use their accelerators
D. that takes place at an intersection where there is a traffic light

25. The above passage states that a driver who watches the light instead of paying attention to traffic may 25.____
A. be involved in an accident
B. end up in jail
C. lose his license
D. develop bad driving habits

KEY (CORRECT ANSWERS)

1.	B	11.	D
2.	B	12.	A
3.	B	13.	B
4.	A	14.	C
5.	C	15.	C
6.	B	16.	C
7.	B	17.	B
8.	D	18.	D
9.	D	19.	A
10.	C	20.	B

21.	C
22.	D
23.	D
24.	B
25.	A

TEST 2

DIRECTIONS: Each question or incomplete statement is followed by several suggested answers or completions. Select the one that BEST answers the question or completes the statement. *PRINT THE LETTER OF THE CORRECT ANSWER IN THE SPACE AT THE RIGHT.*

Questions 1-4.

DIRECTIONS: Each of the statements in this section is followed by several labeled choices. In the space at the right, write the letter of the sentence which means MOST NEARLY what is stated or implied in the passage.

1. It may be said that the problem in adult education seems to be not the piling up of facts but practice in thinking. 1.____
   This statement means MOST NEARLY that
   A. educational methods for adults and young people should differ
   B. adults seem to think more than young people
   C. a well-educated adult is one who thinks but does not have a store of information
   D. adult education should stress ability to think

2. Last year approximately 19,000 fatal accidents were sustained in industry. There were approximately 130 non-fatal injuries to each fatal injury. 2.____
   According to the above statement, the number of non-fatal accidents was
   A. 146,000 B. 190,000 C. 1,150,000 D. 2,500,000

3. No employer expects his stenographer to be a walking encyclopedia, but it is not unreasonable for him to expect her to know where to look for necessary information on a variety of topics. 3.____
   The above statement means MOST NEARLY that the stenographer should
   A. be a college graduate
   B. be familiar with standard office reference books
   C. keep a scrapbook of all interesting happenings
   D. go to the library regularly

4. For the United States, Canada has become the most important country in the world, yet there are few countries about which Americans know less. Canada is the third largest country in the world; only Russia and China are larger. The area of Canada is more than a quarter of the whole British Empire. 4.____
   According to the above statement, the
   A. British Empire is smaller than Russia or China
   B. territory of China is greater than that of Canada
   C. Americans know more about Canada than they do about China or Russia
   D. Canadian population is more than one-quarter the population of the British Empire

Questions 5-8.

DIRECTIONS: Questions 5 through 8 are to be answered SOLELY on the basis of the following paragraph.

A few people who live in old tenements have had the bad habit of throwing garbage out of their windows, especially if there is an empty lot near their building. Sometimes the garbage is food; sometimes the garbage is half-empty soda cans. Sometimes the garbage is a little bit of both mixed together. These people just don't care about keeping the lot clean.

5. The above paragraph states that throwing garbage out of windows is a 5.____
   A. bad habit
   B. dangerous thing to do
   C. good thing to do
   D. good way to feed rats

6. According to the above paragraph, an empty lot next to an old tenement is sometimes used as a place to 6.____
   A. hold local gang meetings
   B. play ball
   C. throw garbage
   D. walk dogs

7. According to the above paragraph, which of the following throw garbage out of their windows? 7.____
   A. Nobody
   B. Everybody
   C. Most people
   D. Some people

8. According to the above paragraph, the kinds of garbage thrown out of windows are 8.____
   A. candy and cigarette butts
   B. food and half-empty soda cans
   C. fruit and vegetables
   D. rice and bread

Questions 9-12.

DIRECTIONS: Questions 9 through 12 are to be answered SOLELY on the basis of the following paragraph.

The game that is recognized all over the world as an all-American game is the game of baseball. As a matter of fact, baseball heroes like Joe DiMaggio, Willie Mays, and Babe Ruth were as famous in their day as movie stars Robert Redford, Paul Newman, and Clint Eastwood are now. All these men have had the experience of being mobbed by fans whenever they put in an appearance anywhere in the world. Such unusual popularity makes it possible for stars like these to earn at least as much money off the job as on the job. It didn't take manufacturers and advertising men long to discover that their sales of shaving lotion, for instance, increased when they got famous stars to advertise their product for them on radio and television.

9. According to the above paragraph, baseball is known everywhere as a(n) _____ game. 9.____
   A. all-American
   B. fast
   C. unusual
   D. tough

10. According to the above paragraph, being so well known means that it is possible for people like Willie Mays and Babe Ruth to 10.____
    A. ask for anything and get it
    B. make as much money off the job as on it
    C. travel anywhere free of charge
    D. watch any game free of charge

11. According to the above paragraph, which of the following are known all over the world? 11.____
    A. Baseball heroes
    B. Advertising men
    C. Manufacturers
    D. Basketball heroes

12. According to the above paragraph, it is possible to sell much more shaving lotion on television and radio if 12.____
    A. the commercials are in color instead of black and white
    B. you can get a prize with each bottle of shaving lotion
    C. the shaving lotion makes you smell nicer than usual
    D. the shaving lotion is advertised by famous stars

Questions 13-15.

DIRECTIONS: Questions 13 through 15 are to be answered SOLELY on the basis of the following passage.

That music gives pleasure is axiomatic. Because this is so, the pleasures of music may seem a rather elementary subject for discussion. Yet the source of that pleasure, our musical instinct, is not at all elementary. It is, in fact, one of the prime puzzles of consciousness. Why is it that we are able to make sense out of these nerve signals so that we emerge from engulfment in the orderly presentation of sound stimuli as if we had lived through an image of life?

If music has impact for the mere listener, it follows that it will have much greater impact for those who sing it or play it themselves with proficiency. Any educated person in Elizabethan times was expected to read musical notation and take part in a madrigalsing. Passive listeners, numbered in the millions, are a comparatively recent innovation.

Everyone is aware that so-called serious music has made great strikes in general public acceptance in recent years, but the term itself still connotes something forbidding and hermetic to the mass audience. They attribute to the professional musician a kind of initiation into secrets that are forever hidden from the outsider. Nothing could be more misleading. We all listen to music, professionals, and non-professionals alike in the same sort of way, in a dumb sort of way, really, because simple or sophisticated music attracts all of us in the first instance, on the primordial level of sheer rhythmic and sonic appeal. Musicians are flattered, no doubt, by the deferential attitude of the layman in regard to what he imagines to be our secret understanding of music. But in all honesty, we musicians know that in the main we listen basically as others do, because music hits us with an immediacy that we recognize in the reactions of the most simple minded of music listeners.

13. A suitable title for the above passage would be 13.____
    A. HOW TO LISTEN TO MUSIC
    B. LEARNING MUSIC APPRECIATION
    C. THE PLEASURES OF MUSIC
    D. THE WORLD OF THE MUSICIAN

14. The author implies that the passive listener is one who 14.____
    A. cannot read or play music
    B. does not appreciate serious music
    C. does not keep time to the music by hand or toe tapping
    D. will not attend a concert if he has to pay for the privilege

15. The author of the above passage is apparently inconsistent when he discusses 15.____
    A. the distinction between the listener who pays for the privilege and the one who does not
    B. the historical development of musical forms
    C. the pleasures derived from music by the musician
    D. why it is that we listen to music

Questions 16-18.

DIRECTIONS: Questions 16 through 18 are to be answered SOLELY on the basis of the following passage.

Who are the clerisy? They are people who like to read books. The use of a word so unusual, so out of fashion, can only be excused on the ground that it has no familiar synonym. The word is little known because what it describes has disappeared, though I do not believe is gone forever. The clerisy are those who read for pleasure, but not for idleness; who read for pastime, but not to kill time; who love books, but do not live by books.

Let us consider the actual business of reading—the interpretive act of getting the words off the age and into your head in the most effective way. The most effective way is not the quickest way of reading; and for those who think that speed is the greatest good, there are plenty of manuals on how to read a book which profess to tell how to strip off the husk and guzzle the milk, like a chimp attacking a coconut. Who among today's readers would whisk through a poem, eyes aflicker, and say that he had read it? The answer to that last question must unfortunately be: far too many. For reading is not respected for the art it is.

Doubtless there are philosophical terms for the attitude of mind of which nasty reading is one manifestation, but here let us call it end-gaining, for its victims put ends before means; they value not reading, but having read. In this, the end-gainers make mischief and spoil all they do; end-gaining is one of the curses of our nervously tense, intellectually flabby civilization. In reading, as in all arts, it is the means, and not the end, which gives delight and brings the true reward. Not straining forward toward the completion, but the pleasure of every page as it comes, is the secret of reading. We must desire to read a book, rather than to have read it. This change in attitude, so simple to describe, is by no means simple to achieve,, if one has lived the life of an end-gainer.

16. A suitable title for the above passage would be 16.____
    A. READING FOR ENLIGHTENMENT
    B. THE ART OF RAPID READING
    C. THE WELL-EDUCATED READER
    D. VALUES IN READING

17. The author does NOT believe that most people read because they 17.____
    A. are bored
    B. have nothing better to do
    C. love books
    D. wish to say that they have read certain books

18. The change in attitude to which the author refers in the last sentence of the above passage implies a change from 18.____
    A. dawdling while reading so that the reader can read a greater number of books
    B. reading light fiction to reading serious fiction and non-fiction
    C. reading works which do not amuse the reader
    D. skimming through a book to reading it with care

Questions 19-22.

DIRECTIONS: Questions 19 through 22 are to be answered SOLELY on the basis of the following passage.

Violence is not new to literature. The writings of Shakespeare and Cervantes are full of it. But those classic writers did not condone violence. They viewed it as a just retribution for sins against the divine order or as a sacrifice sanctioned by heroism. What is peculiar to the modern literature is violence for the sake of violence. Perhaps our reverence for life has been dulled by mass slaughter, though mass slaughter has not been exceptional in the history of mankind. What is exceptional is the boredom that now alternates with war. The basic emotion in peacetime has become a horror of emptiness: a fear of being alone, of having nothing to do, a neurosis whose symptoms are restlessness, an unmotivated and undirected rage, sinking at times into vapid listlessness. This neurotic syndrome is intensified by the prevailing sense of insecurity. The threat of atomic war has corrupted our faith in life itself.

This universal neurosis has developed with the progress of technology. It is the neurosis of men whose chief expenditure of energy is to pull a lever or push a button, of men who have ceased to make things with their hands. Such inactivity applies not only to muscles and nerves but to the creative processes that once engaged the mind. If one could contrast visually, by time-and-motion studies, the daily actions of an eighteenth-century carpenter with a twentieth-century machinist, the latter would appear as a confined, repetitive clot, the former as a free and even fantastic pattern. But the most significant contrast could not be visualized—the contrast between a mind suspended aimlessly above an autonomous movement and a mind consciously bent on the shaping of a material substance according to the persistent evidence of the senses.

19. A suitable title for the above passage would be 19.____
    A. INCREASING PRODUCTION BY MEANS OF SYSTEMATIZATION
    B. LACK OF A SENSE OF CREATIVENESS AND ITS CONSEQUENCE
    C. TECHNOLOGICAL ACHIEVEMENT IN MODERN SOCIETY
    D. WHAT CAN BE DONE ABOUT SENSELESS VIOLENCE

20. According to the author, Shakespeare treated violence as a 20.____
    A. basically sinful act not in keeping with religious thinking
    B. just punishment of transgressors against moral law
    C. means of achieving dramatic excitement
    D. solution to a problem provided no other solution was available

21. According to the author, boredom may lead to 21.____
    A. a greater interest in leisure-time activities
    B. chronic fatigue
    C. senseless anger
    D. the acceptance of a job which does not provide a sense of creativity

22. The underlined phrase refers to the 22.____
    A. hand movements made by the carpenter
    B. hand movements made by the machinist
    C. relative ignorance of the carpenter
    D. relative ignorance of the machinist

23. The concentration of women and female-headed families in the city is both cause and consequence of the city's fiscal woes. Women live in cities because it is easier and cheaper for them to do so, but because fewer women are employed, and those that are receive lower pay than men, they do not make the same contribution to the tax base that an equivalent population of men would. Concomitantly, they are more dependent on public resources, such as transportation and housing. For these reasons alone, urban finances would be improved by increasing women's employment opportunities and pay. Yet nothing in our current urban policy is specifically geared to improving women's financial resources. There are some proposed incentives to create more jobs, but not necessarily ones that would utilize the skills women currently have. The most innovative proposal was a tax credit for new hires from certain groups with particularly high unemployment rates. None of the seven targeted groups were women. 23.____
    Which sentence is BEST supported by the above paragraph?
    A. Innovative programs are rapidly improving conditions for seven targeted groups with traditionally high unemployment rates.
    B. The contribution of women to a city's tax base reflects their superior economic position.
    C. Improving the economic position of women who live in cities would help the financial conditions of the cities themselves.
    D. Most women in this country live in large cities.

24. None of this would be worth saying if Descartes had been right in positing a one-to-one correspondence between stimuli and sensations. But we know that nothing of the sort exists. The perception of a given color can be evoked by an infinite number of differently combined wavelengths. Conversely, a given stimulus can evoke a variety of sensations, the image of a duck in one recipient, the image of a rabbit in another. Nor are responses like these entirely innate. One can learn to discriminate colors or patterns which were indistinguishable prior to training. To an extent still unknown, the production of data from stimuli is a learned procedure. After the learning process, the same stimulus evokes a different datum. I conclude that, though data are the minimal elements of our individual experience, they need be shared responses to a given stimulus only within the membership of a relatively homogeneous community: educational, scientific, or linguistic. 24.____

Which sentence is BEST supported by the above paragraph?

A. One stimulus can give rise to a number of different sensations.
B. There is a one-to-one correspondence between stimuli and sensations.
C. It is not possible to produce data from stimuli by using a learned procedure.
D. It is not necessary for a group to be relatively homogeneous in order to share responses to stimuli.

25. Workers who want to move in the direction of participative structures will need to confront the issues of power and control. The process of change needs to be mutually shared by all involved, or the outcome will not be a really participative model. The demand for a structural redistribution of power is not sufficient to address the problem of change toward a humanistic, as against a technological, workplace. If we are to change our institutional arrangements from hierarchy to participation, particularly in our workplaces, we will need to look to transformations in ourselves as well. As long as we are imbued with the legitimacy of hierarchical authority, with the sovereignty of the status quo, we will never be able to generate the new and original forms that we seek. This means if we are to be equal to the task of reorganizing our workplaces, we need to think about how we can reeducate ourselves and become aware of our assumptions about the nature of our social life together. Unless the issue is approached in terms of these complexities, I fear that all the worker participation and quality of work life efforts will fail. 25.____

According to the above paragraph, which of the following is NOT true?

A. Self-education concerning social roles must go hand in hand with workplace reorganization.
B. The structural changing of the workplace, alone, will not bring about the necessary changes in the quality of work life.
C. Individuals can easily overcome their attitudes towards hierarchical authority.
D. Changing the quality of work life will require the participation of all involved.

KEY (CORRECT ANSWERS)

1. D
2. D
3. B
4. B
5. A

6. C
7. D
8. B
9. A
10. B

11. A
12. D
13. C
14. A
15. C

16. D
17. C
18. D
19. B
20. B

21. C
22. B
23. C
24. A
25. C

PREPARING WRITTEN MATERIAL

PARAGRAPH REARRANGEMENT COMMENTARY

The sentences that follow are in scrambled order. You are to rearrange them in proper order and indicate the letter choice containing the correct answer at the space at the right.

Each group of sentences in this section is actually a paragraph presented in scrambled order. Each sentence in the group has a place in that paragraph; no sentence is to be left out. You are to read each group of sentences and decide upon the best order in which to put the sentences so as to form a well-organized paragraph.

The questions in this section measure the ability to solve a problem when all the facts relevant to its solution are not given.

More specifically, certain positions of responsibility and authority require the employee to discover connection between events sometimes, apparently, unrelated. In order to do this, the employee will find it necessary to correctly infer that unspecified events have probably occurred or are likely to occur. This ability becomes especially important when action must be taken on incomplete information.

Accordingly, these questions require competitors to choose among several suggested alternatives, each of which presents a different sequential arrangement of the events. Competitors must choose the MOST logical of the suggested sequences.

In order to do so, they may be required to draw on general knowledge to infer missing concepts or events that are essential to sequencing the given events. Competitors should be careful to infer only what is essential to the sequence. The plausibility of the wrong alternatives will always require the inclusion of unlikely events or of additional chains of events which are NOT essential to sequencing the given events.

It's very important to remember that you are looking for the best of the four possible choices, and that the best choice of all may not even be one of the answers you're given to choose from.

There is no one right way to solve these problems. Many people have found it helpful to first write out the order of the sentences, as they would have arranged them, on their scrap paper before looking at the possible answers. If their optimum answer is there, this can save them some time. If it isn't, this method can still give insight into solving the problem. Others find it most helpful to just go through each of the possible choices, contrasting each as they go along. You should use whatever method feels comfortable and works for you.

While most of these types of questions are not that difficult, we've added a higher percentage of the difficult type, just to give you more practice. Usually there are only one or two questions on this section that contain such subtle distinctions that you're unable to answer confidently. And you then may find yourself stuck deciding between two possible choices, neither of which you're sure about.

PREPARING WRITTEN MATERIAL

EXAMINATION SECTION

TEST 1

DIRECTIONS: The following groups of sentences need to be arranged in an order that makes sense. Select the letter preceding the sequence that represents the BEST sentence order. *PRINT THE LETTER OF THE CORRECT ANSWER IN THE SPACE AT THE RIGHT.*

1. I. A large Naval station on Alameda Island, near Oakland, held many warships in port, and the War Department was worried that if the bridge were to be blown up by the enemy, passage to and from the bay would be hopelessly blocked. 1.____
   II. Though many skeptics were opposed to the idea of building such an enormous bridge, the most vocal opposition came from a surprising source: the United States War Department.
   III. The War Department's concerns led to a showdown at San Francisco City Hall between Strauss and the Secretary of War, who demanded to know what would happen if a military enemy blew up the bridge.
   IV. In 1933, by submitting a construction cost estimate of $17 million, an engineer named Joseph Strauss won the contract to build the Golden Gate Bridge of San Francisco, which would then become one of the world's largest bridges.
   V. Strauss quickly ended the debate by explaining that the Golden Gate Bridge was to be a suspension bridge, whose roadway would hang in the air from cables strung between two huge towers, and would immediately sink into three hundred feet of water if it were destroyed.

   The BEST order is:
   A. II, III, I, IV, V B. I, II, III, V, IV C. IV, II, I, III, V D. IV, I, III, V, II

2. I. Plastic surgeons have already begun to use virtual reality to map out the complex nerve and tissue structures of a particular patient's face, in order to prepare for delicate surgery. 2.____
   II. A virtual reality program responds to these movements by adjusting the images that a person sees on a screen or through goggles, thereby creating an "interactive" world in which a person can see and touch three-dimensional graphic objects.
   III. No more than a computer program that is designed to build and display graphic images, the virtual reality program takes graphic programs a step further by sensing a person's head and body movements.
   IV. The computer technology known as virtual reality, now in its very first stages of development, is already revolutionizing some aspects of contemporary life.
   V. Virtual reality computers are also being used by the space program, most recently to simulate conditions for the astronauts who were launched on a repair mission to the Hubble telescope.

The BEST order is:
A. IV, II, I, V, III B. III, I, V, II, IV C. IV, III, II, I, V D. III, I, II, IV, V

3. I. Before you plant anything, the soil in your plant bed should be carefully raked level, a small section at a time, and any clods or rocks that can't be broken up should be removed. 3.____
II. Your plant should be placed in a hole that will position it at the same level it was at the nursery, and a small indentation should be pressed into the soil around the plant in order to hold water near its roots.
III. Before placing the plant in the soil, lightly separate any roots that may have been matted together in the container, cutting away any thick masses that can't be separated, so that the remaining roots will be able to grow outward.
IV. After the bed is ready, remove your plant from its container by turning it upside down and tapping or pushing on the bottom —never remove it by pulling on the plant.
V. When you bring home a small plant in an individual container from the nursery, there are several things to remember while preparing to plant it in your own garden.
The BEST order is:
A. V, IV, III, II, I B. V, II, IV, III, II C. I, IV, II, III, V D. I, IV, V, II, III

4. I. The motte and its tower were usually built first, so that sentries could use it as a lookout to warn the castle workers of any danger that might approach the castle. 4.____
II. Though the moat and palisade offered the bailey a good deal of protection, it was linked to the motte by a set of stairs that led to a retractable drawbridge at the motte's gate, to enable people to evacuate onto the motte in case of an attack.
III. The motte of these early castles was a fortified hill, sometimes as high as one hundred feet, on which stood a palisade and tower.
IV. The bailey was a clear, level spot below the motte, also enclosed by a palisade, which in turn was surrounded by a large trench or moat.
V. The earliest castles built in Europe were not the magnificent stone giants that still tower over much of the European landscape, but simpler wooden constructions called motte-and-bailey castles.
The BEST order is:
A. V, III, I, IV, II B. V, IV, I, II, III C. I, IV, III, II, V D. I, III, II, IV, V

5. I. If an infant is left alone or abandoned for a short while, its immediate response is to cry loudly, accompanying its screams with aggressive flailing of its legs and limbs. 5.____
II. If a child has been abandoned for a longer period of time, it becomes completely still and quiet, as if realizing that now its only chance for survival is to shut its mouth and remain motionless.
III. Along with their intense fear of the dark, the crying behavior of human infants offers insights into how prehistoric newborn children might have evolved instincts that would prevent them from becoming victims of predators.

IV. This behavior often surprises people who enter a hospital's maternity ward for the first time and encounter total silence from a roomful of infants.
V. This violent screaming response is quite different from an infant's cries of discomfort or hunger, and seems to serve as either the child's first line of defense against an unwanted intruder, or a desperate attempt to communicate its position to the mother.

The BEST order is:
A. III, II, IV, I, V B. III, I, V, II, IV C. I, V, IV, II, III D. II, IV, I, V, III

6. I. When two cats meet who are strangers, their first actions and gestures determine who the "dominant" cat will be, at least for the time being. 6.____
II. Unlike dogs, cats are typically a solitary animal species who avoid social interaction, but they do display specific social responses to each other upon meeting.
III. This is unlikely, however; before such a point of open hostility is reached, one of the cats will usually take the "submissive" position of crouching down while looking away from the other dat.
IV. If a cat desires dominance or sees the other cat as a threat to its territory, it will stare directly at the intruder with a lowered tail.
V. If the other cat responds with a similar gesture, or with the strong defensive posture of an arched back, laid-back ears and raised tail, a fight or chase is likely if neither cat gives in.

The BEST order is:
A. IV, II, I, V, III B. I, II, IV, V, III C. I, IV, V, III, II D. II, I, IV, V, III

7. I. A star or planet's gravitational force can best be explained in this way: anything passing through this "dent" in space will veer toward the star or planet as if it were rolling into a hole. 7.____
II. Objects that are massive or heavy, such as stars or planets, "sink" into this surface, creating a sort of dent or concavity in the surrounding space.
III. Black holes, the most massive objects known to exist in space, create dents so large and deep that the space surrounding them actually folds in on itself, preventing anything that falls in —even light —from ever escaping again.
IV. The sort of dent a star or planet makes depends on how massive it is; planets generally have weak gravitational pulls, but stars, which are larger and heavier, make a bigger "dent" that will attract more matter.
V. In outer space, the force of gravity works as if the surrounding space is a soft, flat surface.

The BEST order is:
A. III, V, II, I, IV B. III, IV, I, V, II C. V, II, I, IV, III D. I, V, II, IV, III

8. I. Eventually, the society of Kyoto gave the world one of its first and greatest novels when Japan's most promising writer, Lady Murasaki Shikibu, wrote her chronicle of Kyoto's society, *The Tale of Genji*, which preceded the first European novels by more than 500 years. 8.____
II. The society of Kyoto was dedicated to the pleasures of art; the courtiers experimented with new and colorful methods of sculpture, painting, writing, decorative gardening, and even making clothes.

III. Japanese culture began under the powerful authority of Chinese Buddhism, which influenced every aspect of Japanese life from religion to politics and art.
IV. This new, vibrant culture was so sophisticated that all the people in Kyoto's imperial court considered themselves poets, and the line between life and art hardly existed —lovers corresponded entirely through written verses, and even government officials communicated by writing poems to each other.
V. In the eighth century, when the emperor established the town of Kyoto as the capital of the Japanese empire, Japanese society began to develop its own distinctive style.

The BEST order is:
A. V, II, IV, I, III B. II, I, V, IV, III C. V, III, IV, I, II D. III, V, II, IV, I

9. I. Instead of wheels, the HSST uses two sets of magnets, one which sits on the track, and another that is carried by the train; these magnets generate an identical magnetic field which forces the two sets apart. 9.____
II. In the last few decades, railway travel has become less popular throughout the world, because it is much slower than travel by airplane, and not much less expensive.
III. The HSST's designers say that the train can take passengers from one town to another as quickly as a jet plane —while consuming less than half the energy.
IV. This repellent effect is strong enough to lift the entire train above the trackway, and the train, literally traveling on air, rockets along at speeds of up to 300 miles per hour.
V. The revolutionary technology of magnetic levitation, currently being tested by Japan's experimental HSST (High Speed Surface Transport), may yet bring passenger trains back from the dead.

The BEST order is:
A. II, V, I, IV, III B. II, I, IV, III, V C. V, II, III, I, IV D. V, I, III, IV, II

10. I. When European countries first began to colonize the African continent, their impression of the African people was of a vast group of loosely organized tribal societies, without any great centralized source of power or wealth. 10.____
II. The legend of Timbuktu persisted until the nineteenth century, when a French adventurer visited Timbuktu and found that raids by neighboring tribesmen had made the city a shadow of its former self.
III. In the fifteenth century, when the stories of travelers who had traveled Africa's Sudan region began circulating around Europe, this impression began to change.
IV. In 1470, an Italian merchant named Benedetto Dei traveled to Timbuktu and confirmed these rumors, describing a thriving metropolis where rich and poor people worshipped together in the city's many ornate mosques — there was even a university in Timbuktu, much like its European counterparts, where African scholars pursued their studies in the arts and sciences.

V. The travelers' legends told of an enormous city in the western Sudan, Timbuktu, where the streets were crowded with goods brought by faraway caravans, and where there was a stone palace as large as any in Europe.

The BEST order is:

A. III, V, I, IV, II B. I, II, IV, III, V C. I, III, V, IV, II D. II, I, III, IV, V

11. I. Also, our reference points in sighting the moon make us believe that its size is changing; when the moon is rising through the trees, it seems huge, because our brains unconsciously compare the size of the moon with the size of the trees in the foreground. 11.____

II. To most people, the sky itself appears more distant at the horizon than directly overhead, and if the moon's size—which remains constant—is projected from the horizon, the apparent distance of the horizon makes the moon look bigger.

III. Up higher in the sky, the moon is set against tiny stars in the background, which will make the moon seem smaller.

IV. People often wonder why the moon becomes bigger when it approaches the horizon, but most scientists agree that this is a complicated optical illusion, produced by at least three factors.

V. The moon illusion may also be partially explained by a phenomenon that has nothing to do with errors in our perception—light that enters the earth's atmosphere is sometimes refracted, and so the atmosphere may act as a kind of magnifying glass for the moon's image.

The BEST order is:

A. IV, III, V, II, I B. IV, II, I, III, V C. V, II, I, III, IV D. II, I, III, IV, V

12. I. When the Native Americans were introduced to the horses used by white explorers, they were amazed at their new alternative—here was an animal that was strong and swift, would patiently carry a person or other loads on its back, and they later discovered, was right at home on the plains. 12.____

II. Before the arrival of European explorers to North America, the natives of the American plains used large dogs to carry their travois-long lodgepoles loaded with clothing, gear, and food.

III. These horses, it is now known, were not really strangers to North America; the very first horses originated here, on this continent, tens of thousands of years ago, and migrated into Asia across the Bering Land Bridge, a strip of land that used to link our continent with the Eastern world.

IV. At first, the natives knew so little about horses that at least one tribe tried to feed their new animals pieces of dried meat and animal fat, and were surprised when the horses turned their heads away and began to eat the grass of the prairie.

V. The American horse eventually became extinct, but its Asian cousins were reintroduced to the New World when the European explorers brought them to live among the Native Americans.

The BEST order is:

A. II, I, IV, III, V B. II, IV, I, III, V C. I, II, IV, III, V D. I, III, V, II, IV

13. I. The dress worn by the dancer is believed to have been adorned in the past by shells which would strike each other as the dancer performed, creating a lovely sound. 13.____
II. Today's jingle-dress is decorated with the tin lids of snuff cans, which are rolled into cones and sewn onto the dress,
III. During the jingle-dress dance, the dancer must blend complicated footwork with a series of gentle hos that cause the cones to jingle in rhythm to a drumbeat.
IV. When contemporary Native American tribes meet for a pow-wow, one of the most popular ceremonies to take place is the women's jingle-dress dance.
V. Besides being more readily available than shells, the lids are thought by many dancers to create a softer, more subtle sound.
The BEST order is:
A. II, IV, V, I, III B. IV, II, I, III, V C. II, I, III, V, IV D. IV, I, II, V, III

14. I. If a homeowner lives where seasonal climates are extreme, deciduous shade trees—which will drop their leaves in the winter and allow sunlight to pass through the windows—should be planted near the southern exposure in order to keep the house cool during the summer. 14.____
II. This trajectory is shorter and lower in the sky than at any other time of year during the winter, when a house most requires heating; the northern-facing parts of a house do not receive any direct sunlight at all.
III. In designing an energy-efficient house, especially in colder climates, it is important to remember that most of the house's windows should face south.
IV. Though the sun always rises in the east and sets in the west, the sun of the northern hemisphere is permanently situated in the southern portion of the sky.
V. The explanation for why so many architects and builders want this "southern exposure" is related to the path of the sun in the sky.
The BEST order is:
A. III, I, V, IV, II B. III, V, IV, II, I C. I, III, IV, II, V D. I, II, V, IV, III

15. I. His journeying lasted twenty-four years and took him over an estimated 75,000 miles, a distance that would not be surpassed by anyone other than Magellan—who sailed around the world—for another six hundred years. 15.____
II. Perhaps the most far-flung of these lesser-known travelers was Ibn Batuta, an African Moslem who left his birthplace of Tangier in the summer of 1325.
III. Ibn Batuta traveled all over Africa and Asia, from Niger to Peking, and to the islands of Maldive and Indonesia.
IV. However, a few explorers of the Eastern world logged enough miles and adventures to make Marco Polo's voyage look like an evening stroll.
V. In America, the most well-known of the Old World's explorers are usually Europeans such as Marco Polo, the Italian who brought many elements of Chinese culture to the Western world.
The BEST order is:
A. V, IV, II, III, I B. V, IV, III, II, I C. III, II, I, IV, V D. II, III, I, IV, V

16. I. In the rainforests of South America, a rare species of frog practices a reproductive method that is entirely different from this standard process. 16.____
II. She will eventually carry each of the tadpoles up into the canopy and drop each into its own little pool, where it will be easy to locate and safe from most predators.
III. After fertilization, the female of the species, who lives almost entirely on the forest floor, lays between 2 and 16 eggs among the leaf litter at the base of a tree, and stands watch over these eggs until they hatch.
IV. Most frogs are pond-dwellers who are able to deposit hundreds of eggs in the water and then leave them alone, knowing that enough eggs have been laid to insure the survival of some of their offspring.
V. Once the tadpoles emerge, the female backs in among them, and a tadpole will wriggle onto her back to be carried high into the forest canopy, where the female will deposit it in a little pool of water cupped in the leaf of a plant.
The BEST order is:
A. I, IV, III, II, V B. I, III, V, II, IV C. IV, III, II, V, I D. IV, I, III, V, II

17. I. Eratosthenes had heard from travelers that at exactly noon on June 21, in the ancient city of Aswan, Egypt, the sun cast no shadow in a well, which meant that the sun must be directly overhead. 17.____
II. He knew the sun always cast a shadow in Alexandria, and so he figured that if he could measure the length of an Alexandria shadow at the time when there was no shadow in Aswan, he could calculate the angle of the sun, and therefore the circumference of the earth.
III. The evidence for a round earth was not new in 1492; in fact, Eratosthenes, an Alexandrian geographer who lived nearly sixteen centuries before Columbus's voyage (275-195 B.C.), actually developed a method for calculating the circumference of the earth that is still in use today.
IV. Eratosthenes's method was correct, but his result—28,700 miles—was about 15 percent too high, probably because of the inaccurate ancient methods of keeping time, and because Aswan was not due south of Alexandria, as Eratosthenes had believed.
V. When Christopher Columbus sailed across the Atlantic Ocean for the first time in 1492, there were still some people in the world who ignored scientific evidence and believed that the earth was flat, rather than round.
The BEST order is:
A. I, II, V, III, IV B. V, III, IV, I, II C. V, III, I, II, IV D. III, V, I, II, IV

18. I. The first name for the child is considered a trial naming, often impersonal and neutral, such as the Ngoni name *Chabwera*, meaning "it has arrived." 18.____
II. This sort of name is not due to any parental indifference to the child, but is a kind of silent recognition of Africa's sometimes high infant death rate; most parents ease the pain of losing a child with the belief that it is not really a person until it has been given a final name.
III. In many tribal African societies, families often give two different names to their children, at different periods in time.
IV. After the trial naming period has subsided and it is clear that the child will survive, the parents choose a final name for the child, an act that symbolically completes the act of birth.

V. In fact, some African first-given names are explicitly uncomplimentary, translating as "I am dead" or "I am ugly," in order to avoid the jealousy of ancestral spirits who might wish to take a child that is especially healthy or attractive.

The BEST order is:

A. III, I, II, V, IV B. III, IV, II, I, V C. IV, III, I, II, V D. IV, V, III, I, II

19. I. Though uncertain of the definite reasons for this behavior, scientists believe the birds digest the clay in order to counteract toxins contained in the seeds of certain fruits that are eaten by macaws. 19.____

II. For example, all macaws flock to riverbanks at certain times of the year to eat the clay that is found in river mud.

III. The macaws of South America are not only among the largest and most beautifully colored of the world's flying birds, but they are also one of the smartest.

IV. It is believed that macaws are forced to resort to these toxic fruits during the dry season, when foods are more scarce.

V. The macaw's intelligence has led to intense study by scientists, who have discovered some macaw behaviors that have not yet been explained.

The BEST order is:

A. III, IV, I, II, V B. III, V, II, I, IV C. V, II, I, IV, III D. IV, I, II, III, V

20. I. Although Maggie Kuhn has since passed away, the Gray Panthers are still waging a campaign to reinstate the historical view of the elderly as people whose experience allows them to make their greatest contribution in their later years. 20.____

II. In 1972, an elderly woman named Maggie Kuhn responded to this sort of treatment by forming a group called the Gray Panthers, an organization of both old and young adults with the common goal of creating change.

III. This attitude is reflected strongly in the way elderly people are treated by our society; many are forced into early retirement, or are placed in rest homes in which they are isolated from their communities.

IV. Unlike most other cultures around the world, Americans tend to look upon old age with a sense of dread and sadness.

V. Kuhn believed that when the elderly are forced to withdraw into lives that lack purpose, society loses one of its greatest resources: people who have a lifetime of experience and wisdom to offer their communities.

The BEST order is:

A. IV, III, II, V, I B. IV, II, I, III, V C. II, IV, III, V, I D. II, I, IV, III, V

21. I. The current theory among most anthropologists is that humans evolved from apes who lived in trees near the grasslands of Africa. 21.____

II. Still, some anthropologists insist that such an invention was necessary for the survival of early humans, and point to the Kung Bushmen of central Africa as a society in which the sling is still used in this way.

III. Two of these inventions—fire, and weapons such as spears and clubs—were obvious defenses against predators, and there is archaeological evidence to support the theory of their use.

IV. Once people had evolved enough to leave the safety of trees and walk upright, they needed the protection of several inventions in order to survive.
V. But another invention, a feather or fiber sling that allowed mothers to carry children while leaving their hands free to gather roots or berries, would certainly have decomposed and left behind no trace of itself.

The BEST order is:

A. I, II, III, V, IV B. IV, I, II, III, V C. I, IV, III, V, II D. IV, III, V, II, I

22. I. The person holding the bird should keep it in hot water up to its neck, and the person cleaning should work a mild solution of dishwashing liquid into the bird's plumage, paying close attention to the head and neck. 22.____
II. When rinsing the bird, after all the oil has been removed, the running water should be directed against the lay of its feathers, until water begins to bead off the surface of the feathers—a sign that all the detergent has been rinsed out.
III. If you have rescued a sea bird from an oil spill and want to restore it to clean and normal living, you need a large sink, a constant supply of running hot water (a little over 100ºF), and regular dishwashing liquid.
IV. This cleaning with detergent solution should be repeated as many times as it takes to remove all traces of oil from the bird's feathers, sometime over a period of several days.
V. But before you begin to clean the bird, you must find a partner because cleaning an oiled bird is a two-person job.

The BEST order is:

A. III, I, II, IV, V B. III, V, I, IV, II C. III, I, IV, V, II D. III, IV, V, I, II

23. I. The most difficult time of year for the Tsaatang is the spring calving, when the reindeer leave their wintering ground and rush to their accustomed calving place, without stopping by night or by day. 23.____
II. Reindeer travel in herds, and though some animals are tamed by the Tsaatang for riding or milking, the herds are allowed to roam free.
III. This journey is hard for the Tsaatang, who carry all their possessions with them, but once it's over it proves worthwhile; the Tsaatang can immediately begin to gather milk from reindeer cows who have given birth.
IV. The Tsaatang, a small tribe who live in the far northwest corner of Mongolia, practice a lifestyle that is completely dependent on the reindeer, their main resource for food, clothing, and transport.
V. The people must follow their yearly migrations, living in portable shelters that resemble Native American tepees.

The BEST order is:

A. I, III, II, V, IV B. I, IV, II, V, III C. IV, I, III, V, II D. IV II, V, I, III

24. I. The Romans later improved this system by installing these heated pipe networks throughout walls and ceilings, supplying heat to even the uppermost floors of a building—a system that, to this day, hasn't been much improved. 24.____
II. Air-conditioning, the method by which humans control indoor temperatures, was practiced much earlier than most people think.

III. The earliest heating devices other than open fires were used in 350 B.C. by the ancient Greeks, who directed air that had been heated by underground fires into baked clay pipes that ran under the floor.
IV. Ironically, the first successful cooling system, patented in England in 1831, used fire as its main energy source—fires were lit in the attic of a building, creating an updraft of air that drew cool air into the building through ducts that had underground openings near the river Thames.
V. Cooling buildings was more of a challenge, and wasn't attempted until 1500: a water-based system, designed by Leonardo da Vinci, does not appear to have been successful, since it was never used again.

The BEST order is:
A. III, V, IV, I, II B. III, I, II, V, IV C. II, III, I, V, IV D. IV, II, III, I, V

25. I. Cold, dry air from Canada passes over the Rocky Mountains and sweeps down onto the plains, where it collides with warm, moist air from the waters of the Gulf of Mexico, and when the two air masses meet, the resulting disturbance sometimes forms a violent funnel cloud that strikes the earth and destroys virtually everything in its path. 25.____
II. Hurricanes, storms which are generally not this violent and last much longer, are usually given names by meteorologists, but this tradition cannot be applied to tornados, which have a life span measured in minutes and disappear in the same way as they are born—unnamed.
III. A tornado funnel forms rotating columns of air whose speed reaches three hundred miles an hour—a speed that can only be estimated, because no wind-measuring devices in the direct path of a storm have ever survived.
IV. The natural phenomena known as tornados occur primarily over the Midwestern grasslands of the United States.
V. It is here, meteorologists tell us, that conditions for the formation of tornados are sometimes perfect during the spring months.

The BEST order is:
A. II IV, V, I, III B. II, III, I, V, IV C. IV, V, I, III, II D. IV, III, I, V, II

KEY (CORRECT ANSWERS)

1.	C	11.	B
2.	C	12.	A
3.	B	13.	D
4.	A	14.	B
5.	B	15.	A
6.	D	16.	D
7.	C	17.	C
8.	D	18.	A
9.	A	19.	B
10.	C	20.	A

21.	C
22.	B
23.	D
24.	C
25.	C

PREPARING WRITTEN MATERIAL

EXAMINATION SECTION

TEST 1

DIRECTIONS: Each short paragraph below is followed by four restatements or summaries of the information contained within it. Select the one that most completely and accurately restates the information given in the paragraph. *PRINT THE LETTER OF THE CORRECT ANSWER IN THE SPACE AT THE RIGHT.*

1. India's night jasmine, or hurshinghar, is different from most flowering plants, in that its flowers are closed during the day, and open after dark. The scientific reason for this is probably that the plant has avoided competing with other flowers for pollinating insects and birds, and relies instead on the service of nocturnal bats that are drawn to the flower's nectar. According to an old Indian legend, however, the flowers sprouted from the funeral ashes of a beautiful young girl who had fallen hopelessly in love with the sun. 1.____
   A. Despite the Indian legend that explains why the hurshinghar's flowers open at dusk, scientists believe it has to do with competition for available pollinators.
   B. The Indian hurshinghar's closure of its flowers during the day is due to a lack of available pollinators.
   C. The hurshinghar of India has evolved an unhealthy dependency on nocturnal bats.
   D. Like most myths, the Indian legend of the hurshinghar's night-flowering has been disproved by science.

2. Charles Lindbergh's trans-Atlantic flight from New York to Paris made him an international hero in 1927, but he lived nearly another fifty years, and by most accounts they weren't terribly happy ones. The two greatest tragedies of his life—the 1932 kidnapping and murder of his oldest son, and an unshakeable reputation as a Nazi sympathizer during World War II—he blamed squarely on the rabid media hounds who stalked his every move. 2.____
   A. Despite the fact that Charles Lindbergh had a hand in the two greatest tragedies of his life, he insisted on blaming the media for his problems.
   B. Charles Lindbergh lived a largely unhappy life after the glory of his 1927 trans-Atlantic flight, and he blamed his unhappiness on media attention
   C. Charles Lindbergh's later life was marked by despair and disillusionment.
   D. Because of the rabid media attention sparked by Charles Lindbergh's 1927 trans-Atlantic flight, he would later consider it the last happy event of his life

3. The United States, one of the world's youngest nations in the early twentieth century, had yet to spread its wings in terms of foreign affairs, preferring to remain isolated and opposed to meddling in the affairs of others. But the fact remained that as a young nation situated on the opposite side of the globe from Europe, Africa, and Asia, the United States had much work to do in 3.____

establishing relations with the rest of the world. So, too, as the European colonial powers continued to battle for influence in North and South America, did the United States come to believe that it was proper for them to keep these nations from encroaching into their sphere of influence.

A. The roots of the Monroe Doctrine can be traced to the foreign policy shift of the United States during the early nineteenth century.
B. In the early nineteenth century, the United States shifted its foreign policy to reflect a growing desire to actively protect its interests in the Western Hemisphere.
C. In the early nineteenth century, the United States was too young and undeveloped to have devised much in the way of foreign policy.
D. The United States adopted a more aggressive foreign policy in the early nineteenth century in order to become a diplomatic player on the world stage.

4. Hertha Ayrton, a nineteenth-century Englishwoman, pursued a career in science during a time when most women were not given the opportunity to go to college. Her series of successes led to her induction into the Institution of Electrical Engineers in 1899, when she was the first woman to receive this professional honor. Her most noted accomplishment was the research and invention of an anti-gas fan that the British War Office used in the trench warfare of World War I. 4.____

A. The British Army's success in World War I can be partly attributed to Hertha Ayrton, a groundbreaking British scientist.
B. Hertha Ayrton was the first woman to be inducted into the Institution of Electrical Engineers.
C. The injustices of nineteenth-century England were no match for the brilliant mind of Hertha Ayrton.
D. Hertha Ayrton defied the restrictions of her society by building a successful scientific career.

5. Scientists studying hyenas in Tanzania's Ngorongoro Crater have observed that hyena clans have evolved a system of territoriality that allows each clan a certain space to hunt within the 100-square-mile area. These territories are not marked by natural boundaries, but by droppings and excretions from the hyenas' scent glands. Usually, the hyenas take these boundary lines very seriously; some hyena clans have been observed abandoning their pursuit of certain prey after the prey has crossed into another territory, even though no members of the neighboring clan are anywhere in sight. 5.____

A. The hyenas of Ngorongoro Crater illustrate that the best way to peacefully co-exist within a limited territory is to strictly delineate and defend territorial borders.
B. While most territorial boundaries are marked using geographical features, the hyenas of Ngorongoro Crater have devised another method.
C. The hyena clans of Ngorongoro Crater, in order to co-exist within a limited hunting territory, have developed a method of marking strict territorial boundaries.
D. As with most species, the hyenas of Ngorongoro Crater have proven the age-old motto: "To the victor go the spoils."

6. The flood control policy of the U.S. Army Corps of Engineers has long been an obvious feature of the American landscape—the Corps seeks to contain the nation's rivers with an enormous network of dams and levees, "channelizing" rivers into small, confined routes that will stay clear of settled flood—plains when rivers rise. As a command of the U.S. Army, the Corps seems to have long seen the nation's rivers as an enemy to be fought; one of the agency's early training films speaks of the Corps' "battle" with its adversary, Mother Nature. 6.____
   A. The dams and levees built by the U.S. Army Corps of Engineers have at least defeated their adversary, Mother Nature.
   B. The flood control policy of the U.S. Army Corps of Engineers has often reflected a military point of view, making the nation's rivers into enemies that must be defeated.
   C. When one realizes that the flood policy of the U.S. Army Corps of Engineers has always relied on a kind of military strategy, it is only possible to view the Corps' efforts as a failure.
   D. By damming and channelizing the nation's rivers, the U.S. Army Corps of Engineers have made America's flood plains safe for farming and development.

7. Frogs with extra legs or missing legs have been showing up with greater frequency over the past decade, and scientists have been baffled by the cause. Some researchers have concluded that pesticide runoff from farms is to blame; others say a common parasite, the trematode, is the culprit. Now, a new study suggests that both these factors in combination have disturbed normal development in many frogs, leading to the abnormalities. 7.____
   A. Despite several studies, scientists still have no idea what is causing the widespread incidence of deformities among aquatic frogs.
   B. In the debate over what is causing the increase in frog deformities, environmentalists tend to blame pesticide runoff, while others blame a common parasite, the trematode.
   C. A recent study suggests that both pesticide runoff and natural parasites have contributed to the increasing rate of deformities in frogs.
   D. Because of their aquatic habitat, frogs are among the most susceptible organisms to chemical ad environmental change, and this is illustrated by the increasing rate of physical deformities among frog populations.

8. The builders of the Egyptian pyramids, to insure that each massive structure was built on a completely flat surface, began by cutting a network of criss-crossing channels into the pyramid's mapped-out ground space and partly filling the channels with water. Because the channels were all interconnected, the water was distributed evenly throughout the channel system, and all the workers had to do to level their building surface was cut away any rock above the waterline. 8.____
   A. The modern carpenter's level uses a principle that was actually invented several centuries ago by the builders of the Egyptian pyramids.
   B. The discovery of the ancient Egyptians' sophisticated construction techniques is a quiet argument against the idea that they were built by slaves.

C. The use of water to insure that the pyramids were level mark the Egyptians as one of the most scientifically advanced of the ancient civilizations.
D. The builders of the Egyptian pyramids used a simple but ingenious method for ensuring a level building surface with interconnected channels of water

9. Thunderhead Mountain, a six-hundred-foot-high formation of granite in the Black Hills of South Dakota, is slowly undergoing a transformation that will not be finished for more than a century, when what remains of the mountain will have become the largest sculpture in the world. The statue, begun in 1947 by a Boston Sculptor named Henry Ziolkowski, is still being carved and blasted by his wife and children into the likeness of Crazy Horse, the legendary chief of the Sioux tribe of American natives. The enormity of the sculpture—the planned length of one of the figure's arms is 263 feet—is understandable, given the historical greatness of Crazy Horse. 9.____
   A. Only a hero as great as Crazy Horse could warrant a sculpture so large that it will take morae than a century to complete.
   B. In 1947, sculptor Henry Ziolkowski began work on what he imagined would be the largest sculpture in the world—even though he knew he would not live to see it completed.
   C. The huge Black Hills sculpture of the great Sioux chief Crazy Horse, still being carried out by the family of Henry Ziolkowski, will some day be the largest sculpture in the world.
   D. South Dakota's Thunderhead Mountain will soon be the site of the world's largest sculpture, a statue of the Sioux chief Crazy Horse.

10. Because they were some of the first explorers to venture into the western frontier of North America, the French were responsible for the naming of several native tribes. Some of these names were poorly conceived—the worst of which was perhaps Eskimo, the name for the natives of the far North, which translates roughly as "eaters of raw flesh." The name is incorrect; these people have always cooked their fish and game, and they now call themselves the Inuit, a native term that means "the people." 10.____
   A. The first to explore much of North America's western frontier were the French, and they usually gave improper or poorly-informed names to the native tribes.
   B. The Eskimos of North America have never eaten raw flesh, so it is curious that the French would give them a name that means "eaters of raw flesh."
   C. The Inuit have fought for many years to overcome the impression that they eat raw flesh.
   D. Like many native tribes, the Inuit were once incorrectly named by French explorers, but they have since corrected the mistake themselves.

11. Of the 30,000 species of spiders worldwide, only a handful are dangerous to human beings, but this doesn't prevent many people from having a powerful fear of all spiders, whether they are venomous or not. The leading scientific theory about arachnophobia, as this fear is known, is that far in our evolutionary past, some species of spider must have presented a serious enough threat to people that the sight of a star-shaped body or an eight-legged walk was coded into our genes as a danger signal. 11.____
    A. Scientists theorize that peoples' widespread fear of spiders can be traced to an ancient spider species that was dangerous enough to trigger this fearful reaction.
    B. The fear known as arachnophobia is triggered by the sight of a star-shaped body or an eight-legged walk.
    C. Because most spiders have a uniquely shaped body that triggers a human fear response, many humans are afflicted with the fear of spiders known as arachnophobia.
    D. Though only a few of the planet's 30,000 spider species are dangerous to people, many people have an unreasonable fear of them.

12. From the 1970s to the 1990s, the percentage of Americans living in the suburbs climbed from 37% to 47%. In the latter part of the 1990s, a movement emerged that questioned the good of such a population shift—or at least, the good of the speed and manner in which this suburban land was being developed. Often, people began to argue, the planning of such growth was flawed, resulting in a phenomenon that has become known as suburban "sprawl," or the growth of suburban orbits around cities at rates faster than infrastructures could support, and in ways that are damaging to the environment 12.____
    A. The term "urban sprawl" was coined in the 1990s, when the movement against unchecked suburban development began to gather momentum.
    B. In the 1980s and 1990s, home builders benefited from a boom in their most favored demographic segment, suburban new home buyers.
    C. Suburban development tends to suffer from poor planning, which can lead to a lower quality of life for residents
    D. The surge in suburban residences in the late twentieth century was criticized by many as "sprawl" that could not be supported by existing resources

13. Medicare, a $200 billion-a-year program, processes 1 billion claims annually, and in the year 2000, the computer system that handles these claims came under criticism. The General Accounting Office branded Medicare's financial management system as outdated and inadequate—one in a series of studies and reports warning that the program is plagued with duplication, overcharges, double billings, and confusion among users. 13.____
    A. The General Accounting Office's 2000 report proves that Medicare is bloated bureaucracy in need of substantial reform.
    B. Medicare's confusing computer network is an example of how the federal government often neglects the programs that mean the most to average American citizens.

C. In the year 2000, the General Accounting Office criticized Medicare's financial accounting network as inefficient and outdated.
D. Because it has to handle so many claims each year, Medicare's financial accounting system often produces redundancies and errors.

14. The earliest known writing materials were thin clay tablets, used in Mesopotamia more than 5,000 years ago. Although the tablets were cheap and easy to produce, they had two major disadvantages: they were difficult to store, and once the clay had dried and hardened, a person could not write on them. The ancient Egyptians later discovered a better writing material—the thin bark of the papyrus reed, a plant that grew near the mouth of the Nile River, which could be peeled into long strips, woven into a mat-like layer, pounded flat with heavy mallets, and then dried in the sun. 14.____
A. The Egyptians, after centuries of frustration with clay writing tablets, were finally forced to invent a better writing surface.
B. With the bark of the papyrus reed, ancient Egyptians made a writing material that overcame the disadvantages of clay tablets.
C. The Egyptian invention of the papyrus scroll was necessitated in part by a relative lack of available clay.
D. The word "paper" can be traced to the innovations of the Egyptians, who made the first paper-like writing material from the bark of papyrus plant.

15. In 1850, the German pianomaker Heinrich Steinweg and his family stepped off an immigrant ship in New York City, threw themselves into competition with dozens of other established craftsmen, and defeated them all by reinventing the instrument. The company they created commanded the market for nearly the next century and a half, while their competitors—some of the most acclaimed pianomakers in the business—faded into obscurity. And all the while, Steinway & Sons, through their sponsorship and encouragement of the world's most distinguished pianists, helped define the cultural life of the young United States. 15.____
A. The Steinways capitalized on weak competition during the mid-nineteenth century to capture the American piano market.
B. Because of their technical and cultural innovations, the Steinways had an advantage over other American pianomakers.
C. Heinrich Steinweg founded the Steinway piano empire in 1850.
D. From humble immigrant origins, the Steinway family rose to dominate both the pianomaking industry and American musical culture.

16. Feng Shui, the ancient Chinese science of studying the natural environment's effect on a person's well-being, has gained new popularity in the design and decoration of buildings. Although a complex area of study, a basic premise of Feng Shui is that each building creates a unique field of energy which affects the inhabitants of that building or home. In recent years, decorators and realtors have begun to offer services which include a diagnosis of a building's Feng Shui, or energy. 16.____
A. Feng Shui, the Chinese science of balancing environmental energies, has been given more aesthetic quality by recent practitioners.

B. Generally, practitioners of Feng Shui work to create balance within a room, carefully arranging sharp and soft surfaces to create a positive environment that suits the room's primary purpose.
C. The idea behind the Chinese "science" of Feng Sui objects give off certain energies that affect a building's inhabitants has been a difficult one for most Westerners to accept, but it is gaining in popularity.
D. The ancient Chinese science of Feng Shui, which studies the balance of energies in a person's environment, has become popular among those who design and decorate buildings.

17. Because the harsh seasonal variations of the Kansas plains make survival difficult for most plant life, the area is dominated by tall, sturdy grasses. The only tree that has been able to survive and prosper throughout the wide expanse of prairie is the cottonwood, which can take root and grow in the most extreme climatic conditions. Sometimes a storm will shear off a living branch and carry it downstream, where it may snag along a sandbar and take root. 17.____
A. Among the plant life of the Kansas plains, the only tree is the cottonwood.
B. The only prosperous tree on the Kansas plains is the cottonwood, which can take root and grow in a wide range of conditions.
C. Only the cottonwood, whose branches can grow after being broken off and washed down a river, is capable of surviving the climatic extremes of the Kansas plains.
D. Because it is the most widespread and hardiest tree on the Kansas plains, the cottonwood had become a symbol of pioneer grit and fortitude.

18. In the twenty-first century, it's easy to see the automobile as the keystone of American popular culture. Subtract linen dusters, driving goggles, and women's *crepe de chine* veils from our history, and you've taken the Roaring out of the Twenties. Take away the ducktail haircuts, pegged pants, and upturned collars from the teen Car Cult of the Fifties, and the decade isn't nearly as Fabulous. Were the chromed and tailfinned muscle cars of the automobile' Golden Age modeled after us, or were we mimicking them? 18.____
A. Ever since its invention, the automobile has shaped American culture.
B. Many of the familiar names we give historical era, such as "Roaring Twenties" and "Fabulous Fifties," were given because of the predominance of the automobile.
C. Americans' tastes in clothing have been determined primarily by the cars they drive.
D. Teenagers have had a fascination for automobiles ever since the motorcar was first invented.

19. Since the 1960s, an important issue for Canada has been the status of minority French-speaking Canadians, especially in the province of Quebec, whose inhabitants make up 30% of the Canadian population and trace their ancestry back to a Canada that preceded British influence. In response to pressure from Quebec nationalists, the government in 1982 added a Charter of Rights to the constitution, restoring important rights that dated back to the time of aboriginal treaties. Separatism is still a prominent issue, though successive 19.____

referendums and constitutional inquiries have not resulted in any realistic progress toward Quebec's independence.

A. Despite the fact that Quebec's inhabitants have their roots in Canada's original settlers, they have been constantly oppressed by the descendants of those who came later, the British.
B. It seems unavoidable that Quebec's linguistic and cultural differences with the rest of Canada will some day lead to its secession.
C. French-speaking Quebec's activism over the last several decades has led to concessions by the Canadian government, but it seems that Quebec will remain a part of the country for some time.
D. The inhabitants of Quebec are an aboriginal culture that has been exploited by the Canadian government for years, but they are gradually winning back their rights.

20. For years, musicians and scientists have tried to discover what it is about an eighteenth-century Stradivarius violin—which may sell for more than $1 million on today's market—that gives it its unique sound. In 1977, American scientist Joseph Nagyvary discovered that the Stradivarius is made of a spruce wood that came from Venice, where timber was stored beneath the sea, and unlike the dry-seasoned wood from which other violins were made, this spruce contains microscopic holes which add resonance to the violin's sound. Nagyvary also found the varnish used on the Stradivarius to be equally unique, containing tiny mineral crystals that appear to have come from ground-up gemstones, which would filter out high-pitched tones and give the violin a smoother sound. 20.____

A. After carefully studying Stradivarius violins to discover the source of their unique sound, an American scientist discovered two qualities in the construction of them that set them apart from other instruments: the wood from which they were made, and the varnish used to coat the wood.
B. The two qualities that give the Stradivarius violin such a unique sound are the wood, which adds resonance, and the finish, which filters out high-pitched tones.
C. The Stradivarius violin, because of the unique wood and finish used in its construction, is widely regarded as the finest string instrument ever manufactured in the world.
D. A close study of the Stradivarius violin has revealed that the best wood for making violins is Venetian spruce, stored underwater.

21. People who watch the display of fireflies on a clear summer evening are actually witnessing a complex chemical reaction called "bioluminescence," which turns certain organisms into living light bulbs. Organisms that produce this light undergo a reaction in which oxygen combines with a chemical called lucerfin and an enzyme called luciferase. Depending on the organism, the light produced from this reaction can range from the light green of the firefly to the bright red spots of a railroad worm. 21.____

A. Although the function of most displays of bioluminescence is to attract mates, as is the case with fireflies, other species rely on bioluminescence for different purposes.

B. Bioluminescence, a phenomenon produced by several organisms, is the result of a chemical reaction that takes place within the body of the organism.
C. Of all the organisms in the world, only insects are capable of displaying bioluminescence.
D. Despite the fact that some organisms display bioluminescence, these reactions produce almost no heat, which is why the light they create is sometimes referred to as cold light.

22. The first of America's "log cabin" presidents, Andrew Jackson rose from humble backcountry origins to become a U.S. congressman and senator, a renowned military hero, and the seventh president of the United States. Among many Americans, especially those of the western frontier, he was acclaimed as a symbol of the "new" American: self-made, strong through closeness to nature, and endowed with a powerful moral courage. 22.____
A. Andrew Jackson was the first American president to rise from modest origins.
B. Because he was born poor, President Andrew Jackson was more popular among Americans of the western frontier.
C. Andrew Jackson's humble background, along with his outstanding achievements, made him into a symbol of American strength and self-sufficiency.
D. Andrew Jackson achieved success as a legislator, soldier, and president because he was born humbly and had to work for every honor he ever received.

23. In the past few decades, while much of the world's imagination has focused on the possibilities of outer space, some scientists have been exploring a different frontier—the ocean floor. Although ships have been sailing the oceans for centuries, only recently have scientists developed vehicles strong enough to sustain the pressure of deep-sea exploration and observation. These fiberglass vehicles, called submersibles, are usually just big enough to take two or three people to the deepest parts of the oceans' floors. 23.____
A. Modern submersible vehicles, thanks to recent technological innovations, are now exploring underwater cliffs, crevices, and mountain ranges that were once unreachable.
B. While most people tend to fantasize about exploring outer space, they should be turning toward a more accessible realm—the depths of the earth's oceans.
C. Because of the necessarily small size of submersible vehicles, exploration of the deep ocean is not a widespread activity.
D. Recent technological developments have helped scientists to turn their attention from deep space to the deep ocean.

24. The panda—a native of the remote mountainous regions of China—subsists almost entirely on the tender shoots of the bamboo plant. This restrictive diet has allowed the panda to evolve an anatomical structure that is completely different from that of other bears, whose paws are aligned for running, stabbing, and scratching. The panda's paw has an over-developed wrist bone that juts out below the other claws like a thumb, and the panda uses this "thumb" to grip bamboo shoots while it strips them of their leaves. 24.____

   A. The panda is the only bear-like animal that feeds on vegetation, and it has a kind of thumb to help it grip bamboo shoots.
   B. The panda's limited diet of bamboo has led it to evolve a thumb-like appendage for grasping bamboo shoots.
   C. The panda's thumb-like appendage is a factor that limits its diet to the shoots of the bamboo plant.
   D. Because bamboo shoots must be held tightly while eaten, the panda's thumb-like appendage ensure that it is the only bear-like animal that eats bamboo.

25. The stability and security of the Balkan region remains a primary concern for Greece in post-Cold War Europe, and Greece's active participation in peacekeeping and humanitarian operations in Georgia, Albania, and Bosnia are substantial examples of this commitment. Due to its geopolitical position, Greece believes it necessary to maintain, at least for now, a more nationalized defense force than other European nations. It is Greece's hope that the new spirit of integration and cooperation will help establish a common European foreign affairs and defense policy that might ease some of these regional tensions, and allow a greater level of Greek participation in NATO's integrated military structure. 25.____

   A. Greece's proximity to the unstable Balkan region has led it to keep a more nationalized military, though it hopes to become more involved in a common European defense force.
   B. The Balkan states present a greater threat to Greece than any other European nation, and Greece has adopted a highly nationalist military force as a result.
   C. Greece, the only Balkan state to belong to NATO, has an isolationist approach to defense, but hopes to achieve greater integration in the organization's combined forces.
   D. Greece's failure to become more militarily integrated with the rest of Europe can be attributed to the failure to establish a common European defense policy.

KEY (CORRECT ANSWERS)

1. A
2. B
3. B
4. D
5. C

6. B
7. C
8. D
9. C
10. D

11. A
12. D
13. C
14. B
15. D

16. D
17. B
18. A
19. C
20. A

21. B
22. C
23. D
24. B
25. A

PROGRAM EVALUATION

Table of Contents

PROGRAM EVALUATION

Program Evaluation Strategy

MANAGING FOR SUCCESS

An essential component of any successful organization is its ability to continually assess and evaluate its performance. To establish effective and efficient programs, managers need fundamental information regarding the position and progress of their programs, and what improvements can be made to enhance the overall quality of their operations.

In identifying this need, the PTO's Office of Planning and Evaluation (P&E) has developed an evaluation strategy for the Patent and Trademark Office. Our goal is to support PTO in planning, assessing, and improving its program activities, so that managers have the information and support they need to continually develop and advance their programs.

TYPES OF PROGRAM EVALUATION

Program evaluation is based on the fundamental idea that programs should have a demonstrable benefit.

In its simplest terms, program evaluation is defined as a systematic approach to assessing the performance of a program or service. Program evaluations are most commonly referred to as either summative or formative in nature. Summative evaluations make a judgment about a program's operations and usefulness, whereas formative evaluations describe a program's operations in order to improve the way in which it functions.

In recent years, the formative approach to evaluating has evolved into what has come to be called "evaluation research."

Evaluation research includes:

- Design of programs
- Ongoing monitoring of how well programs are functioning
- Assessment of program impact
- Analysis of benefits relative to costs.

This approach seems to be the most productive. As internal evaluators, our goal is not only to report to managers on their program's current situation, but also assist them in developing and enhancing the resources they need for continual operational improvement.

JUDGING VS. COACHING

In conducting formative evaluations, the goal is not to judge a program's worth or usefulness, rather the goal is to provide recommendations for program improvements in addition to assessing impacts and results.

A program evaluation trainer, uses the example of a world-class figure-skating champion to differentiate the roles of a coach and judge. As a skater performs, both the judge and the coach are meticulously assessing the skaters every move; however, each has a different motive for evaluating the performance. The judge looks at the performance and impassively scores the skater against the competition, providing little, if any, feedback to the skater. The coach on the other hand, goes a step beyond assessing the performance by actually working with the skater to improve his or her performance. The judge's objective is to score the skater's single performance, whereas the coach's objective is to help the skater achieve his or her fullest potential for future performances.

The coaching perspective helps programs become as efficient and effective as possible, while reaching their fullest potential. Using the example, the coach can work with and recommend improvements to the skater, but it is the skater who is responsible for making the improvements and for eventually becoming a guide and example for others that follow. By diagnosing, consulting and informing programs on their performance, we not only help programs gain a better understanding of what works well within their organization, we also maintain PTO's strategic goal of providing our customers with the highest level of quality and service in all aspects of PTO operations.

Conducting a Program Evaluation

In order to be effective, every evaluation must be tailored to the individual program or organization.

The following are stages in conducting a program evaluation. These stages are designed to adapt to individual needs, interests and the stage of development of the organization or program being evaluated.

THE NEED FOR PLANNING

Ideally, a successful evaluation will provide the best information possible on all key issues within a given set of constraints, such as available time, staff and budget resources. This makes it important to consider at the outset that the design of the evaluation needs to be done carefully, since criticism of the findings will likely focus on the methodology used.

Given the constraints we are all under these days, you may very well ask why you should spend precious resources on planning and designing your evaluation. The answer is precisely because of those constraints. In addition to increasing credibility in the product, a careful and sound design:

- increases overall quality,
- contains costs,
- ensures timeliness of findings,
- increases the strength and specificity of findings and recommendations,
- decreases criticism of methodology,
- improves customer satisfaction, and
- results in less resources required to carry out the evaluation.

STAGE 1: EVALUABILITY ASSESSMENT

Program evaluation is essentially a process in which questions are asked about a program or activity and answers are actively sought. In order to have an effective evaluation--which will result in improved program performance--first, the right questions must be asked, and second, the evaluation team must assure that the questions can be accurately answered.

Before conducting any formal evaluation, an evaluability assessment is conducted. The purpose of the evaluability assessment is to identify the program's goals, performance indicators and data sources, which will be used to conduct the evaluation. The evaluability assessment not only answers the question of whether a program can be meaningfully evaluated, but whether the evaluation is likely to contribute to improved program performance.

During the evaluability assessment there is usually a clear indication of whether a program is ready to be evaluated. If the necessary information (goals, objectives, performance measurements, etc.) is available and is identified by the evaluators and intended users as clear, concise and realistic (given resource allocations and restrictions), the evaluation can proceed. However, if the goals, objectives and performance indicators are found to be either underdeveloped or undefined, the program office is advised to first focus on developing or redefining their performance measurements before continuing with the evaluation.

The foremost question is whether or not the program can be evaluated in a meaningful way based on what currently exists.

Program evaluations are generally concerned with whether a program or policy is achieving its intended goal or purpose. Frequently though, the goals and purposes were to attract as much support as possible for the proposed project, but may lack consistency or be too ambitious given the realities of program functions. Programs and policies that do not have clear and consistent goals can not be evaluated for their effectiveness. Thus, uncovering those goals and purposes is generally the starting point of most evaluations. This first stage of an evaluation is necessary to determine whether they can be evaluated.

Program Evaluation Criteria

- Program goals and objectives, important side effects, and priority information needs are well defined.
- Program goals and objectives are plausible.
- Relevant performance data can be obtained.
- The intended users of the evaluation results have agreed on how they will use the information.

Performance Measurement

Performance measurement is a process by which a program objectively measures how it is accomplishing its mission through the delivery of its products, services, or processes. It is a self-assessment, goal-setting, and progress monitoring tool, which provides on-going performance feedback to both management and staff. A good performance measurement system is designed to provide information which helps clarify goals and motivates performance, solves problems, and corrects deviations or alters planned directions.

Performance Measurement is crucial to the overall management of programs because of one basic principle: "What gets measured, gets done."

Mission, Goals and Objectives

The first step in performance measurement is identifying the mission, goals and objectives. The following is a brief description of each:

The mission is the purpose for which a program or organization was created. A mission answers the following questions:

- Who are we?
- What do we do?
- For whom do we do it?
- Why do we do it?

Goals are statements, usually general and abstract, about how the program expects to accomplish its mission. Goals may be quantitative ("Increase production") or qualitative ("Improve worker morale").

Tips on Goal Setting

- Goals may be general or specific and may encompass time spans ranging from a few months to several years.
- Goals may be set for the entire organization, programs, and individuals.
- Goals at the various organizational levels must be coordinated if the organization is to achieve its intended overall purpose.
- There must be coordination of the long-term goals of the organization with the short term goals of departments and programs, and of both of these with the personal goals of workers
- Involve both management and staff when developing goals.

Objectives are the means for accomplishing goals. They must be quantifiable containing specific statements detailing the desired accomplishments of a program's goals.

Rules for Writing Objectives

- Use a single issue per objective.
- Define measurable objectives using a verb-noun structure ("Increase productivity by 15 percent by fiscal year 2015").
- Specify an expected time for achievement.

Performance Indicators

Once goals and objectives have been established, performance indicators are developed. Performance indicators track and measure whether the goals and objectives have been reached, or how well the program is progressing toward achieving them.

In the classical sense, a performance indicator is defined as a ratio where the output of an effort is divided by the inputs (labor, energy, time, etc.) required to produce it. . For example:

$$\frac{\text{\# of customers helped}}{\text{\# of service reps}}$$

$$\frac{\text{\# of acceptable documents produced}}{\text{hours expanded for documents}}$$

Customer Requirements and Stakeholder Requirements are the Building Blocks for Measurement Ratios. When designing indicators ask the question: How Do We Know We Met Customer Requirements?

Two integral components of performance indicators are effectiveness and efficiency. Effective production is defined as producing the desired results, whereas efficient production is defined as producing the desired outputs with a minimum level of input. Simply stated, effectiveness is doing the right things, and efficiency is doing things right.

Effectiveness and efficiency are both critical measures of performance and success. Organizations can temporarily survive without perfect efficiency, but would most likely die if they were ineffective. When designing performance measurements, it is essential that an organization considers both effectiveness and efficiency. Omitting either would result in performance measurements that provide inaccurate and often costly productivity information.

It bears repeating that if a program has not clearly identified its goals and objectives and set effectiveness and efficiency measures, it will be difficult to evaluate.

Four Criteria for Measurement Effectiveness and Efficiency

1. **Quality-** The measure must define and reflect quality of production or services as well as quantity. A measure that assesses only quantity outputs can lead to reduced productivity.

2. **Mission and goals-** The measure must define and assess only outputs and services that are integrated with the organizational mission and strategic goals. Measures directed to products and services that are not consistent with mission and goals threaten productivity.

3. **Rewards and Incentives-** Measures must be integrated with performance incentives, reward systems and practices. Measures that have no important contingencies will not work to improve productivity.

4. **Employee Involvement-** There must be involvement of employees and other direct stakeholders in the definition and construction of productivity measures. When lack of involvement has not resulted in commitment and buy-in, results from the measures are not likely to be received favorably or to have any impact on future productivity.

STAGE 2: DESIGNING THE EVALUATION

What's worth knowing?
How will we get it?
How will it be used?

By the time you have an idea of the evaluation capacity of your program, you may have the answers to many of the questions that lead to the design. Every question asked by an evaluation can be looked at with varying levels of intensity and thoroughness. When great precision is needed and resources are available, the most powerful of evaluations may be conducted, on the other hand when time and resources are limited and only approximate answers are needed, the level of the evaluation will differ. Given the diversity of programs, policies and projects to be evaluated, the number of questions to be answered, and the differing availability of resources, there can be no single recipe for a successful evaluation. However, these simple guidelines, once tailored, should provide a solid framework for conducting an evaluation.

In determining the design of an evaluation, the following questions are answered and an Evaluation Design Proposal is drafted.

1. Why are we doing this evaluation?

Clarify what the overall purpose of the evaluation is and what specific objectives will be accomplished. Focus not only on what the evaluation will do, but also identify what the evaluation will NOT do.

2. For whom are we doing this evaluation?

It is essential to identify who the audience is so that their needs, perspectives and constraints can be assessed. Identify both the primary audience and secondary audiences.

Who is sponsoring the evaluation? Who is authorizing the expenditure of funds and human resources? Who will be approving the report?

3. What are we evaluating?

Discuss the issues of the evaluation. Are we studying the need for a program or activity? The operations of a program or activity? The effects of a program or activity? Define the specific questions to be answered during the evaluation.

4. How are we doing this evaluation?

Make a list of the information needed to conduct the evaluation. Once the information needs are defined, identify the data collection techniques. Examples of Data Collection Techniques:

Surveys
Interviews
Focus Group Sessions
Case Studies
Tests
Observations
Document Reviews
Production Reports
Computerized databases

5. When are we doing this evaluation?

Establish both the beginning and completion dates and interim deadlines. It may be helpful to set up a project plan to track the dates and resources.

6. Where are we doing this evaluation?

Determine the location of the evaluation. Will a special staff be pulled together? Will they need space for meetings? For working? For storage of files?

7. Who is doing this evaluation?

Assess the skills and resources needed to conduct the evaluation. Identify possible training needs and establish roles and responsibilities for each team member (Hendricks, 1994).

Tips on Building an Effective
Study Team

- Keep teams small.
- Acknowledge team members' need for high performance.
- Reward both team leaders and team members.
- Focus on people, not methodology.
- Keep a skills inventory of team members.
- Make use of project management tools to create benchmarks of success.
- Form a policy group and a work group to involve policy makers, managers, and key staff in the evaluation.

Consider whether the skills and resources are available internally, or whether it might be more economical or beneficial to hire an external contractor to conduct the evaluation. Depending on the nature of the program or project, it may be critical that the results of the evaluation come from an outside, objective source.

One More Thing

After the design is completed, it is helpful to take an overall look at the design.

A well-designed evaluation can usually be recognized by the way it has:

1. Defined and posed questions for study.
2. Developed the methodological strategies for answering those questions.
3. Formulated a data collection plan that anticipates and addresses problems and obstacles that are likely to be encountered.
4. Provided a detailed analysis plan that will ensure that the questions posed will be answered with the appropriate data in the best possible fashion.
5. Established and maintained focus on the usefulness of the product for the intended user.

A sound design reduces downtime deciding what to do next, reduces time spent on collecting and analyzing irrelevant data and strengthens the relevance of the evaluation.

STAGE 3: CONDUCTING THE STUDY

Once the evaluation proposal is drafted and agreed upon by the evaluation team and the evaluation users, the process of collecting and analyzing the relevant data can begin.

DATA COLLECTION AND ANALYSIS

Developing A Data Measurement System

There are two methods of evaluation studies: qualitative and quantitative. Qualitative data collection systems permit the evaluator to study selected issues, cases, or events in depth and detail; data collection is not constrained by predetermined categories of analysis. Quantitative methods use standardized measures that fit diverse opinions and experiences into predetermined response categories. Considering evaluation design alternatives leads directly to consideration of the relative strengths and weaknesses of qualitative and quantitative studies, and the time and resources available for the study.

The advantage of the quantitative approach is that it measures the reactions of a great many people to a limited set of questions, thus facilitating comparison and statistical aggregation of the data. It gives a broad, generalized set of findings. Qualitative methods typically produce a wealth of detailed data about a much smaller number of people and cases. Qualitative data provide depth and detail through direct quotation and careful description of program situations, events, people, interactions, and observed behaviors.

Purposes and functions of qualitative and quantitative data are different, yet can be complementary. The statistics from standardized items make summaries, comparisons, and generalizations quite easy and precise. The narrative comments from open-ended questions are typically meant to provide a forum for elaboration, explanations, meanings, and new ideas.

It is recommended that an evaluation team engage stakeholders early because they have a different perspective, have data the evaluator needs, and can influence the evaluation positively if they are engaged, or negatively if they are ignored or threatened.

Categorizing research questions into major categories can help refine the research agenda of almost any study. Time spent in developing a detailed research design, data collection and analysis plan may improve the quality of the overall results.

Stakeholders include potential users of evaluation information and those with an investment in the organization or unit involved in the study.

Determine Data Availability

Once it has been established what to measure, it must be determined if the data for those measures is available and how to get it. If data is not available, alternative indicators must be identified.

The evaluation team should try to keep its indicators simple and use existing data whenever possible. However, do not compromise the evaluation by discarding indicators the team thinks are meaningful and important before weighing their obtainability.

Data Availability Concerns

1. Does the data currently exist ? If not, can it be developed, and at what effort and cost?
2. If the data exists, what will it cost to retrieve the data?
3. What will it take to get the data converted into the established measurement values?
4. Will a system investment be required? At what cost?
5. Will management support this level of cost? Can a limited version be used?
6. When will data be produced?

Collecting Data

The collection of data addresses the critical issues of making sure the correct data is identified, and a baseline is collected. The baseline data reflects the initial status of the program or process. During this phase, in addition to documenting the method of collection of the data, document any problems with the process, and work to resolve any process problems regularly. Meet with management at the end of an established trial period to evaluate results.

Analyzing Data

Once we have collected the data and before we meet with management, we must analyze the data to make sure that it will provide us with enough information and the right type of information on which to base an evaluation. We must ensure that the data fits the indicators identified to analyze. Agree to finalize the current indicators or revise them as needed, and analyze the baseline data collected for the purpose of setting goals.

DATA PRESENTATION

Once the data has been collected and analyzed, it must be decided how the data and results will be presented. Numbers by themselves are often difficult to understand, they cannot explain circumstances, and they may not easily lead to conclusions. Therefore, it is important to present the information in ways that make it easy to understand, that show relationships to other data, and that allow the information to be used to support decision-making processes. Whenever possible, use graphical tools to present data.

Measures must be shown in context. The most frequent evaluation contexts are: (1) goals compared to actual results, (2) trends in relation to previous periodic results, and (3) comparison of results to other relevant data. Using one or more of these contexts, meaningful conclusions should be drawn about the measurement result with little or no explanation.

REFINING MEASURES

Indicators may need some slight modifications or adjustment to better meet performance information needs of program or executive management. Continually check the usefulness of measurement data and adjust data collection methods if necessary.

Adjusting Measures

Are the measures working well?
What are the measures indicating?
Are additional indicators necessary?
Is data not really available (too difficult or expensive to acquire)?
Is data too difficult to use?

Balance Types Of Measures

One consideration of performance indicator development is that measures are interrelated and cannot be viewed in isolation. Timeliness, quality and cost are always in contention with each other, and the impact of improving any one or two must be weighed in relation to the expense of the third. A balance must be reached between the effectiveness and the economy and efficiency.

Consider Weighting Measures

Not all indicators are equally important. To reflect importance or priorities within measures or categories of measures, weight or index the measures. Weighting or indexing measures is an involved and advanced process and may not be necessary or appropriate for every program. However, weighting measures can provide some valuable insights into program outcomes.

Integrating with Management Process

Once performance results become available, the challenge shifts to presenting and using them effectively.

Establish Goals

Goals should be established based on: (1) policy or administrative priorities, (2) mission (3) customer feedback, (4) past history, (5) forecasted demand and (6) benchmark information.

Determine What The Measurements Say

It is extremely important to understand what the measurements say, as well as what they do not say. The measurements must be compared to performance goals, benchmarks, or past performance. Then variances or changes must be analyzed, and subsequent actions must be planned. In addition to program performance evaluation, the measurement results in the evaluation process can be used for external reporting, planning and budgeting activities and performance appraisal evaluation.

STAGE 4: REPORTING EVALUATION RESULTS

Reporting evaluation results is more of a process than a stage. Beginning on the first day of the evaluation, the evaluators should be continually reporting and discussing their findings with the evaluation users. It is not only important to keep them updated on the evaluation's progress, but also, it is important to keep them informed of any findings and recommendations that can be implemented before the full completion of the evaluation. Remember, the reason for doing an evaluation is to help an organization or program become as effective and efficient as possible. The sooner an organization can implement changes or improvements, the better.

Action-Oriented Reporting

As stated previously, the purpose of an evaluation is to improve a program or an organization's performance. The way in which evaluators do this is by providing recommendations for improvement to management and staff.

The majority of an evaluation report should be devoted to communicating the findings and specific recommendations. Reports should be action-oriented, centered mostly around the findings, but also around the recommendations and suggestions for implementation.

Action-oriented reports are often structured as a series of short reports targeted to specific audiences, rather than one all inclusive document.

Findings and recommendations should be presented clearly and concisely, in a way that meets the informational needs of the audience. In order for recommendations to be accepted by an organization, it must first understand what is being recommended and why it is relevant to their concerns. Evaluation studies are only useful if they are used.

Program Evaluation Report

Generally, an evaluation report should include:

- Executive Summary
  Purpose of Evaluation
  Program Background
  Evaluation Methodology
- Analysis of the Findings
- Recommendations

Tips for Reporting Evaluation Results

- Remember that the burden for effectively reporting results is on the evaluators, not the audience.
- Be aggressive. Instead of waiting for audiences to request information, actively look for opportunities to report results. Report regularly and frequently, appear in person if at all possible, and target multiple reports and briefings to specific audiences and /or issues.
- Simplify, simplify! Audiences are usually busy and their interest is pulled in different directions, so determine and report on the key points. If the core message creates interest, quickly follow up with more details.
- Study the audience. Learn about their backgrounds, interests, concerns, plans, pet peeves, etc.
- Focus on actions. Audiences are rarely interested in general information; they usually want guidance that will help them decide what to do next.
- Report in many different ways. Rather than using only one reporting technique or another, produce several different types of reports. Use written reports, personal briefings, screen show presentations, etc.

STAGE 5: PROGRAM OFFICES IMPLEMENT IMPROVEMENT ACTIVITIES

In this phase of the evaluation process, program office managers implement and monitor the recommendations and action plans originating from the evaluation study. The program manager facilitates the solution of problems by motivating staff and providing technical support. Particular attention must be given to customer and stakeholder requirements.

All employees should be trained in the process improvement recommendations so that they will possess the skills needed to recommend solutions to future problems. Decisions made closer to the customer and occurrence of events save time, reduce errors, and improve morale and service.

STAGE 6: ON-GOING CONSULTATION

Program evaluation is a continuous process of measuring, analyzing and refining an organization or program's performance.

A program evaluation is not an end in itself, rather it is the beginning of a continuous self-evaluation mechanism. With an effective evaluation comes additional data, refined measurements and new initiatives. In order to remain effective, organizations must continually evaluate this information to ensure the achievement of their mission, goals, and objectives.

PRINCIPLES AND PRACTICES, OF ADMINISTRATION, SUPERVISION AND MANAGEMENT

TABLE OF CONTENTS

PRINCIPLES AND PRACTICES, OF ADMINISTRATION, SUPERVISION AND MANAGEMENT

Most people are inclined to think of administration as something that only a few persons are responsible for in a large organization. Perhaps this is true if you are thinking of Administration with a capital *A*, but administration with a lower case *a* is a responsibility of supervisors at all levels each working day.

All of us feel we are pretty good supervisors and that we do a good job of administering the workings of our agency. By and large, this is true, but every so often it is good to check up on ourselves. Checklists appear from time to time in various publications which psychologists say tell whether or not a person will make a good wife, husband, doctor, lawyer, or supervisor.

The following questions are an excellent checklist to test yourself as a supervisor and administrator.

Remember, Administration gives direction and points the way but administration carries the ideas to fruition. Each is dependent on the other for its success. Remember, too, that no unit is too small for these departmental functions to be carried out. These statements apply equally as well to the Chief Librarian as to the Department Head with but one or two persons to supervise.

GENERAL ADMINISTRATION: General Responsibilities of Supervisors

1. Have I prepared written statements of functions, activities, and duties for my organizational unit?

2. Have I prepared procedural guides for operating activities?

3. Have I established clearly in writing, lines of authority and responsibility for my organizational unit?

4. Do I make recommendations for improvements in organization, policies, administrative and operating routines and procedures, including simplification of work and elimination of non-essential operations?

5. Have I designated and trained an understudy to function in my absence?

6. Do I supervise and train personnel within the unit to effectively perform their assignments?

7. Do I assign personnel and distribute work on such a basis as to carry out the organizational unit's assignment or mission in the most effective and efficient manner?

8. Have I established administrative controls by:

    a. Fixing responsibility and accountability on all supervisors under my direction for the proper performance of their functions and duties.

b. Preparations and submitting periodic work load and progress reports covering the operations of the unit to my immediate superior.

c. Analysis and evaluation of such reports received from subordinate units.

d. Submission of significant developments and problems arising within the organizational unit to my immediate superior.

e. Conducting conferences, inspections, etc., as to the status and efficiency of unit operations.

9. Do I maintain an adequate and competent working force?

10. Have I fostered good employee-department relations, seeing that established rules, regulations, and instructions are being carried out properly?

11. Do I collaborate and consult with other organizational units performing related functions to insure harmonious and efficient working relationships?

12. Do I maintain liaison through prescribed channels with city departments and other governmental agencies concerned with the activities of the unit?

13. Do I maintain contact with and keep abreast of the latest developments and techniques of administration (professional societies, groups, periodicals, etc.) as to their applicability to the activities of the unit?

14. Do I communicate with superiors and subordinates through prescribed organizational channels?

15. Do I notify superiors and subordinates in instances where bypassing is necessary as soon thereafter as practicable?

16. Do I keep my superior informed of significant developments and problems?

SEVEN BASIC FUNCTIONS OF THE SUPERVISOR

I. PLANNING

This means working out goals and means to obtain goals. What needs to be done, who will do it, how, when, and where it is to be done.

SEVEN STEPS IN PLANNING

A. Define job or problem clearly.
B. Consider priority of job.
C. Consider time-limit—starting and completing.
D. Consider minimum distraction to, or interference with, other activities.
E. Consider and provide for contingencies—possible emergencies.
F. Break job down into components.

G. Consider the 5 W's and H:
WHY..........is it necessary to do the job? (Is the purpose clearly defined?)
WHAT........needs to be done to accomplish the defined purpose?
.........is needed to do the job? (Money, materials, etc.)
WHO..........is needed to do the job?
..........will have responsibilities?
WHERE......is the work to be done?
WHEN........is the job to begin and end? (Schedules, etc.)
HOW..........is the job to bed done? (Methods, controls, records, etc.)

II. ORGANIZING

This means dividing up the work, establishing clear lines of responsibility and authority and coordinating efforts to get the job done.

III. STAFFING

The whole personnel function of bringing in and training staff, getting the right man and fitting him to the right job—the job to which he is best suited.

In the normal situation, the supervisor's responsibility regarding staffing normally includes providing accurate job descriptions, that is, duties of the jobs, requirements, education and experience, skills, physical, etc.; assigning the work for maximum use of skills; and proper utilization of the probationary period to weed out unsatisfactory employees.

IV. DIRECTING

Providing the necessary leadership to the group supervised. Important work gets done to the supervisor's satisfaction.

V. COORDINATING

The all-important duty of inter-relating the various parts of the work.
The supervisor is also responsible for controlling the coordinated activities. This means measuring performance according to a time schedule and setting quotas to see that the goals previously set are being reached. Reports from workers should be analyzed, evaluated, and made part of all future plans.

VI. REPORTING

This means proper and effective communication to your superiors, subordinates, and your peers (in definition of the job of the supervisor). Reports should be read and information contained therein should be used, not be filed away and forgotten. Reports should be written in such a way that the desired action recommended by the report is forthcoming.

VII. BUDGETING
This means controlling current costs and forecasting future costs. This forecast is based on past experience, future plans and programs, as well as current costs.

You will note that these seven functions can fall under three topics:

Planning) Make a plan Organizing)	Staffing) Directing) Get things done Controlling)	Reporting) Watch it work Budgeting)

PLANNING TO MEET MANAGEMENT GOALS

I. WHAT IS PLANNING?

A. Thinking a job through before new work is done to determine the best way to do it
B. A method of doing something
C. Ways and means for achieving set goals
D. A means of enabling a supervisor to deliver with a minimum of effort, all details involved in coordinating his work

II. WHO SHOULD MAKE PLANS?

Everybody!
All levels of supervision must plan work. (Top management, heads of divisions or bureaus, first line supervisors, and individual employees.) The higher the level, the more planning required.

III. WHAT ARE THE RESULTS OF POOR PLANNING?

A. Failure to meet deadline
B. Low employee morale
C. Lack of job coordination
D. Overtime is frequently necessary
E. Excessive cost, waste of material and manhours

IV. PRINCIPLES OF PLANNING

A. Getting a clear picture of your objectives. What exactly are you trying to accomplish?
B. Plan the whole job, then the parts, in proper sequence.
C. Delegate the planning of details to those responsible for executing them.
D. Make your plan flexible.
E. Coordinate your plan with the plans of others so that the work may be processed with a minimum of delay.
F. Sell your plan before you execute it.
G. Sell your plan to your superior, subordinate, in order to gain maximum participation and coordination.
H. Your plan should take precedence. Use knowledge and skills that others have brought to a similar job.
I. Your plan should take account of future contingencies; allow for future expansion.
J. Plans should include minor details. Leave nothing to chance that can be anticipated.
K. Your plan should be simple and provide standards and controls. Establish quality and quantity standards and set a standard method of doing the job. The controls will indicate whether the job is proceeding according to plan.
L. Consider possible bottlenecks, breakdowns, or other difficulties that are likely to arise.

V. Q. WHAT ARE THE YARDSTICKS BY WHICH PLANNING SHOULD BE MEASURED?
A. Any plan should:
—Clearly state a definite course of action to be followed and goal to be achieved, with consideration for emergencies.
— Be realistic and practical.
— State what's to be done, when it's to be done, where, how, and by whom.
— Establish the most efficient sequence of operating steps so that more is accomplished in less time, with the least effort, and with the best quality results.
— Assure meeting deliveries without delays.
— Establish the standard by which performance is to be judged.

Q. WHAT KINDS OF PLANS DOES EFFECTIVE SUPERVISION REQUIRE?
A. Plans should cover such factors as:
— Manpower: right number of properly trained employees on the job
— Materials: adequate supply of the right materials and supplies
— Machines: full utilization of machines and equipment, with proper maintenance
— Methods: most efficient handling of operations
— Deliveries: making deliveries on time
— Tools: sufficient well-conditioned tools
— Layout: most effective use of space
— Reports: maintaining proper records and reports
— Supervision: planning work for employees and organizing supervisor's own time

MANAGEMENT PRINCIPLES

I. MANAGEMENT
Q. What do we mean by management?
A. Getting work done through others.

Management could also be defined as planning, directing, and controlling the operations of a bureau or division so that all factors will function properly and all persons cooperate efficiently for a common objective.

II. MANAGEMENT PRINCIPLES

A. There should be a hierarchy—wherein authority and responsibility run upward and downward through several levels—with a broad base at the bottom and a single head at the top.

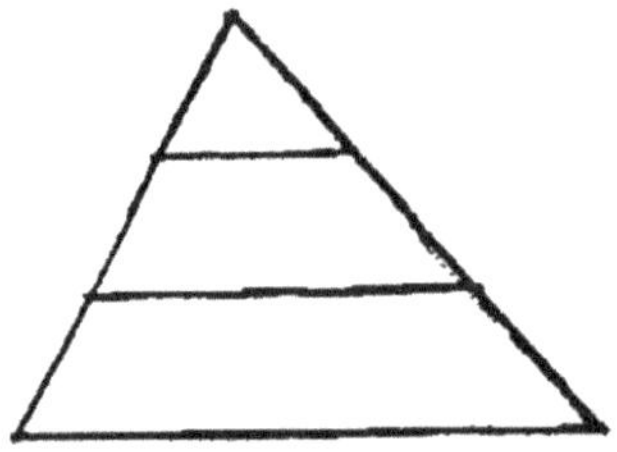

B. Each and every unit or person in the organization should be answerable ultimately to the manager at the apex. In other words, *The buck stops here!*

C. Every necessary function involved in the bureau's objectives is assigned to a unit in that bureau.

D. Responsibilities assigned to a unit are specifically clear-cut and understood.

E. Consistent methods of organizational structure should be applied at each level of the organization.

F. Each member of the bureau from top to bottom knows: to whom he reports and who reports to him.

G. No member of one bureau reports to more than one supervisor. No dual functions.

H. Responsibility for a function is matched by authority necessary to perform that function. Weight of authority.

I. Individuals or units reporting to a supervisor do not exceed the number which can be feasibly and effectively coordinated and directed. Concept of *span of control*.

J. Channels of command (management) are not violated by staff units, although there should be staff services to facilitate and coordinate management functions.

K. Authority and responsibility should be decentralized to units and individuals who are responsible for the actual performance of operations.
Welfare – down to Welfare Centers
Hospitals – down to local hospitals

L. Management should exercise control through attention to policy problems of exceptional performance, rather than through review of routine actions of subordinates.

M. Organizations should never be permitted to grow so elaborate as to hinder work accomplishments.

III. ORGANIZATION STRUCTURE

Types of Organizations
The purest form is a leader and a few followers, such as:

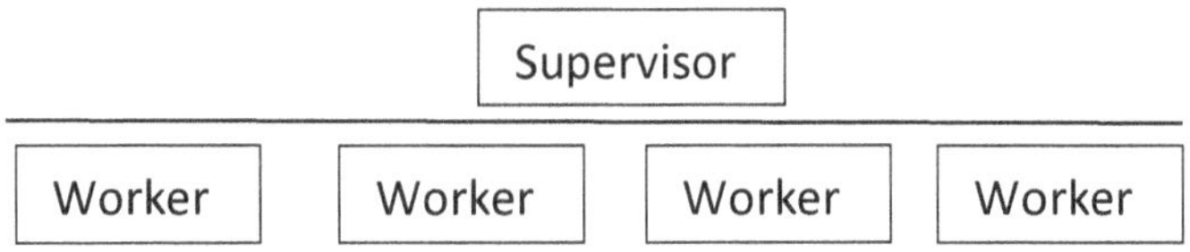

(Refer to organization chart) from supervisor to workers.

The line of authority is direct, The workers know exactly where they stand in relation to their boss, to whom they report for instructions and direction.

Unfortunately, in our present complex society, few organizations are similar to this example of a pure line organization. In this era of specialization, other people are often needed in the simplest of organizations. These specialists are known as staff. The sole purpose for their existence (staff) is to assist, advise, suggest, help or counsel line organizations. Staff has no authority to direct line people—nor do they give them direct instructions.

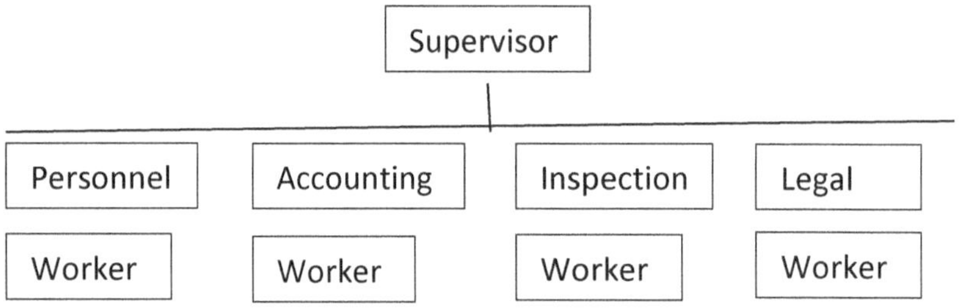

<u>Line Functions</u>
1. Directs
2. Orders
3. Responsibility for carrying out activities from beginning to end
4. Follows chain of command
5. Is identified with what it does
6. Decides when and how to use staff advice
7. Line executes

<u>Staff Functions</u>
1. Advises
2. Persuades and sells
3. Staff studies, reports, recommends but does not carry out
4. May advise across department lines
5. May find its ideas identified with others
6. Has to persuade line to want its advice
7. Staff: Conducts studies and research. Provides advice and instructions in technical matters. Serves as technical specialist to render specific services.

<u>Types and Functions of Organization Charts</u>
An organization chart is a picture of the arrangement and inter-relationship of the subdivisions of an organization.

A. Types of Charts:
   1. Structural: basic relationships only
   2. Functional: includes functions or duties
   3. Personnel: positions, salaries, status, etc.
   4. Process Chart: work performed
   5. Gantt Chart: actual performance against planned
   5. Flow Chart: flow and distribution of work

B. Functions of Charts:
   1. Assist in management planning and control
   2. Indicate duplication of functions
   3. Indicate incorrect stressing of functions
   4. Indicate neglect of important functions
   5. Correct unclear authority
   6. Establish proper span of control

C. Limitations of Charts:
   1. Seldom maintained on current basis
   2. Chart is oversimplified
   3. Human factors cannot adequately be charted

D. Organization Charts should be:
   1. Simple
   2. Symmetrical
   3. Indicate authority
   4. Line and staff relationship differentiated
   5. Chart should be dated and bear signature of approving officer
   6. Chart should be displayed, not hidden

ORGANIZATION

There are four basic principles of organization:

1. Unity of command
2. Span of control
3. Uniformity of assignment
4. Assignment of responsibility and delegation of authority

I. UNITY OF COMMAND

Unity of command means that each person in the organization should receive orders from one, and only one, supervisor. When a person has to take orders from two or more people, (a) the orders may be in conflict and the employee is upset because he does not know which he should obey, or (b) different orders may reach him at the same time and he does not know which he should carry out first.

Equally as bad as having two bosses is the situation where the supervisor is bypassed. Let us suppose you are a supervisor whose boss bypasses you (deals directly with people reporting to you). To the worker, it is the same as having two bosses; but to you, the supervisor, it is equally serious. Bypassing on the part of your boss will undermine your authority, and the people under you will begin looking to your boss for decisions and even for routine orders.

You can prevent bypassing by telling the people you supervise that if anyone tries to give them orders, they should direct that person to you.

II. SPAN OF CONTROL

Span of control on a given level involves:

A. The number of people being supervised
B. The distance
C The time involved in supervising the people. (One supervisor cannot supervise too many workers effectively.)

Span of control means that a supervisor has the right number (not too many and not too few) of subordinates that he can supervise well.

III. UNIFORMITY OF ASSIGNMENT

In assigning work, you as the supervisor should assign to each person jobs that are similar in nature. An employee who is assigned too many different types of jobs will waste time in going from one kind of work to another. It takes time for him to get to top production in one kind of task and, before he does so, he has to start on another.
When you assign work to people, remember that:

A. Job duties should be definite. Make it clear from the beginning what they are to do, how they are to do it, and why they are to do it. Let them know how much they are expected to do and how well they are expected to do it.
B. Check your assignments to be certain that there are no workers with too many unrelated duties, and that no two people have been given overlapping responsibilities. Your aim should be to have every task assigned to a specific person with the work fairly distributed and with each person doing his part.

IV. ASSIGNMENT OF RESPONSIBILITY AND DELEGATION OF AUTHORITY

A supervisor cannot delegate his final responsibility for the work of his department. The experienced supervisor knows that he gets his work done through people. He can't do it all himself. So he must assign the work and the responsibility for the work to his employees. Then they must be given the authority to carry out their responsibilities.

By assigning responsibility and delegating authority to carry out the responsibility, the supervisor builds in his workers initiative, resourcefulness, enthusiasm, and interest in their work. He is treating them as responsible adults. They can find satisfaction in their work, and they will respect the supervisor and be loyal to the supervisor.

PRINCIPLES OF ORGANIZATION

I. DEFINITION

Organization is the method of dividing up the work to provide the best channels for coordinated effort to get the agency's mission accomplished.

II. PURPOSE OF ORGANIZATION

A. To enable each employee within the organization to clearly know his responsibilities and relationships to his fellow employees and to organizational units
B. To avoid conflicts of authority and overlapping of jurisdiction.
C. To ensure teamwork.

III. BASIC CONSIDERATIONS IIN ORGANIZATIONAL PLANNING

A. The basic plans and objectives of the agency should be determined, and the organizational structure should be adapted to carry out effectively such plans and objectives.
B. The organization should be built around the major functions of the agency and not individuals or groups of individuals.

C. The organization should be sufficiently flexible to meet new and changing conditions which may be brought about from within or outside the department.
D. The organizational structure should be as simple as possible and the number of organizational units kept at a minimum.
E. The number of levels of authority should be kept at a minimum. Each additional management level lengthens the chain of authority and responsibility and increases the time for instructions to be distributed to operating levels and for decisions to be obtained from higher authority.
F. The form of organization should permit each executive to exercise maximum initiative within the limits of delegated authority.

IV. BASES FOR ORGANIZATION

A. Purpose (Examples: education, police, sanitation)
B. Process (Examples: accounting, legal, purchasing)
C. Clientele (Examples: welfare, parks, veteran)
D. Geographic (Examples: borough offices, precincts, libraries)

V. ASSIGNMENTS OF FUNCTIONS

A. Every function of the agency should be assigned to a specific organizational unit. Under normal circumstances, no single function should be assigned to more than one organizational unit.
B. There should be no overlapping, duplication, or conflict between organizational elements.
C. Line functions should be separated from staff functions, and proper emphasis should be placed on staff activities.
D. Functions which are closely related or similar should normally be assigned to a single organizational unit.
E. Functions should be properly distributed to promote balance, and to avoid overemphasis of less important functions and underemphasis of more essential functions.

VI. DELEGATION OF AUTHORITY AND RESPONSIBILITY

A. Responsibilities assigned to a specific individual or organizational unit should carry corresponding authority, and all statements of authority or limitations thereof should be as specific as possible.
B. Authority and responsibility for action should be decentralized to organizational units and individuals responsible for actual performance to the greatest extent possible, without relaxing necessary control over policy or the standardization of procedures. Delegation of authority will be consistent with decentralization of responsibility but such delegation will not divest an executive in higher authority of his overall responsibility.
C. The heads of organizational units should concern themselves with important matters and should delegate to the maximum extent details and routines performed in the ordinary course of business.
D. All responsibilities, authorities, and relationships should be stated in simple language to avoid misinterpretation.
E. Each individual or organizational unit charged with a specific responsibility will be held responsible for results.

VII. EMPLOYEE RELATIONSHIPS

A. The employees reporting to one executive should not exceed the number which can be effectively directed and coordinated. The number will depend largely upon the scope and extent of the responsibilities of the subordinates.
B. No person should report to more than one supervisor. Every supervisor should know who reports to him, and every employee should know to whom he reports. Channels of authority and responsibility should not be violated by staff units.
C. Relationships between organizational units within the agency and with outside organizations and associations should be clearly stated and thoroughly understood to avoid misunderstanding.

DELEGATING

I. WHAT IS DELEGATING?
Delegating is assigning a job to an employee, giving him the authority to get that job done, and giving him the responsibility for seeing to it that the job is done.

A. What To Delegate
1. Routine details
2. Jobs which may be necessary and take a lot of time, but do not have to be done by the supervisor personally (preparing reports, attending meetings, etc.)
3. Routine decision-making (making decisions which do not require the supervisor's personal attention)

B. What Not To Delegate
1. Job details which are *executive functions* (setting goals, organizing employees into a good team, analyzing results so as to plan for the future)
2. Disciplinary power (handling grievances, preparing service ratings, reprimands, etc.)
3. Decision-making which involves large numbers of employees or other bureaus and departments
4. Final and complete responsibility for the job done by the unit being supervised

C. Why Delegate?
1. To strengthen the organization by developing a greater number of skilled employees
2. To improve the employee's performance by giving him the chance to learn more about the job, handle some responsibility, and become more interested in getting the job done
3. To improve a supervisor's performance by relieving him of routine jobs and giving him more time for *executive functions* (planning, organizing, controlling, etc.) which cannot be delegated

II. TO WHOM TO DELEGATE
People with abilities not being used. Selection should be based on ability, not on favoritism.

REPORTS

I. DEFINITION
A report is an orderly presentation of factual information directed to a specific reader for a specific purpose

II. PURPOSE
The general purpose of a report is to bring to the reader useful and factual information about a condition or a problem. Some specific purposes of a report may be:

A. To enable the reader to appraise the efficiency or effectiveness of a person or an operation
B. To provide a basis for establishing standards
C. To reflect the results of expenditures of time, effort, and money
D. To provide a basis for developing or altering programs

III. TYPES

A. Information Report: Contains facts arranged in sequence
B. Summary (Examination) Report: Contains facts plus an analysis or discussion of the significance of the facts. Analysis may give advantages and disadvantages or give qualitative and quantitative comparisons
C. Recommendation Report: Contains facts, analysis, and conclusion logically drawn from the facts and analysis, plus a recommendation based upon the facts, analysis, and conclusions

IV. FACTORS TO CONSIDER BEFORE WRITING REPORT

A. Why write the report?: The purpose of the report should be clearly defined.
B. Who will read the report?: What level of language should be used? Will the reader understand professional or technical language?
C. What should be said?: What does the reader need or want to know about the subject?
D. How should it be said?: Should the subject be presented tactfully? Convincingly? In a stimulating manner?

V. PREPARATORY STEPS

A. Assemble the facts: Find out who, why, what, where, when, and how.
B. Organize the facts: Eliminate unnecessary information
C. Prepare an outline: Check for orderliness, logical sequence
D. Prepare a draft: Check for correctness, clearness, completeness, conciseness, and tone
E. Prepare it in final form: Check for grammar, punctuation, appearance

VI. OUTLINE FOR A RECOMMENDATION REPORT

Is the report:
A. Correct in information, grammar, and tone?
B. Clear?
C. Complete?

D. Concise?
E. Timely?
F. Worth its cost?

Will the report accomplish its purpose?

MANAGEMENT CONTROLS

I. CONTROL

What is control? What is controlled? Who controls?

The essence of control is action which adjusts operations to predetermined standards, and its basis is information in the hands of managers. Control is checking to determine whether plans are being observed and suitable progress toward stated objectives is being made, and action is taken, if necessary, to correct deviations.

We have a ready-made model for this concept of control in the automatic systems which are widely used for process control in the chemical land petroleum industries. A process control system works this way. Suppose, for example, it is desired to maintain a constant rate of flow of oil through a pipe at a predetermined or set-point value. A signal, whose strength represents the rate of flow, can be produced in a measuring device and transmitted to a control mechanism. The control mechanism, when it detects any deviation of the actual from the set-point signal, will reposition the value regulating flow rate.

II. BASIS FOR CONTROL

A process control mechanism thus acts to adjust operations to predetermined standards and does so on the basis of information it receives. In a parallel way, information reaching a manager gives him the opportunity for corrective action and is his basis for control. He cannot exercise control without such information, and he cannot do a complete job of managing without controlling.

III. POLICY

What is policy?

Policy is simply a statement of an organization's intention to act in certain ways when specified types of circumstances arise. It represents a general decision, predetermined and expressed as a principle or rule, establishing a normal pattern of conduct for dealing with given types of business events—usually recurrent. A statement is therefore useful in economizing the time of managers and in assisting them to discharge their responsibilities equitably and consistently.

Policy is not a means of control, but policy does generate the need for control.

Adherence to policies is not guaranteed nor can it be taken on faith. It has to be verified. Without verification, there is no basis for control. Policy and procedures, although closely related and interdependent to a certain extent, are not synonymous. A policy may be adopted, for example, to maintain a materials inventory not to exceed one million dollars.

A procedure for inventory control could interpret that policy and convert it into methods for keeping within that limit, with consideration, too, of possible but foreseeable expedient deviation.

IV. PROCEDURE

What is procedure?

A procedure specifically prescribes:
A. What work is to be performed by the various participants
B. Who are the respective participants
C. When and where the various steps in the different processes are to be performed
D. The sequence of operations that will insure uniform handling of recurring transactions
E. The paper that is involved, its origin, transition, and disposition

Necessary appurtenances to a procedure are:
A. Detailed organizational chart
B. Flow charts
C. Exhibits of forms, all presented in close proximity to the text of the procedure

V. BASIS OF CONTROL – INFORMATION IN THE HANDS OF MANAGERS

If the basis of control is information in the hands of managers, then reporting is elevated to a level of very considerable importance.

Types of reporting may include:
A. Special reports and routine reports
B. Written, oral, and graphic reports
C. Staff meetings
D. Conferences
E. Television screens
F. Non-receipt of information, as where management is by exception
G. Any other means whereby information is transmitted to a manager as a basis for control action

FRAMEWORK OF MANAGEMENT

I. ELEMENTS

A. Policy: It has to be verified, controlled.

B. Organization is part of the giving of an assignment. The organizational chart gives to each individual in his title, a first approximation of the nature of his assignment and orients him as being accountable to a certain individual. Organization is not in a true sense a means of control. Control is checking to ascertain whether the assignment is executed as intended and acting on the basis of that information.

C. Budgets perform three functions:
   1. They present the objectives, plans, and programs of the organization in financial terms.

2. They report the progress of actual performance against these predetermined objectives, plans, and programs.
3. Like organizational charts, delegations of authority, procedures, and job descriptions, they define the assignments which have flowed from the Chief Executive. Budgets are a means of control in the respect that they report progress of actual performance against the program. They provide information which enables managers to take action directed toward bringing actual results into conformity with the program.

D. Internal Check provides in practice for the principle that the same person should not have responsibility for all phases of a transaction. This makes it clearly an aspect of organization rather than of control. Internal Check is static, or built-in.

E. Plans, Programs, Objectives
People must know what they are trying to do. Objectives fulfill this need. Without them, people may work industriously and yet, working aimlessly, accomplish little. Plans and Programs complement Objectives, since they propose how and according to what time schedule the objectives are to be reached.

F. Delegations of Authority
Among the ways we have for supplementing the titles and lines of authority of an organizational chart are delegations of authority. Delegations of authority clarify the extent of authority of individuals and in that way serve to define assignments. That they are not means of control is apparent from the very fact that wherever there has been a delegation of authority, the need for control increases. This could hardly be expected to happen if delegations of authority were themselves means of control.

II. MANAGER'S RESPONSIBILITY

Control becomes necessary whenever a manager delegates authority to a subordinate because he cannot delegate and then simply sit back and forget4 about it. A manager's accountability to his own superior has not diminished one whit as a result of delegating part of his authority to a subordinate. The manager must exercise control over actions taken under the authority so delegated. That means checking serves as a basis for possible corrective action.

Objectives, plans, programs, organizational charts, and other elements of the managerial system are not fruitfully regarded as either controls or means of control. They are pre-established standards or models of performance to which operations are adjusted by the exercise of management control. These standards or models of performance are dynamic in character for they are constantly altered, modified, or revised. Policies, organizational set-up, procedures, delegations, etc. are constantly altered but, like objectives and plans, they remain in force until they are either abandoned or revised. All of the elements (or standards or models of performance), objectives, plans, and programs, policies, organization, etc. can be regarded as a *framework of management*.

III. CONTROL TECHNIQUES

Examples of control techniques:
A. Compare against established standards
B. Compare with a similar operation
C. Compare with past operations
D. Compare with predictions of accomplishment

IV. WHERE FORECASTS FIT

Control is after-the-fact while forecasts are before. Forecasts and projections are important for setting objectives and formulating plans.

Information for aiming and planning does not have to be before-the-fact. It may be an after-the-fact analysis proving that a certain policy has been impolitic in its effect on the relation of the company or department with customer, employee, taxpayer, or stockholder; or that a certain plan is no longer practical, or that a certain procedure is unworkable.

The prescription here certainly would not be in control (in these cases, control would simply bring operations into conformity with obsolete standards) but the establishment of new standards, a new policy, a new plan, and a new procedure to be controlled too.

Information is, of course, the basis for all communication in addition to furnishing evidence to management of the need for reconstructing the framework of management.

PROBLEM SOLVING

The accepted concept in modern management for problem solving is the utilization of the following steps:

A. Identify the problem
B. Gather data
C. List possible solutions
D. Test possible solutions
E. Select the best solution
F. Put the solution into actual practice

Occasions might arise where you would have to apply the second step of gathering data before completing the first step.

You might also find that it will be necessary to work on several steps at the same time.

I. IDENTIFY THE PROBLEM

Your first step is to define as precisely as possible the problem to be solved. While this may sound easy, it is often the most difficult part of the process.

It has been said of problem solving that you are halfway to the solution when you can write out a clear statement of the problem itself.

Our job now is to get below the surface manifestations of the trouble and pinpoint the problem. This is usually accomplished by a logical analysis, by going from the general to the particular; from the obvious to the not-so-obvious cause.

Let us say that production is behind schedule. WHY? Absenteeism is high. Now, is absenteeism the basic problem to be tackled, or is it merely a symptom of low morale among the workforce? Under these circumstances, you may decide that production is not the problem; the problem is *employee morale*.

In trying to define the problem, remember there is seldom one simple reason why production is lagging, or reports are late, etc.

Analysis usually leads to the discovery that an apparent problem is really made up of several subproblems which must be attacked separately.

Another way is to limit the problem, and thereby ease the task of finding a solution, and concentrate on the elements which are within the scope of your control.

When you have gone this far, write out a tentative statement of the problem to be solved.

II. GATHER DATA

In the second step, you must set out to collect all the information that might have a bearing on the problem. Do not settle for an assumption when reasonable fact and figures are available.

If you merely go through the motions of problem-solving, you will probably shortcut the information-gathering step. Therefore, do not stack the evidence by confining your research to your own preconceived ideas.

As you collect facts, organize them in some form that helps you make sense of them and spot possible relationships between them. For example, plotting cost per unit figures on a graph can be more meaningful than a long column of figures.

Evaluate each item as you go along. Is the source material absolutely, reliable, probably reliable, or not to be trusted.

One of the best methods for gathering data is to go out and look the situation over carefully. Talk to the people on the job who are most affected by this problem.

Always keep in mind that a primary source is usually better than a secondary source of information.

III. LIST POSSIBLE SOLUTIONS

This is the creative thinking step of problem solving. This is a good time to bring into play whatever techniques of group dynamics the agency or bureau might have developed for a joint attack on problems.

Now the important thing for you to do is: Keep an open mind. Let your imagination roam freely over the facts you have collected. Jot down every possible solution that occurs to you. Resist the temptation to evaluate various proposals as you go along. List seemingly absurd ideas along with more plausible ones. The more possibilities you list during this step, the less risk you will run of settling for merely a workable, rather than the best, solution.

Keep studying the data as long as there seems to be any chance of deriving additional ideas, solutions, explanations, or patterns from it.

IV. TEST POSSIBLE SOLUTIONS

Now you begin to evaluate the possible solutions. Take pains to be objective. Up to this point, you have suspended judgment but you might be tempted to select a solution you secretly favored all along and proclaim it as the best of the lot.

The secret of objectivity in this phase is to test the possible solutions separately, measuring each against a common yardstick. To make this yardstick try to enumerate as many specific criteria as you can think of. Criteria are best phrased as questions which you ask of each possible solution. They can be drawn from these general categories:

Suitability – Will this solution do the job?
Will it solve the problem completely or partially?
Is it a permanent or a stopgap solution?

Feasibility - Will this plan work in actual practice?
Can we afford this approach?
How much will it cost?

Acceptability - Will the boss go along with the changes required in the plan?
Are we trying to drive a tack with a sledge hammer?

V. SELECT THE BEST SOLUTION

This is the area of executive decision.

Occasionally, one clearly superior solution will stand out at the conclusion of the testing process. But often it is not that simple. You may find that no one solution has come through all the tests with flying colors.

You may also find that a proposal, which flunked miserably on one of the essential tests, racked up a very high score on others.

The best solution frequently will turn out to be a combination.

Try to arrange a marriage that will bring together the strong points of one possible solution with the particular virtues of another. The more skill and imagination that you apply, the greater is the likelihood that you will come out with a solution that is not merely adequate and workable, but is the best possible under the circumstances.

VI. PUT THE SOLUTION INTO ACTUAL PRACTICE

As every executive knows, a plan which works perfectly on paper may develop all sorts of bugs when put into actual practice.

Problem-solving does not stop with selecting the solution which looks best in theory. The next step is to put the chosen solution into action and watch the results. The results may point towards modifications.

If the problem disappears when you put your solution into effect, you know you have the right solution.

If it does not disappear, even after you have adjusted your plan to cover unforeseen difficulties that turned up in practice, work your way back through the problem-solving solutions.

Would one of them have worked better?
Did you overlook some vital piece of data which would have given you a different slant on the whole situation? Did you apply all necessary criteria in testing solutions? If no light dawns after this much rechecking, it is a pretty good bet that you defined the problem incorrectly in the first place.

You came up with the wrong solution because you tackled the wrong problem.

Thus, step six may become step one of a new problem-solving cycle.

COMMUNICATION

I. WHAT IS COMMUNICATION?
We communicate through writing, speaking, action, or inaction. In speaking to people face-to-face, there is opportunity to judge reactions and to adjust the message. This makes the supervisory chain one of the most, and in many instances the most, important channels of communication.

In an organization, communication means keeping employees informed about the organization's objectives, policies, problems, and progress. Communication is the free interchange of information, ideas, and desirable attitudes between and among employees and between employees and management.

II. WHY IS COMMUNICATION NEEDED?

A. People have certain social needs
B. Good communication is essential in meeting those social needs
C. While people have similar basic needs, at the same time they differ from each other
D. Communication must be adapted to these individual differences

An employee cannot do his best work unless he knows why he is doing it. If he has the feeling that he is being kept in the dark about what is going on, his enthusiasm and productivity suffer.

Effective communication is needed in an organization so that employees will understand what the organization is trying to accomplish; and how the work of one unit contributes to or affects the work of other units in the organization and other organizations.

III. HOW IS COMMUNICATION ACHIEVED?

Communication flows downward, upward, sideways.

A. Communication may come from top management down to employees. This is downward communication.

Some means of downward communication are:
1. Training (orientation, job instruction, supervision, public relations, etc.)
2. Conferences
3. Staff meetings
4. Policy statements
5. Bulletins
6. Newsletters
7. Memoranda
8. Circulation of important letters

In downward communication, it is important that employees be informed in advance of changes that will affect them.

B. Communications should also be developed so that the ideas, suggestions, and knowledge of employees will flow upward to top management.

Some means of upward communication are:
1. Personal discussion conferences
2. Committees
3. Memoranda
4. Employees suggestion program
5. Questionnaires to be filled in giving comments and suggestions about proposed actions that will affect field operations.

Upward communication requires that management be willing to listen, to accept, and to make changes when good ideas are present. Upward communication succeeds when there is no fear of punishment for speaking out or lack of interest at the top. Employees will share their knowledge and ideas with management when interest is shown and recognition is given.

C. The advantages of downward communication:
1. It enables the passing down of orders, policies, and plans necessary to the continued operation of the station.
2. By making information available, it diminishes the fears and suspicions which result from misinformation and misunderstanding.
3. It fosters the pride people want to have in their work when they are told of good work.
4. It improves the morale and stature of the individual to be *in the know.*

5. It helps employees to understand, accept, and cooperate with changes when they know about them in advance.

D. The advantages of upward communication:
1. It enables the passing upward of information, attitudes, and feelings.
2. It makes it easier to find out how ready people are to receive downward communication.
3. It reveals the degree to which the downward communication is understood and accepted.
4. It helps to satisfy the basic social needs.
5. It stimulates employees to participate in the operation of their organization.
6. It encourage employees to contribute ideas for improving the efficiency and economy of operations.
7. It helps to solve problem situations before they reach the explosion point.

IV. WHY DOES COMMUNICATION FAIL?

A. The technical difficulties of conveying information clearly
B. The emotional content of communication which prevents complete transmission
C. The fact that there is a difference between what management needs to say, what it wants to day, and what it does say
D. The fact that there is a difference between what employees would like to say, what they think is profitable or safe to say, and what they do say

V. HOW TO IMPROVE COMMUNICATION

As a supervisor, you are a key figure in communication. To improve as a communicator, you should:

A. Know: Knowing your subordinates will help you to recognize and work with individual differences.
B. Like: If you like those who work for you and those for whom you work, this will foster the kind of friendly, warm, work atmosphere that will facilitate communication.
C. Trust: Showing a sincere desire to communicate will help to develop the mutual trust and confidence which are essential to the free flow of communication.
D. Tell: Tell your subordinates and superiors *what's doing.* Tell your subordinates *why* as well as *how.*
E. Listen: By listening, you help others to talk and you create good listeners. Don't forget that listening implies action.
F. Stimulate: Communication has to be stimulated and encouraged. Be receptive to ideas and suggestions and motivate your people so that each member of the team identifies himself with the job at hand.
G. Consult: The most effective way of consulting is to let your people participate, insofar as possible, in developing determinations which affect them or their work.

VI. HOW TO DETERMINE WHETHER YOU ARE GETTING ACROSS

A. Check to see that communication is received and understood
B. Judge this understanding by actions rather than words
C. Adapt or vary communication, when necessary
D. Remember that good communication cannot cure all problems

VII. THE KEY ATTITUDE

Try to see things from the other person's point of view. By doing this, you help to develop the permissive atmosphere and the shared confidence and understanding which are essential to effective two-way communication.

Communication is a two-way process:

A. The basic purpose of any communication is to get action.
B. The only way to get action is through acceptance.
C. In order to get acceptance, communication must be humanly satisfying as well as technically efficient.

HOW ORDERS AND INSTRUCTIONS SHOULD BE GIVEN

I. CHARACTERISTICS OF GOOD ORDERS AND INSTRUCTIONS

A. Clear
Orders should be definite as to
—What is to be done
—Who is to do it
—When it is to be done
—Where it is to be done
—How it is to be done

B. Concise
Avoid wordiness. Orders should be brief and to the point.

C. Timely
Instructions and orders should be sent out at the proper time and not too long in advance of expected performance.

D. Possibility of Performance
Orders should be feasible:
1. Investigate before giving orders
2. Consult those who are to carry out instructions before formulating and issuing them

E. Properly Directed
Give the orders to the people concerned. Do not send orders to people who are not concerned. People who continually receive instructions that are not applicable to them get in the habit of neglecting instructions generally.

F. Reviewed Before Issuance
Orders should be reviewed before issuance:
1. Test them by putting yourself in the position of the recipient
2. If they involve new procedures, have the persons who are to do the work review them for suggestions.

G. Reviewed After Issuance
Persons who receive orders should be allowed to raise questions and to point out unforeseen consequences of orders.

H. Coordinated
Orders should be coordinated so that work runs smoothly.

I. Courteous
Make a request rather than a demand. There is no need to continually call attention to the fact that you are the boss.

J. Recognizable as an Order
Be sure that the order is recognizable as such.

K. Complete
Be sure recipient has knowledge and experience sufficient to carry out order. Give illustrations and examples.

A DEPARTMENTAL PERSONNEL OFFICE IS RESPONSIBLE FOR THE FOLLOWING FUNCTIONS

1. Policy
2. Personnel Programs
3. Recruitment and Placement
4. Position Classification
5. Salary and Wage Administration
6. Employee performance Standards and Evaluation
7. Employee Relations
8. Disciplinary Actions and Separations
9. Health and Safety
10. Staff Training and Development
11. Personnel Records, Procedures, and Reports
12. Employee Services
13. Personnel Research

SUPERVISION

I. LEADERSHIP

All leadership is based essentially on authority. This comes from two sources: It is received from higher management or it is earned by the supervisor through his methods of supervision. Although effective leadership has always depended upon the leader's using his authority in such a way as to appeal successfully to the motives of the people supervised, the conditions for making this appeal are continually changing. The key to today's problem of leadership is flexibility and resourcefulness on the part of the leader in meeting changes in conditions as they occur.

Three basic approaches to leadership are generally recognized:

A. The Authoritarian Approach
   1. The methods and techniques used in this approach emphasize the *I* in leadership and depend primarily on the formal authority of the leader. This authority is sometimes exercised in a hardboiled manner and sometimes in a benevolent

manner, but in either case the dominating role of the leader is reflected in the thinking, planning, and decisions of the group.

2. Group results are to a large degree dependent on close supervision by the leader. Usually, the individuals in the group will not show a high degree of initiative or acceptance of responsibility and their capacity to grow and develop probably will not be fully utilized. The group may react with resentment or submission, depending upon the manner and skill of the leader in using his authority.
3. This approach develops as a natural outgrowth of the authority that goes with the leader's job and his feeling of sole responsibility for getting the job done. It is relatively easy to use and does not require must resourcefulness.
4. The use of this approach is effective in times of emergencies, in meeting close deadline as a final resort, in settling some issues, in disciplinary matters, and with dependent individuals and groups.

B. The Laissez-Faire or Let 'em Alone Approach

1. This approach generally is characterized by an avoidance of leadership responsibility by the leader. The activities of the group depend largely on the choice of its members rather than the leader.
2. Group results probably will be poor. Generally, there will be disagreements over petty things, bickering, and confusion. Except for a few aggressive people, individuals will not show much initiative and growth and development will be retarded. There may be a tendency for informal leaders to take over leadership of the group.
3. This approach frequently results from the leader's dislike of responsibility, from his lack of confidence, from failure of other methods to work, from disappointment or criticism. It is usually the easiest of the three to use and requires both understanding and resourcefulness on the part of the leader.
4. This approach is occasionally useful and effective, particularly in forcing dependent individuals or groups to rely on themselves, to give someone a chance to save face by clearing his own difficulties, or when action should be delayed temporarily for good cause.

C. The Democratic Approach

1. The methods and techniques used in this approach emphasize the *we* in leadership and build up the responsibility of the group to attain its objectives. Reliance is placed largely on the earned authority of the leader.
2. Group results are likely to be good because most of the job motives of the people will be satisfied. Cooperation and teamwork, initiative, acceptance of responsibility, and the individual's capacity for growth probably will show a high degree of development.
3. This approach grows out of a desire or necessity of the leader to find ways to appeal effectively to the motivation of his group. It is the best approach to build up inside the person a strong desire to cooperate and apply himself to the job. It is the most difficult to develop, and requires both understanding and resourcefulness on the part of the leader.
4. The value of this approach increases over a long period where sustained efficiency and development of people are important. It may not be fully effective in all situations, however, particularly when there is not sufficient time to use it properly or where quick decisions must be made.

All three approaches are used by most leaders and have a place in supervising people. The extent of their use varies with individual leaders, with some using one approach predominantly. The leader who uses these three approaches, and varies their use with time and circumstance, is probably the most effective. Leadership which is used predominantly with a democratic approach requires more resourcefulness on the part of the leader but offers the greatest possibilities in terms of teamwork and cooperation.

The one best way of developing democratic leadership is to provide a real sense of participation on the part of the group, since this satisfies most of the chief job motives. Although there are many ways of providing participation, consulting as frequently as possible with individuals and groups on things that affect them seems to offer the most in building cooperation and responsibility. Consultation takes different forms, but it is most constructive when people feel they are actually helping in finding the answers to the problems on the job.

There are some requirements of leaders in respect to human relations which should be considered in their selection and development. Generally, the leader should be interested in working with other people, emotionally stable, self-confident, and sensitive to the reactions of others. In addition, his viewpoint should be one of getting the job done through people who work cooperatively in response to his leadership. He should have a knowledge of individual and group behavior, but, most important of all, he should work to combine all of these requirements into a definite, practical skill in leadership.

II. NINE POINTS OF CONTRAST BETWEEN *BOSS* AND *LEADER*

A. The boss drives his men; the leader coaches them.
B. The boss depends on authority; the leader on good will.
C. The boss inspires fear; the leader inspires enthusiasm.
D. The boss says I; the leader says *We*.
E. The boss says *Get here on time*; the leader gets there ahead of time.
F. The boss fixes the blame for the breakdown; the leader fixes the breakdown.
G. The boss knows how it is done; the leader shows how.
H. The boss makes work a drudgery; the leader makes work a game.
I. The boss says *Go*; the leader says *Let's go.*

EMPLOYEE MORALE

Employee morale is the way employees feel about each other, the organization or unit in which they work, and the work they perform.

I. SOME WAYS TO DEVELOP AND MAINTAIN GOOD EMPLYEE MORALE

A. Give adequate credit and praise when due.
B. Recognize importance of all jobs and equalize load with proper assignments, always giving consideration to personality differences and abilities.
C. Welcome suggestions and do not have an *all-wise* attitude. Request employees' assistance in solving problems and use assistants when conducting group meetings on certain subjects.
D. Properly assign responsibilities and give adequate authority for fulfillment of such assignments.

E. Keep employees informed about matters that affect them.
F. Criticize and reprimand employees privately.
G. Be accessible and willing to listen.
H. Be fair.
I. Be alert to detect training possibilities so that you will not miss an opportunity to help each employee do a better job, and if possible with less effort on his part.
J. Set a good example.
K. Apply the golden rule.

II. SOME INDICATIONS OF GOOD MORALE

A. Good quality of work
B. Good quantity
C. Good attitude of employees
D. Good discipline
E. Teamwork
F. Good attendance
G. Employee participation

MOTIVATION

DRIVES

A drive, stated simply, is a desire or force which causes a person to do or say certain things. These are some of the most usual drives and some of their identifying characteristics recognizable in people motivated by such drives:

A. Security (desire to provide for the future)
Always on time for work
Works for the same employer for many years
Never takes unnecessary chances
Seldom resists doing what he is told

B. Recognition (desire to be rewarded for accomplishment)
Likes to be asked for his opinion
Becomes very disturbed when he makes a mistake
Does things to attract attention
Likes to see his name in print

C. Position (desire to hold certain status in relation to others)
Boasts about important people he knows
Wants to be known as a key man
Likes titles
Demands respect
Belongs to clubs, for prestige

D. Accomplishment (desire to get things done)
Complains when things are held up
Likes to do things that have tangible results
Never lies down on the job
Is proud of turning out good work

E. Companionship (desire to associate with other people)
Likes to work with others
Tells stories and jokes
Indulges in horseplay
Finds excuses to talk to others on the job

F. Possession (desire to collect and hoard objects)
Likes to collect things
Puts his name on things belonging to him
Insists on the same location

Supervisors may find that identifying the drives of employees is a helpful step toward motivating them to self-improvement and better job performance. For example: An employee's job performance is below average. His supervisor, having previously determined that the employee is motivated by a drive for security, suggests that taking training courses will help the employee to improve, advance, and earn more money. Since earning more money can be a step toward greater security, the employee's drive for security would motivate him to take the training suggested by the supervisor. In essence, this is the process of charting an employee's future course by using his motivating drives to positive advantage.

EMPLOYEE PARTICIPATION

I. WHAT IS PARTICIPATION

Employee participation is the employee's giving freely of his time, skill, and knowledge to an extent which cannot be obtained by demand.

II. WHY IS IT IMPORTANT?

The supervisor's responsibility is to get the job done through people. A good supervisor gets the job done through people who work willingly and well. The participation of employees is important because:

A. Employees develop a greater sense of responsibility when they share in working out operating plans and goals.
B. Participation provides greater opportunity and stimulation for employees to learn, and to develop their ability.
C. Participation sometimes provides better solutions to problems because such solutions may combine the experience and knowledge of interested employees who want the solutions to work.
D. An employee or group may offer a solution which the supervisor might hesitate to make for fear of demanding too much.

E. Since the group wants to make the solution work, they exert pressure in a constructive way on each other.
F. Participation usually results in reducing the need for close supervision.

II. HOW MAY SUPERVISORS OBTAIN IT?

Participation is encouraged when employees feel that they share some responsibility for the work and that their ideas are sincerely wanted and valued. Some ways of obtaining employee participation are:

A. Conduct orientation programs for new employees to inform them about the organization and their rights and responsibilities as employees.
B. Explain the aims and objectives of the agency. On a continuing basis, be sure that the employees know what these aims and objectives are.
C. Share job successes and responsibilities and give credit for success.
D. Consult with employees, both as individuals and in groups, about things that affect them.
E. Encourage suggestions for job improvements. Help employees to develop good suggestions. The suggestions can bring them recognition. The city's suggestion program offers additional encouragement through cash awards.

The supervisor who encourages employee participation is not surrendering his authority. He must still make decisions and initiate action, and he must continue to be ultimately responsible for the work of those he supervises. But, through employee participation, he is helping his group to develop greater ability and a sense of responsibility while getting the job done faster and better.

STEPS IN HANDLING A GRIEVANCE

1. Get the Facts
   a. Listen sympathetically
   b. Let him talk himself out
   c. Get his story straight
   d. Get his point of view
   e. Don't argue with him
   f. Give him plenty of time
   g. Conduct the interview privately
   h. Don't try to shift the blame or pass the buck

2. Consider the Facts
   a. Consider the employee's viewpoint
   b. How will the decision affect similar cases
   c. Consider each decision as a possible precedent
   d. Avoid snap judgments—don't jump to conclusions

3. Make or Get a Decision
   a. Frame an effective counter-proposal
   b. Make sure it is fair to all
   c. Have confidence in your judgment
   d. Be sure you can substantiate your decision

4. Notify the Employee of Your Decision
Be sure he is told; try to convince him that the decision is fair and just.

5. Take Action When Needed and If Within Your Authority
Otherwise, tell employee that the matter will be called to the attention of the proper person or that nothing can be done, and why it cannot.

6. Follow through to see that the desired result is achieved.

7. Record key facts concerning the complaint and the action taken.

8. Leave the way open to him to appeal your decision to a higher authority.

9. Report all grievances to your superior, whether they are appealed or not.

DISCIPLINE

Discipline is training that develops self-control, orderly conduct, and efficiency.

To discipline does not necessarily mean to punish.

To discipline does mean to train, to regulate, and to govern conduct.

I. THE DISCIPLINARY INTERVIEW

Most employees sincerely want to do what is expected of them. In other words, they are self-disciplined. Some employees, however, fail to observe established rules and standards, and disciplinary action by the supervisor is required.

The primary purpose of disciplinary action is to improve conduct without creating dissatisfaction, bitterness, or resentment in the process.

Constructive disciplinary action is more concerned with causes and explanations of breaches of conduct than with punishment. The disciplinary interview is held to get at the causes of apparent misbehavior and to motivate better performance in the future.

It is important that the interview be kept on an impersonal a basis as possible. If the supervisor lets the interview descend to the plane of an argument, it loses its effectiveness.

II. PLANNING THE INTERVIEW

Get all pertinent facts concerning the situation so that you can talk in specific terms to the employee.

Review the employee's record, appraisal ratings, etc.

Consider what you know about the temperament of the employee. Consider your attitude toward the employee. Remember that the primary requisite of disciplinary action is fairness.

Don't enter upon the interview when angry.

Schedule the interview for a place which is private and out of hearing of others.

III. CONDUCTING THE INTERVIEW

A. Make an effort to establish accord.
B. Question the employee about the apparent breach of discipline. Be sure that the question is not so worded as to be itself an accusation.
C. Give the employee a chance to tell his side of the story. Give him ample opportunity to talk.
D. Use understanding—listening except where it is necessary to ask a question or to point out some details of which the employee may not be aware. If the employee misrepresents facts, make a plain, accurate statement of the facts, but don't argue and don't engage in personal controversy.
E. Listen and try to understand the reasons for the employee's (mis)conduct. First of all, don't assume that there has been a breach of discipline. Evaluate the employee's reasons for his conduct in the light of his opinions and feelings concerning the consistency and reasonableness of the standards which he was expected to follow. Has the supervisor done his part in explaining the reasons for the rule? Was the employee's behavior unintentional or deliberate? Does he think he had real reasons for his actions? What new facts is he telling? Do the facts justify his actions? What causes, other than those mentioned, could have stimulated the behavior?
F. After listening to the employee's version of the situation, and if censure of his actions is warranted, the supervisor should proceed with whatever criticism is justified. Emphasis should be placed on future improvement rather than exclusively on the employee's failure to measure up to expected standards of job conduct.
G. Fit the criticism to the individual. With one employee, a word of correction may be all that is required.
H. Attempt to distinguish between unintentional error and deliberate misbehavior. An error due to ignorance requires training and not censure.
I. Administer criticism in a controlled, even tone of voice, never in anger. Make it clear that you are acting as an agent of the department. In general, criticism should refer to the job or the employee's actions and not to the person. Criticism of the employee's work is not an attack on the individual.
J. Be sure the interview does not destroy the employee's self-confidence. Mention his good qualities and assure him that you feel confident that he can improve his performance.
K. Wherever possible, before the employee leaves the interview, satisfy him that the incident is closed, that nothing more will be said on the subject unless the offense is repeated.

BASIC FUNDAMENTALS OF LIBRARY SCIENCE

TABLE OF CONTENTS

BASIC FUNDAMENTALS OF LIBRARY SCIENCE

The problem of classifying' all human knowledge has produced a branch of learning called "library science." A lasting contribution to a simple and understandable method of locating a book on any topic was designed by Melvil Dewey in 1876. His plan divided all knowledge into ten large classes and then dubdivided each class according to related groups.

DEWEY DECIMAL SYSTEM

1. Subject Classification

The Dewey Decimal Classification System is the accepted and most widely used subject classification system in libraries throughout the world.

2. Classification by Three (3) Groups

There are three groups of classification in the system. A basic group of ten (10) classifications arranges all knowledge as represented by books within groups by classifications numbered 000-900.

The second group is the "100 division"; each group of the basic "10 divisions" is again divided into 9 sub-sctions allowing for more detailed and specialized subjects not identified in the 10 basic divisions.

3. There is a third, still further specialized "One thousand" group where each of the "100" classifications are further divided by decimalized, more specified, subject classifications. The "1,000" group is mainly used by highly specialized scientific and much diversified libraries.

These are the subject classes of the Dewey System:

000-099	General works (included bibliography, encyclopedias, collections, periodicals, newspapers,etc.)
100-199	Philosophy (includes psychology, logic, ethics, conduct, etc.) 200-299 Religion (includes mythology, natural theology, Bible, church history, etc.)
300-399	Social Science (includes economics, government, law, education, commerce, etc.)
400-499	Language (includes dictionaries, grammars, philology, etc.) 500-599 Science (includes mathematics, chemistry, physics, astronomy, geology, etc.) 600-699 Useful Arts (includes agriculture, engineering, aviation, medicine, manufactures, etc.) 700-799 Fine Arts (includes sculpture, painting, music, photography, gardening, etc.)
800-899	Literature (includes poetry, plays, orations, etc.) 900-999 History (includes geoegraphy, travel, biography, ancient and modern history, etc.)

PREPARING TO USE THE LIBRARY

Your ability to use the library and its resources is an important factor in determining your success. Skill and efficiency in finding the library materials you need for assignments and research papers will increase the amount of time you have to devote to reading or organizing information.

These are some of the preparations you can make now.

1. Develop skill in using your local library. You can increase your familiarity with the card catalog and the periodical indexes,such as the *Readers' Guide to Periodical Literature, in* any library.
2. Take the *Test in Library Science* to see how you can improve your knowledge of the library.
3. Read in such books as *Books, Libraries and You* by Jessie Edna Boyd, *The Library Key* by Margaret G.Cook, and *Making Books Work, a Guide to the Use of Libraries* by Jennie Maas Flexner.

You can find other titles by looking under the subject heading LIBRARIES AND READERS in the card catalog of your library. THREE TYPES OF BOOK CARDS

Here are the three general types of cards which are used to represent a book in the main catalog.

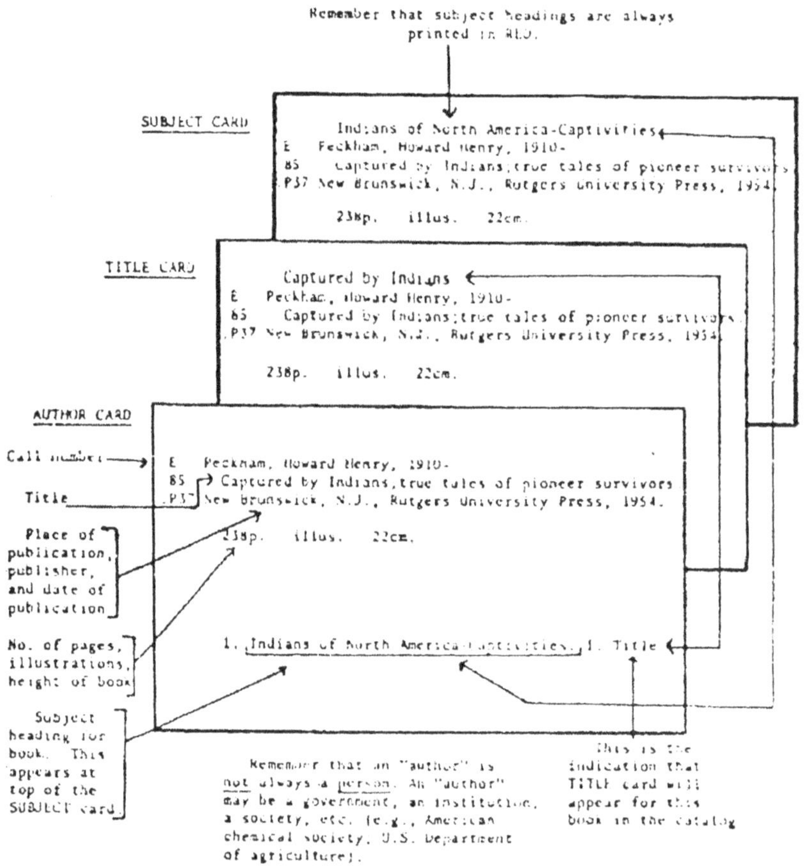

CARD CATALOG

The Card Catalog lists all books in the library by author. The majority of books also have title and subject cards.

<u>Author card</u>

If the author is known, look in the catalog under the author's name. The "author" for some works may be a society, an institution, or a government department.

<u>Title card</u>

Books with distinctive titles, anonymous works and periodicals will have a title card.

Subject card

To find books on a specific subject, look in the catalog under that subject heading. (Subject headings are printed in red on the Catalog Card.)

Call number

The letters and numbers in the upper left-hand corner *of the* Catalog Card are the book's call number. Copy this call number accurately, for it will determine the shelf location of the book. The word "Reference" marked in red in the upper right-hand corner of the catalog card indicates that the item is shelved in the Reference Section,and "Periodical "marked in yellow on the Catalog Card indicates that the item is shelved in the Periodicals Section. PERIODICALS

All magazines are arranged in alphabetical order by title. PERIODICALS FILE

To determine whether the Library has a specific magazine, consult the Periodicals File. Check the title of the magazine needed, and note that there are two cards for each title.

The bottom card lists the current issues available. The top card lists back bound volumes.

Those marked "Ask at Ref.Desk" may be obtained from the Reference Librarian. PERIODICAL INDEXES

Material in magazines is more up-to-date than books and is a valuable source of information. To find articles on a chosen subject, use the periodical indexes.

The Readers' Guide to Periodical Literature is the most familiar of these indexes. In the front of each volume is a list of the periodicals indexed and a key to abbreviations. Similar aids appear in the front of other periodical indexes.

Sample entry: WEASELS

WONDERFUL WHITE WEASEL. R.Beck. il OUTDOOR LIFE 135:48-9+ Ja '65

Explanation : An illustrated article on the subject WEASELS entitled WONDERFUL WHITE WEASEL, by R.Beck,will be found in volume 135 of OUTDOOR LIFE, pages 48-9 (continued on later pages of the same issue), the January 1965 number.

Major libraries subscribe to the following indexes:

Art Index

Biography Index

Book Review Index

British Humanities Index

Essay and General Literature Index

This is helpful for locating criticism of works of literature.

An Index to Book Reviews in the Humanities

International Index ceased publications June, 1965 and continued as Social Science and Humanities Index

The Music Index The New York

Times Index Nineteenth Century Readers' Guide

Poole's Index

Poverty and Human Resources Abstracts

Psychological Abstracts

Public Affairs Information Service.Bulletin of the (PAIS) is a subject index to current books,pamphlets,periodical articles, government documents, and other library materials in economics and public affairs.

Readers' Guide to Periodical Literature
Social Science and Humanities Index a continuation of the International Index
Sociological Abstracts

Do you have the basic skills for using a library efficiently? You should be able to answer AT LEAST 33 of the following questions correctly. *CHECK YOUR ANSWERS BY TURNING TO THE ANSWER KEY AT THE BACK OF THIS SECTION.*

USING A CARD CATALOG

Questions 1-9.

DIRECTIONS: An author card (or "main entry" card) is shown below. Identify each item on the card by selecting the CORRECT letters for them. *PRINT THE LETTER OF THE CORRECT ANSWER IN THE SPACE AT THE RIGHT.*

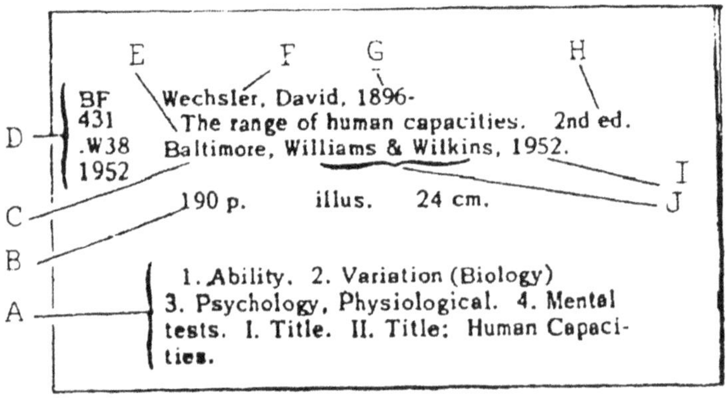

Sample Answer:

0. F

1. Date book was published. 1.___
2. Number of pages in book. 2.___
3. Title. 3.___
4. Place of publication. 4.___
5. Call number. 5.___
6. Year author was born 6.___
7. Edition. 7.___
8. Publisher. 8.___
9. Other headings under which cards for this book may be found. 9.___

Questions 10-13.

DIRECTIONS: Select the letter preceding the word or phrase which completes each of the following statements correctly.

10. The library's title card for the book THE LATE GEORGE APLEY can be found by looking in the card catalog under 10.____

A. Apley, George B. The C. Late D. George E. Apley

11. A catalog card for a book by John F. Kennedy would be found in the drawer labelled 11.____

A. JEFFERSON-JOHNSON,ROY
B. PRESCOTT-PRICELESS
C. KIERNAN-KLAY
D. U.S.PRESIDENT-U.S.SOCIAL SECURITY
E. KENNEBEC-KIERKEGAARD

12. The title cards for these three periodicals would be found in the card catalog arranged in which of the following orders: 12.____

A. NEW YORKER, NEWSWEEK, NEW YORK TIMES MAGAZINE
B. NEWSWEEK, NEW YORKER, NEW YORK TIMES MAGAZINE
C. NEW YORK TIMES MAGAZINE, NEW YORKER, NEWSWEEK
D. NEW YORKER, NEW YORK TIMES MAGAZINE, NEWSWEEK
E. NEWSWEEK, NEW YORK TIMES MAGAZINE, NEW YORKER

13. A card for a copy of the U.N.Charter would be found in the catalog drawer marked 13.____

A. TWENTIETH-UNAMUNO
B. UNITED MINE WORKERS-UNITED SHOE MACHINERY
C. U.S.BUREAU-U.S. CONGRESS
D. U.S.SOCIAL POLICY-UNIVERSITAS
E. CHANCEL-CIARDI

II. UNDERSTANDING ENTRIES IN A PERIODICAL INDEX

Questions 14-25.

DIRECTIONS: The following items are excerpts from THE READERS' GUIDE TO PERIODICAL LITERATURE. Identify each lettered section of the entries by placing the correct letters in the spaces.(There are more letters than spaces, so some of the letters will not be used.)

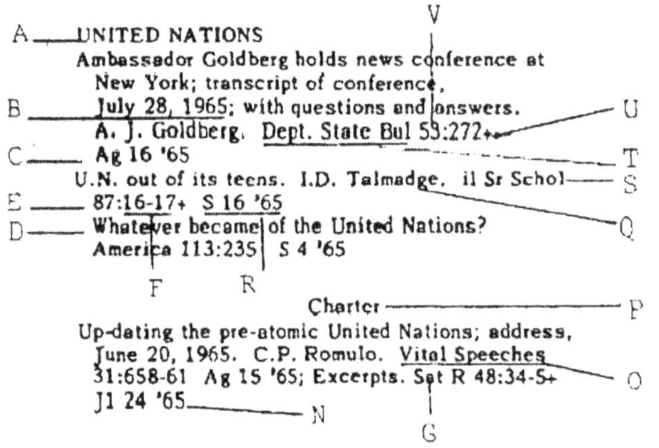

14. Title of magazine containing a transcript of a news con-conference held by U.N.Ambassador Arthur Goldberg. 14.____

15. Magazine in which the full text of C.P.Romulo's address on the U.N. appears. 15.____

16. Author of an article titled U.N. OUT OF ITS TEENS. 16.____

17. Date on which Ambassador Goldberg wrote a letter urging the Security Council to respond to the challenge of southeast Asia. 17.____

18. Title of an article for which no author is listed. 18.____

19. Date of the SATURDAY REVIEW issue which contains excerptsl of a speech called "Up-Dating the Pre-Atomic United Nations." 19.____

20. Pages in the DEPARTMENT OF STATE BULLETIN on which Ambassador Goldberg's letter appears. 20.____

21. Symbol indicating that the letter is continued on a later page. 21.____

22. Volume number of the magazine in which the article by I.D.Talmadge is printed. 22.____

23. Symbols meaning September 16,1965. 23.____

24. The general subject heading under which all five articles are listed. 24.____

25. A subject heading subdivision. 25.____

Questions 26-27.

DIRECTIONS: Select the letter preceding the phrase which completes each of the following statements correctly.

26. To determine whether or not the library has THE MAGAZINE OF AMERICAN HISTORY, check in 26.____

   A. the list of magazine titles in the front of THE READERS' GUIDE TO PERIODICAL LITERATURE
   B. the library's card catalog

C. Ulrich's GUIDE TO PERIODICALS
D. SATURDAY REVIEW
E. THE LIBRARY JOURNAL

27. THE READERS' GUIDE is a good place to look for material on the Job Corps because it 27.____

A. indexes only the best books and magazines in each field
B. is a guide to articles on many subjects appearing in all of the library's periodicals
C. indexes recent discussions on the subject in many magazines
D. specializes in official government information
E. does all of the above

III. IDENTIFYING LIBRARY TERMS

Questions 28-32.

DIRECTIONS: Match the correct definitions with these terms by placing the correct letters in the blanks. (Some of the letters will not be used.)

28. Bibliography	A. Word or phrase printed in A. Word or phrase printed in log to indicate the major log to indicate the major	28.____
29. Anthology	B. Brief written summary of the major ideas presented in an article or book	29.____
30. Index	C. List of books and/or articles on one subject or by one author	30.____
31. Abstract	D. Collection of selections from the writings of one or several authors	31.____
32. Subject heading	E. Written account of a person's life	32.____
	F. Alphabetical list of subjects with the pages on which they are to be found in a book or periodical	
	G. Subordinate, usually explanatory title, additional to the main title and usually printed below it	

IV. FINDING A BOOK BY ITS CALL NUMBER

Questions 33-38.

DIRECTIONS: The Library of Congress classification system call numbers shown below are arranged in order, just as the books bearing those call numbers would be arranged on the shelves. To show where other call numbers would be located, select the letter of the CORRECT ANSWER.

A.	B.	C.	D.	E.	F.	G.	H.	I.	J.	K.
PS 201 .L67 1961	PS 201 .M44	PS 208 .B87 1944	PS 351 .D7	PS 351 .D77	PS 3513 .A2	PS 3515 .D72	PS 3515.3 A66	PS 3526 .N21	PS 3526.17 P2	PS 3526.37 A10

L.	M.	N.
PS 3526.37 C20	PS 3526.37 C37	PT 1 .R2

33. A book with the call number PS would be shelved 33.____
201
.L67

A. Before A B. Between A & B C. Between B & C
D. Between C & D E. Between D & E

34. A book with the call number PS would be shelved 34.____
208
.B87
1944a

A. Between A & B B. Between C & D C. Between B & C
D. Between C & D E. Between D & E

35. A book with the call number PS would be shelved 35.____
351
D8

A. Between C & D B. Between D & E C. Between E & F
D. Between F & G E. Between G & H

36. A book with the call number PS would be shelved 36.____
3526.3
M53

A. Between L & M B. Between J & K C. Between K & L
D. Between M & 0 E. Between 0 & P

37. A book with the call number PS would be shelved 37.____
3526.37
C205

A. Between L & M B. Between N & 0 C. Between M & N
D. Between 0 & P E. Between P & Q

38. A book with the call number PS would be shelved 38.____
3526.37
C3

A. Between M & N B. Between L & M C. Between N & 0
D. Between 0 & P E. Between P & Q

V. General

Questions 39-40.

DIRECTIONS: Each question or incomplete statement is followed by several suggested answers or completions. Select the one that BEST answers the question or completes the statement. *PRINT THE LETTER OF THE CORRECT ANSWER IN TEE SPACE AT THE RIGHT.*

39. When it is finished (in 610 volumes), the ______ will be the MOST monumental national bibliography in the world. 39.____

A. UNION LIST OF SERIALS IN LIBRARIES OF THE UNITED STATES AND CANADA
B. UNITED STATES CATALOG
C. READERS' GUIDE TO PERIODICAL LITERATURE
D. NATIONAL UNION CATALOG

40. For those who wish to investigate the publishing companies and the people who control them, to locate the date a company was founded, who owned it, when it changed hands, what firm succeeded it, and other information of a similar nature, the periodical ______ is clearly invaluable. 40.____

A. PUBLISHERS' TRADE LIST ANNUAL (PTLA)
B. CUMULATIVE BOOK INDEX
C. AMERICAN BOOKTRADE DIRECTORY
D. PUBLISHERS WEEKLY

KEY (CORRECT ANSWERS)

1. I
2. B
3. E
4. C
5. D
6. G
7. H
8. J
9. A
10. C - The first word of the title which is not an article.
11. E - Every book in the library is listed in the card catalog under the author's name. (Warning: The "author" may be a society, a university, or some other institution.)
12. C - A title is alphabetized word-by-word; therefore, "New" comes before "Newsweek," "New York" before "New Yorker."
13. B - The United Nations, not an individual, is the author of this work.
14. T 16. Q 18. D 20. J 22. E 24. A 26. B 28. C 30. F 32. A
15. 0 17. M 19. N 21. K 23. R 25. P/H 27. C 29. D 31. B
33. A - When two call numbers are identical except that one has a year or some other figure added at its end, the shorter call numbers comes first.
34. B
35. C - The numbers which follow a. are regarded as decimals; therefore, .D77 precedes .D8.
36. B - 3526.3 precedes 3526.37
37. A - .C20 precedes .C205
38. B - .C3 precedes .C37 (Read the call number line-by-line, and put a J before a P, before a PB, etc. Put a lower number before a greater one.)
39. D
40. D

www.ingramcontent.com/pod-product-compliance
Lightning Source LLC
Chambersburg PA
CBHW081802300426
44116CB00014B/2213
9781799313465